1983

An OPUS book

The Modern American Novel

Malcolm Bradbury

The Modern American Novel

Two bodies of modern literature seem to me to have come
to the real verge: the Russian and the American. ... The
furthest frenzies of French modernism or futurism have not
yet reached the pitch of extreme consciousness that Poe,
Melville, Hawthorne, Whitman reached. The Europeans
were all *trying* to be extreme. The great Americans I
mention just were it. Which is why the world has funked
them, and funks them today.

D. H. Lawrence, *Studies in Classic
American Literature* (1923)

Oxford New York

OXFORD UNIVERSITY PRESS

1983

Oxford University Press, Walton Street, Oxford OX2 6DP

London Glasgow New York Toronto
Delhi Bombay Calcutta Madras Karachi
Kuala Lumpur Singapore Hong Kong Tokyo
Nairobi Dar es Salaam Cape Town
Melbourne Auckland
and associates in
Beirut Berlin Ibadan Mexico City Nicosia

British Library Cataloguing in Publication Data
Bradbury, Malcolm
The Modern American Novel.
1. American fiction–19th century–History
and criticism 2. American fiction–20th
century–History and criticism
I. Title
813'. 5'09 PS379
ISBN 0-19-212591-5

Library of Congress Cataloging in Publication Data
Bradbury, Malcolm 1932-
The Modern American Novel. (OPUS)
Bibliography: P. Includes index.
1. American fiction–20th century–History
and criticism. I. Title. II. Series.
PS379.B67 1983 813'.5'09 82-12567
ISBN 0-19-212591-5

Set by Datamove Ltd
Printed in Great Britain by
William Clowes (Beccles) Ltd
Beccles and London

Preface and Acknowledgements

This book covers the American novel from the 1890s, when western fiction saw the first stirrings of the tendency we have come to call 'modernism', to the immediate present, when the talk is of a successor movement we are coming to call 'postmodernism'. Between the two comes a story of enormous development and change, not only in the nature of American fiction but in its importance on the global map of fiction. It is a process not easy to record, since it is made up not just of those larger patterns of movement and counter-movement, influence and reaction, which constitute the history of any serious literary form. Modernity in fiction has taken many shapes and arisen from many artistic conflicts: this is one of the themes of this book. But another is the central role that American writing has played in any adequate conception of the modern novel. That high judgement is itself a modern one – in the 1890s American fiction was still regarded as an offshoot of British fiction; major figures like Herman Melville died in neglect during the decade; a novelist like Henry James preferred to work in England to have access to art's cosmopolitanism. Not until the 1920s did a generation of writers emerge in America – the generation of Hemingway, Fitzgerald, Faulkner, and Dos Passos – whose work seemed to have world impact, creating both a usable present and a sense of a usable past; not until 1930 did the Nobel Prize for Literature go to an American novelist, Sinclair Lewis, with Theodore Dreiser as close contender.

By that time, however, it had come to seem that an old prophecy was fulfilling itself. In 1820 Sydney Smith had asked, in the *Edinburgh Review*, 'Who reads an American book?' Melville was later to reply that one day everyone would, and that, moreover, that book would be a new sort of book, the product of a new nation. It was a prophecy still being asserted in the twentieth century: 'And so I say one can have at any moment in one's life all of English literature inside you and behind you and you do not know if there is going to be any more of it. However very likely there is, there is at any rate going to be more American literature. Very likely.'[1] This is (who else?) Gertrude Stein in 1934, claiming American writing as the truly twentieth-century writing: English writers, she said, had the nineteenth century, when they 'had and told', but the twentieth looked like being one 'too many for them'. By the 1930s, American fiction was thriving and exerting a powerful international influence – on the French novel, for example; by the 1950s it was American fiction that seemed to govern the direction of the contemporary novel. Behind all this there was, of course, a shift in the political as well as the cultural balance of power and superpower; as Gore Vidal once said, writers in powerful countries often win far more attention than they deserve. But it is also true that power, influence, and historical modernity express themselves within the texture of writing; and the fact is that the contemporary influence of American novels reflects an extraordinary range and quality of talent, a force of creation, and a historical intervention which merit close attention. It is also true that fiction from powerful countries frequently manifests an internationalism, a cosmopolitan awareness, arising from its cultural contacts; and this cosmopolitanism accounts for much of the interest of contemporary American fiction.

In the 1950s and before, it was conventional to emphasize the distinctiveness of American fiction, and to stress its degree of separateness from the European tradition. As Richard Chase suggested in a notable study, the reason for the relative neglect of nineteenth-century American fiction was that it diverged from the pre-eminently social and moral direction of European fiction, evolving its own tradition of 'romance', concerning itself less with society and custom than with the natural, the metaphysical, the noumenal. It was, said Leslie Fiedler, eminently a 'gothic' fiction; it displayed, said R. W. B. Lewis, a new world fable of prelapsarian man beginning again, the new Adam in the new Eden, existing not in history but mythical space; and other critics enlarged on these distinctions.[2] Since then, however, criticism has grown more

[1] Gertrude Stein, 'What is English Literature?' (1934), reprinted in Gertrude Stein, *Look At Me Now and Here I Am: Writings and Lectures, 1911–45*, ed. Patricia Meyerowitz (1971).

[2] Richard Chase, *The American Novel and Its Tradition* (1957); Leslie A. Fiedler, *Love and Death in the American Novel* (1960, 1967); R. W. B. Lewis, *The American*

comparative, more concerned with the novel as a form; and this has reminded us that the main movements of the American novel have roughly paralleled the general development of the novel in the west. There have been special American weights and emphases: on transcendental romance in the early nineteenth century; on naturalism in the 1890s and the early twentieth century; on spatial and expressionistic modernism in the 1920s. But what has been crucial is that in American hands the novel has been deeply invigorated as a modern form, and has undergone some of its most striking modern recoveries.

All of which suggests the emphasis of this book, which is written with the comparative perspective much in mind. We may still regard the modern American novel as predominantly a product of the culture out of which it is created, as deriving from a distinct history, ideology, landscape, and cast of mind; we may also regard it as a central and flourishing instance of the novel as a living modern genre. I have sought here to balance the two: to take, so to speak, an approach that comes from American Studies, which attempts to see literature in the context of American history, and relate it to one that comes from comparative literature, which looks at the international relation of literary forms. I am concerned with the modern history of American culture; I am also concerned with the broad evolution of the modern novel as a species. I have told the story in both historical and formal stages, beginning with the radical naturalism and the subjective impressionism of the 1890s, considering the collision of naturalist realism and modernism in the 1910s and 1920s, the attempt to recover proletarian naturalism in the 1930s, and thence to the complex formal directions that have marked and continue to mark the post-war era. I have sought at the same time to look in some detail at individual authors; in case my selectivity seems too great, I have offered at the end of the book a fuller list of the modern American novelists whose work seems to me most significant.[3] I hope this book can be read as a critical record of the achievement of

---

Adam: Innocence, Tragedy and Tradition in the Nineteenth Century (1955); Marius Bewley, *The Eccentric Design: Form in the Classic American Novel* (1959); Richard Poirier, *A World Elsewhere: The Place of Style in American Literature* (1966, 1967); Tony Tanner, *City of Words: American Fiction 1950–1970* (1971).

[3] For much fuller coverage of individual authors, and a vaster map, see volume III, *United States and Latin America*, in *The Penguin Companion to Literature*, ed. Malcolm Bradbury, Eric Mottram, and Jean Franco (1971).

American fiction since the turning-point of the 1890s; I also hope it may contribute to our understanding of the modern novel in general.

There are various acknowledgements to be made. I have drawn somewhat on articles I have previously written: in chapters 1 and 2 on '"Years of the Modern": The Rise of Realism and Naturalism', in volume VIII, *American Literature to 1900*, and 'The American Risorgimento: The Coming of the New Arts', written with David Corker, in volume IX, *American Literature since 1900*, both in the *Sphere History of Literature in the English Language*, ed. Marcus Cunliffe (London: Sphere Books, 1975); in chapter 4, on 'Style of Life, Style of Art and the American Novelist in the 1920s', in *The American Novel and the Nineteen Twenties*, ed. Malcolm Bradbury and David Palmer (Stratford-upon-Avon Studies 13; London: Edward Arnold, 1971); for chapter 6 on 'The Novel' in volume III, *1945–1965*, of *The Twentieth Century Mind*, ed. C. B. Cox and A. E. Dyson (London and New York: Oxford University Press, 1972). Though the borrowings are light, acknowledgements to these editors and publishers are due. I am especially indebted to Catharine Carver for her wise and sensitive editing of these critical fictions. For much help and provocation in thinking about the novel in general, the American novel in particular, I am indebted to many colleagues, students, and friends, notably to Christopher Bigsby, Ellman Crasnow, Guido Almansi, David Lodge, John Fletcher, Jonathan Raban, Haideh Daragahi, Lawrence Levine, Ihab Hassan, Marc Chenetier, Lorna Sage, David Corker and Mas'ud Zaverzadeh, as to the University of East Anglia for much assistance.

Norwich
January 1982

Contents

1 Naturalism and Impressionism: The 1890s   1

2 Modernity and Modernism: 1900–1912   20

3 Artists and Philistines: 1912–1920   42

4 Art-Style and Life-Style: The 1920s   57

5 Realism and Surrealism: The 1930s   96

6 Liberal and Existential Imaginations: The 1940s and 1950s   126

7 Postmoderns and Others: The 1960s and 1970s   156

   The American Novel Since 1890: A list of major works   187

   Select Bibliography   196

   Index   201

1 Naturalism and Impressionism: The 1890s

I'm not in a very good mood with 'America' myself. It seems to be the most grotesquely illogical thing under the sun; and I suppose I love it less because it won't let me love it more. I should hardly like to trust pen and ink with all the audacity of my social ideas; but after fifty years of optimistic content with 'civilization' and its ability to come out all right in the end, I now abhor it, and feel that it is coming out all wrong in the end, unless it bases itself anew on a real equality. Meanwhile I wear a fur-lined coat, and live on all the luxury my money can buy.

W. D. Howells, letter to Henry James, 1888

His mind took a mechanical but firm impression, so that afterward everything was pictured and explained to him, save why he himself was there.

Stephen Crane, *The Red Badge of Courage* (1895)

I

In 1893 the American historian Henry Adams, sitting down amid the machinery on display at the World's Columbian Exposition, held in the bursting new skyscraper city of Chicago, felt himself to be confronted by a whole new set of powers. The late-nineteenth-century American wonders could be seen outside: Chicago itself, a village of 250 inhabitants in 1833, was now America's second city, railhead of the plains, hogbutcher of the world, its population over a million. Two American motions met here, the westering motion towards the frontier, the urbanizing motion towards the city; not only European immigrants but migrants off the land, pushed off their homesteads by recurrent agricultural depression, mechaniza-tion, and mortgages flooded into Chicago's factories, stockyards, and ghettos and intensified its social problems. The signs of mechanical development and innovation were everywhere apparent; indeed it was the technological marvels on display, with so much else, at the

Exposition that made Adams sit down in what he called 'helpless reflection', and consider the processes driving American culture, the culture of a nation that seemed to many the image of the modernizing future. 'Chicago', Adams wrote in his ironic, self-doubting, third-person autobiography, *The Education of Henry Adams* (1907) 'asked in 1893 for the first time the question of whether the American people knew where they were driving. . . . Chicago was the first expression of American thought as a unity.' In Adams's view, a new process of history was evolving, with America at its centre; new theories – based on laws of accelerating forces, exponential development, the process of entropy – were needed to explain it. And this process overwhelmed not only the past but past world-views and forms of education, including – hence the irony of his title – Henry Adams's own.

Apocalyptic feelings and rising pessimism about the direction of history were common enough in the west as the turn of the century approached. They were accelerated by the Darwinian legacy, which threatened alike religion and humanism, engendered greater concern with science and social management, and intensified the sense of victimization before dominant processes. Such feelings were particularly strong in the United States, where modernizing was accelerating, technological evolution advancing, and social stress rising at an unprecedented rate. At the same time there were great new excitements. The United States had come to being as a nation little more than a century before; now it was outstripping Great Britain and Germany combined in industrial production, and its new frontiers were technology and the city itself. Pessimism and optimism combined in Adams's response to what he came to call the new 'multiverse': *The Education of Henry Adams*, a novel-like work of extraordinary images, alienation, and self-effacement, displays a deep sense of historical displacement, and is a remarkable endeavour to bridge the space between the world's augmenting scientific and material energy and the capacities, or incapacities, of the human mind to master and unify the processes it had itself released. Adams's point was that changes in the historical process generated pressure on consciousness, that new forms of education were needed to grasp the conditions of contemporary life. As science and Darwin threatened the old teleological order, and socialism the lore of liberal individualism, so psychology and behaviourism were challenging the solidity of the social and the moral self. The structures of expression, the arts of consciousness, were put under extreme strain; the tone shapes the anxious formal structure of Adams's book. It was part of a general epistemological and aesthetic upheaval in all the artistic forms, reshaping not just their subject-matter but their very mode of composition. The last years of the century generated new styles, forms, and movements in the arts, much as they did new technologies and scientific and social theories.

Appropriately, writers too came to the Chicago Exposition, like Hamlin Garland, one of a new generation of scientific realists (he called himself a 'veritist') who were now beginning to dominate the novel. In the changing new society, the old cultured patriciate of the East Coast was fading; Garland saw himself as a modern populist and determinist, reaching towards new geographical as well as literary frontiers, and he looked to the Middle West and West for a new American writing, observing the contrast between the America of plain and prairie and that of technology, unplanned capitalism, new science, and skyscrapers. He thus expressed many of the new notes emerging in the novel – a form which, in America as in Europe, had been steadily moving towards increased realism and naturalism. From the upheavals of 1848 onward, European fiction had been growing ever more representational and attentive to commonplace contemporary life; in America too the symbolist or transcendental romance of Poe, Hawthorne, and Melville had given way to a realism of democratic scepticism, concern with social problems, and fascination with the ordinary life of the expanding continent. 'Is it true? – true to the motives, the impulses, the principles that shape the life of actual men and women?' asked the novelist William Dean Howells, active importer of European realist ideas. For such ideas were, he stressed, essentially democratic and American, and they turned the writer towards the local and the familiar: the evolution of the novel was 'first the provincial, then the national, then the universal'. And, since the Civil War, realism of this kind had prospered in many guises – in the local-colour realism of Edward Eggleston's *A Hoosier Schoolmaster* (1871), or Sarah Orne Jewett's *The Country of the Pointed Firs* (1896); in the novel of progressive social indignation, like Henry Adams's own *Democracy* (1880) or Garland's own *A Spoil of Office* (1892); in the Western vernacular of writers like Bret Harte and Mark Twain.

But now, in Europe and America, even the novel of realism was in question, as old realistic ideas of individualism came under pressure from new world-views. Fiction was becoming less the expression of a common reality all could recognize, more a response to the uncommon realities and systems that lay behind modern life and called for revelation. New modes of discourse, more scientific and systematic, drawn from sociology and biology, suggested the displacement of the individual from the centre of the universe; new formal techniques, more aesthetic and subjective, drawn from a new aesthetics, emphasized the importance of form and impression. Adams in Chicago saw a world of new powers; Garland, speaking in the same place, saw the need for a progressive new form of the novel. In both men, we can see the old ideas and ideals of nineteenth-century thought and art coming into question, and a grasping, in the transitional and *fin de siècle* mood, of those new notions of man and consciousness, those new structures of artistic expression that would transform the twentieth-century novel.

II

As the 1890s started, three novelists dominated American fiction in reputation and influence. All had started their work in or just after the Civil War; all represented different aspects of the realist tradition; and all now seemed to enter an artistic crisis in the new atmosphere of the end of the century. Mark Twain, America's most powerful novelist, had begun as a frontier writer, his vernacular prose insistently mocking the genteel pressures, the formal styles and ideals of 'civilization'. His major novels were written on the East Coast after the war, but they explore the world of the frontier West before it. His main subjects were the Mississippi Valley in that river's key years as the central American artery, and then the move-ment west – themes that carried enormous moral force, for they evoked the innocent morality of a life beyond social rule and genteel convention. The central book was *The Adventures of Huckleberry Finn* (1884), according to Hemingway the book with which American fiction started – a fundamental myth of self-creating American freedom, a vernacular vision of spontaneous open morality won on a river raft despite the enslaving pressures of life beyond. But Twain wrote too of post-war America, in a mixture of violent satire (*The Gilded Age*, 1873, with Charles Dudley Warner) and celebration of American technological potential. The ambivalent tone is summed up in *A Connecticut Yankee in King Arthur's Court* (1889),

which displaces a Hartford, Connecticut, machine-shop superinten-
dent back in time to that late-Victorian wonderland, sixth-century
Camelot, to bring to its world of feudalism, monarchy, and slavery
the modern American blessings – democracy, technology, know-
how, advertising. But the book ends in horrifying irony: Hank's
machinery outruns its creator and murderously destroys all life with
a mechanical holocaust, in a dark predictive image of modernity.
That darkening vision spread through Twain's work of the 1890s
and, though often explained as the result of personal crises, it clearly
also derived from the intellectual crisis of the age – his growing
doubt about the power of 'innocent' morality, his reading in the new
texts of determinism. *Pudd'nhead Wilson* (1894) reverts to the classic
subject-matter, Mississippi Valley life before the Civil War, but sees
it now through the eyes of 1890s pessimism and determinism: an old
story-book fable of two children of different backgrounds exchanged
in the cradle is turned into a plot of devastating ironies. One child is
white and 'free', the other 'black' and a slave; Twain develops the
plot to question all notions of freedom, showing that his characters
are all slaves to something, to heredity or environment, and cannot
assert an independent identity or sustain a moral intent. And that
bitter irony dominates the yet bleaker works that follow: *The Man
Who Corrupted Hadleyburg* (1900), the philosophical tract *What Is
Man?* (1906), the unfinished *The Mysterious Stranger* (posthumous,
1916).

'I have lost my pride in [Man] & can't write gaily nor praisefully
about him anymore,' Twain wrote in 1899 to William Dean
Howells, another Midwesterner who had penetrated the East Coast
citadel by becoming editor of the *Atlantic Monthly*; there he urged
his case for an egalitarian American realism which dealt with the
'smiling aspects' of American life. Howells became, indeed, the
exemplary American realist, producing something like a novel a
year, from morally acute, photographically precise works dealing
with what he called 'the life of small things' to Utopian romances.
To a degree rare in American fiction, his characters were members of
family and community, living out ordinary lives amid the contingency and moral pressure of place, time, and custom. His best-
known book, *The Rise of Silas Lapham* (1885), deals with a simple
Boston paint manufacturer who rises in the post-Civil War industrial
boom, but is drawn into corruption. Scruples intervene, and his
social and business success alike collapse; but his social fall is his

moral rise, a contribution to society's ethical economy. Increasingly, though, Howells's work, like Twain's, revealed a deep ambiguity in its treatment of commercial, corporate, technological America. Thus Lapham's 'virtue' is rooted in his pre-Civil War ethic of agrarian individualism and simplicity; and his failure in the America of trusts and corporatism suggests what powerful pressures threatened Howells's world of domestic decency. Like Twain, then, Howells grew pessimistic, especially after the condemnation of the Haymarket Riot anarchists in 1886. In 1889 he moved from Boston, the old literary capital, to New York City, reflecting this in a new kind of novel, *A Hazard of New Fortunes* (1890), about New York as the modern technological city where social goodwill is collapsing, strife and strikes split the classes, and the form of the novel as he had used it is itself seen under threat. The task of writing about the new world is hence handed on to his character Kendricks, who claims that 'the great American novel, if true, must be incredible'. Howells saw his mode of social realism declining, supported the younger naturalists, and wrote of his despair to the third survivor of realism, Henry James.

James was the most cosmopolitan of the realists, and had moved to realism's fountainhead, in Europe. Earlier, James's expatriation had seemed to Howells an evasion of realism's task, an escape to Europe's 'romance'. In fact James's choice of milieu arose from his need for a dense social order that would set art into motion; and his 'romance' was managed through a realist perception refined by contact with Flaubert, Turgenev, George Eliot. His classic requirement became 'solidity of specification', meaning not a reportorial but a registrative view of art. Art's task was not to record but to *make* life; reality was a constructed, not a recorded, thing; it was in the inherent tension of the novel between empiricism and idealism, realism and romance, naturalism's 'magnificent treadmill of the pigeon-holed and documented' and romance's 'balloon of experience', that the form found itself. This was James's quest of the 1870s and 1880s; but by the beginning of the 1890s he too was beginning to feel under pressure, and he replied to Howells's pessimism with his own. 'I *have* felt, for a long time past,' he wrote in 1895, 'that I have fallen on evil days – every sign or symbol of being in the least *wanted*, anywhere by anyone, having so utterly failed.' Again, his crisis was partly personal, but it was also philosophical and aesthetic; however, for all his doubts, James responded to the aesthetic transformations of the 1890s, and made an extraordinary and innovative recovery. By the time of this letter he was already on a new path that would lead, with *The Spoils of Poynton* and *What Maisie Knew* in 1897, to the remarkable work of his late phase – work in which consciousness severs itself from the world's materiality, changing the entire grammar of fiction. By the century's turn, James was ready, in his essay 'The Future of Fiction', to suggest that the novel might reach a new level of self-realization: 'It has arrived, in truth, the novel, late at self-consciousness, but it has done its utmost ever since to make up for lost opportunities,' he noted, pointing, undoubtedly, to the new achievements that had grown in Europe and America during the nineteenth century's last decade.

III

In America, these ferments are most visible in the work of the remarkable new generation of writers who began to emerge in the 1890s and took on strong character as a generation – partly because they shared aesthetic theories and preoccupations, partly because they shared the tutelage of Howells, partly because most had brief careers and early deaths. Often presented by the critics as strongly American, working, as Alfred Kazin put it, 'on native grounds', they were in fact much influenced by European theories of naturalism – above all those of Emile Zola, who in 1879 had set down his theory of the naturalist novel in *Le Roman expérimental*. For Zola, the word 'experimental' had scientific analogies; the novelist's task was to undertake a social or scientific study, recording facts, styles and systems of behaviour, living conditions, the workings of institutions, and deducing the underlying processes of environmental, genetic, and historical-evolutionary development. Naturalism was thus realism scientized, systematized, taken finally beyond realist principles of fidelity to common experience or of humanistic exploring of individual lives within the social and moral web of existence.

In fact naturalism was, by the 1890s, beginning to decline in Europe, disturbed by new decadent, impressionist, aesthetic tendencies that seemed in tune with contemporary psychology. However in the United States, where technological systems seemed to prevail, evolutionary hopes were strong, the laws of social struggle were apparent, and social Darwinism was a popular creed, it acquired a special dominance. Another reason for the appeal of naturalism, with its scientific, often ironic world-view, was the fascination of the new American cityscape itself. For if the novelist was analogous to the sociologist, so was he to the journalist, the hard-boiled city room reporter or the crusading investigator of social facts, the man who walked in the city, observed, explored, exposed, the man who had been there, in the place of experience – the ghetto, the stockyard, the apartment block, the battlefield, the social jungle. He was like the new photographer, with his hand-held camera, catching sudden vignettes of life. But he was also like the modern painter, preoccupied with shades and acts of perception, the blur and impression of fleeting modern urban reality, the strange angles of vision needed to take in the world of manifold contrasts. Indeed the analogy with painting drew the American naturalist novelists back towards the problems of form and subjectivity which also haunted the 1890s; the tense relation between art and life, impressionism and naturalism, became a dominant theme in the writing and criticism of the most impressive writers of the decade.

These young writers had been bred amid the transitions which ran so powerfully through nineteenth-century American society, making past accountings of experience seem incomplete. Thus Hamlin Garland had been born on the economically depressed prairie, in the 'middle border' area of Wisconsin, Iowa, South Dakota, moved to Boston to immerse himself in new social, political, and economic theories, turning to evolutionary thought to explain the bleak world he had left behind him, then returned to Chicago and the West around 1893. Frank Norris was born in Chicago itself, where a new school of urban sociologists was exploring the hard world of immigrant conflict and social deprivation, and where a similar school of urban novelists would follow. He had bohemian leanings, went to Paris as an art student, and returned with Zola's novels to Berkeley, in California, another new centre of literary activity. And it was a similar bohemian revolt that led Stephen Crane to break with the genteel morality of his religious background – he was born in New Jersey, the son of a Methodist minister – and move to New York, to the 'mean streets' of the Bowery and the Tenderloin, aiming both to report the facts and refine his aesthetic sensibilities. For these writers, confronting a new American social experience, naturalism offered a view which questioned the conviction that man was a conscious and rational creature, that happiness is secured by virtuous behaviour, that the landscape of familiar experience offered all the moral pointers men needed. With this view, they could observe mass and mechanism, touch on unexplored areas of society, the life of working people, the problems of cities, the operations of social and genetic patterns. Their writing drew on the new 'brute fact' of American life; hence their insistence that literature derived from life rather than form. They turned to consciously modern settings – the shock city, the West, the ghettos, depressed homesteads, the sky-scrapers, corporations and department stores – and period themes – the split between culture and materiality, idealism and underlying economic and sexual drives. Naturalism thus became a way of dealing with the fact of a modern America largely unexplored by genteel awareness; but it was also a formal obsession, part of the decade's aesthetic self-consciousness, not merely – as Zola himself emphasized – a reporting system, but an artistic movement.

A conflict between the passion to get at life and the pursuit of form can lead to a dualistic vision. Strikingly, for a generation ostensibly given over to 'life', most of these writers produced works of aesthetic speculation. Norris, in his essays in *The Responsibilities of the Novelist* (1903), urged that art yield to life, 'the honest rough-and-tumble, Anglo-Saxon knockabout that for us means life'; he equally emphasized his 'naturalist' sources and stressed that naturalism was not a mode of report but of romance, requiring scale, exaggeration, and symbolic motifs. Hamlin Garland displayed a similar tension in the essays of his aptly titled *Crumbling Idols* (1894), where he defined his own tendency, 'veritism', as a reaction both against 'romance' and against Zola's sexual explicitness and lack of idealism. Veritism was a form of local realism, dealing with the near-by and the probable; but it also was a form of 'impressionism', a formal response 'based on the moment of experience, actively felt and immediately expressed'. Stephen Crane, a greater artist if a weaker theorist, was obsessed with similar problems. Behind his stories and his one great novel, *The Red Badge of Courage* (1895), the naturalist pieties are evident. In the presentation copies of *Maggie: A Girl of the Streets* (1893), his first published fiction, printed at his own expense, he wrote that it tried to show 'that environment is a tremendous thing in the world and frequently shapes lives regardless'. His settings were the classic ones of naturalism: the big city, the battle-field, man exposed and adrift in a nature that is 'indifferent, flatly indifferent', as he puts it in his fine story 'The Open Boat' (1897). Crane wrote with persistent naturalist assumptions about the failure of religious and genteel explanations of life, and about the ironic status of the human agent. Yet that irony is also a *style*, a form of extreme artistic self-consciousness; and he always stressed that the writer's essential property was his distinctive 'impression' – that key art-word of the period. Like all the better American writers influenced by naturalist thought, Crane in his work mixes an encounter with the 'real thing' – the place, the fact, the experience – with an insistence on the mode by which it is perceived and written about. Appropriately, his move to the garrets, tenements, and brothels of New York City was a move to the two cities dominating the times: the naturalist one of struggles, problems, and conflicts, the decadent bohemia of evanescence and artifice.

IV

For the modern reader it is surely Stephen Crane who best exemplifies the volatile mixture of American fiction in the 1890s. He aptly called his early writings – his initial 'city-sketches', collected in 1900, and his two key urban novellas, *Maggie: A Girl of the Streets: A Story of New York* and its companion piece, *George's Mother* (1896) – 'experiments in misery': the misery is real, but so is the tone of formal experiment. *Maggie* and *George's Mother* are formal naturalism, and take their plots from Victorian melodrama, using methods and tones close to parody. *Maggie* is the story of an innocent – indeed over-innocent – girl from the tenements of Rum Alley who glimpses larger horizons than those among which she lives, becomes sexually attracted to a flashy young man who seems to offer them, and is ruined when he discards her; she then turns to prostitution, suffers moral condemnation from those around her, and kills herself. *George's Mother* is another apparently monitory fable, about a young man from the same tenement who rejects his mother's morality and temperance attitudes, turns to the exciting city, finds its saloons, sinks into alcoholism, and finally fails to register the 'reality' of his mother's death, as he concentrates on realities outside. The stories are conventional, but Crane deflates their sentimental potential with insistent irony, for the lessons in morality occur inside the stories, and are part of the damage. As for the city itself, dominating both stories, it is duplicitous. It is the Darwinian jungle, where, in *Maggie*, the woman of 'brilliance and audacity' rules, snatching Maggie's lover from her and then discarding him for better, where traffic snarls on the streets, and children fight animalistically for victory in tenement yards; it is also the place of dream, wealth, indulgence, the social theatre where ever fresh roles are offered; George longs to 'comprehend it completely, that he might walk understandingly in its great marvels, its mightiest march of life, its sin'. Crane's naturalism is not unwavering: Maggie, inconsistent with her environment, is an innocent romantic who has 'blossomed in a mud-puddle' with none of the dirt of Rum Alley in her veins. What she is consistent with is Crane's need for irony, his devotion to unexpected juxtapositions, his contrastive impressionism. Indeed his characters are impressionists of a sort, living by small acts of consciousness among contingent awarenesses. Over them is the larger condition: the city, dominant, gives rise to their competitive struggles, their fleeting mode of consciousness, their moral void. When George's mother dies in front of him, an 'endless roar, the eternal tramp of the marching city, came mingled with strange cries'. Beyond that is a larger condition still: that of Crane's distinctively toned prose. Concerned to disestablish the centrality of character, to tell the story obliquely, through scenes that pose contrasts and show the ironic displacement of mankind, stylistically he commands every situation.

The short story and the novella, dominant forms in the 1890s, yielded well to this mode of naturalistic impressionism. In *The Red Badge of Courage*, where Crane works at novel length, his problems clearly intensify. Shifting from the city to another naturalist locale, the battlefield, he set the book in the American Civil War, which he had not known; as he explained, 'Of course I have never been in a battle ... I wrote it intuitively. ...' But war was a key naturalist image of life; it was real and existential, a place where human delusions of heroism and power were tested, a field of struggle and competition, and it involved the ironic nullification of the human self, the process of mortal reduction. Crane focused the book on the battle itself: political issues are absent, the characters have designations rather than names (the tall soldier, etc.), and individuals are swamped in the experiential texture. The central character, Henry Fleming, is named only once; otherwise he is called 'The Youth'. The book consists of his impressions over two days of fighting; events and objects become the correlatives of his mood. Henry becomes, in fact, the exemplary experiencer of war as embroilment in flux, movement, sensation, colour, fear and physical pain; the sequence of impressions itself nullifies his initial desire to perform a heroic role. In a sense, the technique itself overwhelms Henry's heroic self-image. His commanding consciousness dissolves; war's impact on him is that of sensation, producing a mechanical response. He encounters the brute fact of death, the indifference of nature; he is pushed to flee, then pushed back into battle again, acquiring, accidentally, his red badge, the initiatory wound, less a mark of heroism than entry into a modern world of exposure. The wound is a token of arbitrary and nihilistic reality, but also a sign of complicity with that reality; Henry ends the book 'a man', an initiate in experience.

The ending is troublesome to many readers (as indeed it was to Crane, who rewrote it several times) because its language suggests that there is a potential for heroism even in the indifferent natural-istic world; Henry leaves the battlefield in tune with 'a world for him', and even indifferent nature seems to agree: 'Over the river a golden ray of sun came through the host of leaden rain clouds.' Given nature's performance in the book, this can be read as irony; what it rather points to is an ambiguity in Crane's impressionism. *The Red Badge* is very much about reality as immediate and hostile, assaulting the formal organization of consciousness, displacing its function into acts of perception, instinct, reaction, immersion, withdrawal. Crane marvellously realizes through Henry the visual instantaneousness of an exposed and naked world:

It seemed to the youth that he saw everything. Each blade of grass was bold and clear. He thought he was aware of every change in the thin, transparent vapour that floated idly by in sheets. The brown or gray trunks of the trees showed each roughness of their surfaces. And the men of the regiment, with their starting eyes and sweating faces, running madly, or falling, as if thrown headlong, to queer, heaped-up corpses – all were comprehended.

Impressionism here moves towards abstraction, posing the scene, making the youth a film-like camera, his angle of vision always relative. The problem is whether impressionism can yield up a logic in experience, a hidden order behind events.

Crane is symbolist enough to want this, desiring, he said, a 'hidden long logic' in his stories. In fact the extraordinary quality of the novel lies in its capacity to present consciousness in half-apprehending motion through a shimmering world of experience: this is the heart of its visionary naturalism. But its symbolism remains less than a logic of experience discovered, turned into wisdom. Such complexities linked Crane's work with that of Conrad's and James's, and indeed in 1897 he moved to England as an expatriate, to be hailed by Conrad as a 'complete impressionist', while Wells noted his crucial selectivity, 'the expression in art of certain enormous repudiations'. Crane was drawn to such company, but also to the life of action; he became, like so many in this decade, a war correspondent, covering the Spanish-American war and the Graeco-Turkish war. His work, caught between two possibilities, varied much in quality, but he is important to his successors and to readers now because he walked the difficult edge of modern writing, trying to decipher the character of acts of consciousness, and processes of artistic perception, in a world from which most of the numinous external significances, the divine signatures of teleology, had been withdrawn.

Hamlin Garland's work shows related tensions; it is significant that we remember him now not for the political novels like *A Spoil of Office* but for the short stories in the two volumes *Main-Travelled Roads: Six Mississippi Valley Stories* (1891; extended 1893) and *Prairie Folks* (1893). Garland's stories are indeed 'impressionist', lyric pieces, portraits of homesteaders and prairie people, trapped in primitive miseries and punitive economic conditions, left behind in America's shift from being a rural to an urban nation. The city shimmers on the edge of these pieces, a force both emancipating and corrupting, a new chance but a threat to the stubborn individuality of the landsmen. Often the focus is on a revenant, a version of Garland himself, returned from the city to survey the roots left behind. But though they deal with social issues the stories avoid overdirect commentary; they are presented through the impression and the tactics of contrast. Indeed compositional artistry turns the circumstantial and deterministic into grounds for wistful hope and expectation – a theme hard to sustain at length, though Garland tries successfully in *Rose of Dutcher's Coolly* (1895). Later, passing beyond his 'veritism', he wrote sentimental Western romances; but the lyrical precision of the earlier stories is his great achievement.

Crane and Garland both qualified and amended naturalism, treating it more as a world-view than a necessary form. But there was one powerful and positive exponent of Zolaesque naturalism in the 1890s, Frank Norris. The essays of *The Responsibilities of the Novelist* set out the most coherent case for the relevance of naturalist

method to contemporary American life and consciousness, presenting it less as a form of social reportage, or an entirely deterministic
world-view, than as a form of modern epic, a drama of the people
which encompassed 'the vast, the monstrous, the tragic', reached
into the unconscious parts of life ('the unplumbed depths of the
human heart, and the mystery of sex'), the great evolutionary cycles
and systems of history, nature, and community. Norris was no
complex theoretician, but he laid down lore that helped establish the
notion of the panoramic popular epic, the Great American Novel,
which preoccupied so many of his successors. His two first ventures
in naturalism came when, in 1894, he went from Berkeley to Lewis
Gates's writing class at Harvard, where he worked on *McTeague: A
Story of San Francisco*, published in 1899, and *Vandover and the
Brute*. *Vandover*, left unfinished at his death, lost in the San
Francisco earthquake, recovered and completed by his brother, and
published in 1914, is naturalism at its most literary, a *fin de siècle* tale
about the artist and his double, a decadent fable about the degeneration of an artist into lycanthropy. Here is the '*bête humaine*' which
so preoccupied the new thought; a much more fundamental and
original treatment of it comes in *McTeague*, probably Norris's most
powerful book. Firmly based in San Francisco poor life, set in a
world of deprivation, immigration, and urbanization, it follows his
own prescription that 'The novel of California must now be a novel
of city life'. But it is also the story of a naturalist process, a
movement towards degeneration; in it, an evolving chain of events,
once set in motion, releases underlying forces, energies, and conflicts
– especially those that come from the primitive, secreted desires of
men and women, and their atavistic sources in the life of the race and
the herd.

The characters are conceived as primitives. McTeague is a San
Francisco dentist come from the mining camps, without a diploma;
his qualification is strength, and he is massive, strong and sluggish, a
dormant beast whose only pleasures are those of eating, smoking,
sleeping, and playing his concertina. 'Mysterious instincts' attract
him to one of his patients, Trina, a girl from a money-obsessed
immigrant Swiss peasant background. Their courtship and marriage
'awaken' his animal sexuality and her avarice, the subconscious
rhythms of their lives, and fate then reinforces their atavism. Trina
wins, appropriately enough in a fatalistic novel, a lottery;
McTeague, denounced by a jealous rival, Marcus, for practising

without a diploma, is deprived of work, his strength turning back to brutality just as Trina's peasant carefulness turns to greed. Functionless, he steals his wife's money, runs away, then returns for the rest of her savings, and is now so debased that he kills her for them. With his canary, he flees back to the mining camps, where his strength is natural, and where his inner instincts lead him to gold. In Death Valley, Marcus, after the gold and the reward, finds him and handcuffs him; McTeague kills him, and the plot of fate and the plot of symbols coalesce, the novel closing with McTeague handcuffed to a corpse, his double, and 'stupidly looking around him, now at the dead horizon, now at the ground, now at the half-dead canary chittering feebly in its little gilt prison'.

It is a plot of clear naturalism, setting its hypotheses about atavistic instincts and desires to work, and pursuing them through an enlarging, expressionistic system in which fate, chance, and process conspire. 'Suddenly the animal stirred and woke,' Norris writes of the moment when McTeague is first tempted by the sight of Trina as she lies helpless under gas in his dental chair, 'the evil instincts that in him were so close to the surface leaped into life, clamoring and shouting.' If crude, this is powerful; Norris, in the language of naturalism, is striving to express the deep undercurrents of sexual energies and unconscious forces for which Freud would shortly provide a deeper explanation and a discourse. Norris is evidently after the psycho-social sum of his characters, in whom culture and nature, the aesthetic and the atavistic, habitually contend; in this sense they are the agents of forces which they do not control. This underlying subject pushes Norris towards a typological, a symbolist, a mythic dimension. And the book's dominant symbol is gold itself, the California metal; when Trina presses coins against her body in bed, so substituting money for sexuality, one desire for another like it, or when McTeague hungers for a gold tooth that will advertise his dentistry parlour, they join a vocabulary of desire and participate in a symbolic system which links and structures the entire novel. *Vandover* and *McTeague* are American variants of pure naturalism, psychologically intense, socially alert, symbolically energetic.

After these early enterprises in bleak naturalism, Norris became a professional journalist and editor. He reported the Spanish-American war for *McClure's*, and turned for a while to more popular romance, to novels in which love and a mild racism replaced his naturalist principles. Then, around the turn of the century, he ventured into a new naturalist stage – less bleakly despairing, more clearly reflecting progressive and muckraking sympathies. He conceived, on the model of Zola's *Rougon-Macquart* cycle, an epic trilogy which would be focused on the cultivation, marketing, and consumption of America's great crop, wheat, 'straight naturalism with all the guts I can get into it'. A move away from the psychological naturalism of *McTeague* towards a sociological and evolutionary theme, concerned with underlying forces in life which are no longer guided by the *bête humaine* but by the outer force of nature, it was to cover the spatial map of America and Europe, the great global movements of life forces, biological and economic. Norris thus conceived not just one form of naturalism, but two: one concentrated, despairing, filled with end-of-the-century unease about human victimization, the other sprawling, an optimistic epic of American energies and resources, filled with progressive expectations and biological vitalism. In the event, however, only two volumes of the 'Wheat Trilogy' were written; before it was finished Norris died suddenly in 1902, from peritonitis. *The Octopus* appeared in 1901, *The Pit* posthumously in 1903, and the third volume, *The Wolf*, dealing with Europe, was never written.

None the less, we can clearly see the nature of the conception. Central to *The Octopus* is a figure of the writer, the poet Presley, who goes out to California to write a 'True Romance' about the Spanish-American past, but instead finds himself throwing bombs in defence of the farmers of the San Joaquin valley, a gigantic land space intruded on by the trusts and the railroads, who are bringing in industrial methods and weakening the farmers by unjust freight tariffs. This is the new True Romance, of modern forces and powers, and of the natural processes of the land – the seeding of the earth, the growing of the wheat crop, the large cyclical motions of the universe. Norris displays his reportorial skills and his indignation, but he also shows exploiters and exploited alike subject to this indurant process, which is ultimately transcendent and displaces the deaths, the greeds and selfishnesses of the human story: the wheat, 'that mighty world-force, that nourisher of nations, wrapped in Nirvanic calm, indifferent to the human swarms, moves onward in its appointed grooves,' displaying that 'all things, surely, inevitably, resistlessly work together for good'. While *The Octopus* deals with the natural landscape of this oceanic vitalism, *The Pit* turns to the railhead of it all, Chicago itself, where, around the wheat-trading 'pit' at the Board of Trade, another epic adventure, that of American business, is taking place. Norris, like some of his naturalist successors, recognizes the figure of the businessman as the modern American hero, and here he explores the warfare in the national existence between the material and the ideal, between economic energies and emotional and aesthetic ones, between commerce and culture, men and women. Again, however, the experiences of individual life – its heroisms, romances, failures, injustices, tragedies – are aspects of larger cosmic cycles which may swamp the individual but nourish the race. Thus, apart from its political, muckraking side, Norris's work activates the American sense that great and noble powers work in the universe, powers which sometimes have a malign face but a grand indifference that finally works for human destiny.

Norris was a novelist both of mixed attitudes and mixed gifts, and his work varied uneasily between popular romance and theoretical naturalism. Yet he is a central figure in the late-nineteenth-century transformation of American fiction; something of his importance can be seen in the transition of a metaphor. 'Nature was, then,' Presley thinks in *The Octopus*, 'a gigantic engine, a vast cyclopean power, huge, terrible, a leviathan with a heart of steel, knowing no compunction, no forgiveness, no tolerance; crushing out the human atom standing in its way, with nirvanic calm.' The world of nature, in which earlier American writers had found an image of extra-social freedom and transcendence, a life in myth and space, was itself now incorporated into the world of the machine that was once set against it. For Norris it was an ambiguous machine: it drives McTeague to his death, it nourishes the race. From this you might derive the optimistic biologism of a John Steinbeck, or the dark aggression in nature that lies behind Ernest Hemingway's world of war and slaughter. Norris's work, certainly, marked the end of an old liberal pastoral, for now nature too was a working process, just as naturalism was now a key part of American literary perception.

V

The fiction of the 1890s creates a new mood in the novel because it was a fiction of that which had been hidden and suppressed. It released into the novel's discourse a vision of the underlying processes men now found in the world, of the conditions and determinants that structured genetic, biological, and social life, of the patterns and instincts that lay within or beneath consciousness. New themes, groups, areas of life begin to be dealt with: in the immigrant novel and the Jewish novel, like Abraham Cahan's *Yekl: A Tale of the New York Ghetto* (1896); in Black fiction, like Paul Laurence Dunbar's *The Uncalled* (1898), about a Black minister losing his faith and convictions in the mess of the modern city and the world of indifference; in the novel of female consciousness striving to break out of the prison of gentility. In Kate Chopin's notable *The Awakening* (1899), a well-to-do and intelligent New Orleans wife, Edna Pontellier, who comes to sense the needs and hidden forces that lie behind the polite fiction of marriage and social life, follows the path of her emotional awakening to her final self-abnegation. Similarly, in Harold Frederic's *The Damnation of Theron Ware* (1896), a minister trapped in the hypocrisy and gentility of small-town life tries to move, unsuccessfully, into a more secular but above all a more aesthetic world, a world of greater emotional wholeness.

The same quest for wholeness is visible in fiction itself, as novels seek to move beyond realism towards some larger concept of form. Some writers moved from naturalism to aestheticism: Henry Harland began, in the 1880s, writing realistic novels of New York ghetto life, like *Mrs Peixada* (1886); he then moved to London, joined bohemia, edited the *Yellow Book*, and began writing exotic, decadent historical romances set in Europe, in which, said Henry James, 'cardinals are a part of the furniture.' Henry Blake Fuller produced, in *The Cliff-Dwellers* (1893) and *With the Procession* (1895), two remarkable novels of Chicago realism; he also wrote high-toned European historical romances of an aesthetic-decadent kind: *The Chevalier of Pensieri Vani* (1890), *The Châtelaine of La Trinité* (1892). Lafcadio Hearn turned to Japan to catch at the fleeting aesthetic moment; at a more popular level, the romance novel, celebrated by Norris, practised by writers like Richard Harding Davis and Winston S. Churchill, was an enormous success. The oscillation between realism and romance, materialism and idealist fantasy, echoed the split in American culture observed by George Santayana, between idealism and realism. It was the split, too, explored by the new American philosophy of pragmatism, which also attempted to heal the division between consciousness and action, between intransitive and transitive being.

The American novelists of the 1890s seem so strongly a generation in part because so many of them died young – Crane, at twenty-nine, on a health trip to Germany; Harold Frederic, at forty-two, an expatriate in England; Frank Norris at thirty-two. Kate Chopin died, a neglected writer, in 1904, Paul Laurence Dunbar, the Black poet who had brought new tones to Black fiction, in 1906. Something of the decade's ferment seems to die too as the century turns, and yet there is an evident deposit of influence. It pointed, in one direction, towards the enlargement of naturalism as a native American philosophy, a form of positivism consonant with American evolution and above all the nation's new movement into the century of the machine, the city, and the struggles of groups and masses; in the other, towards consciousness less as process than as subjective and aesthetic awareness, consciousness as the flux of mind that stirred in the face of the new naturalist world, and as the pressure of the arts toward form. And these signals and preoccupations were to shape American fiction in the years that followed.

2 Modernity and Modernism 1900-1912

The child born in 1900 would, then, be born into a new world which would not be a unity but a multiple. Adams tried to imagine it, and an education that would fit it. He found himself in a land where no one had ever penetrated before; where order was an accidental relation obnoxious to nature; artificial compulsion imposed on motion; against which every free energy of the universe revolted; and which, being merely occasional, resolved back into anarchy at last. He could not deny that the law of the new multiverse explained much that had been most obscure. . . .

Henry Adams, *The Education of Henry Adams* (1907)

Henry James is a combination of two ways of writing and that makes him a general a general who does something. Listen to it.

Gertrude Stein, 'Henry James' (1933)

I

In 1900, as the century turned, Henry Adams attended another major exhibition, the Great Exposition in Paris; Paris, he explained, completed what Chicago had begun. In the intervening seven years, a new world had come: in 1893 Roentgen's X-rays had been discovered, in 1898 radium, 'that metaphysical bomb'; the automobile had become 'a nightmare at a hundred kilometers an hour'. At the Exposition Adams found himself, he said, 'lying in the Gallery of Machines. . ., his historical neck broken by the sudden irruption of forces totally new.' What above all the Gallery displayed was the 'occult mechanism' of the forty-foot dynamo: 'Before the end one began to pray to it; inherited instinct taught the natural expression of man before silent and infinite force.' The old religious world, the world of the Virgin, was over; new powers dominated modern existence. The change affected all societies, but most of all those multiplying energy; above all America was now becoming the 'twenty-million-horse-power society'. This meant a special pressure on the American, who could not, Adams wrily said, 'run his machine and a woman too'. In the new century of the modern multiverse the American must become either 'the child of new forces or the chance sport of nature'. Adams's chiliastic vision of modern proliferation and change, driving modern man into the 'supersensual universe', the modern world into entropy, the modern mind into chaos, is an extraordinary vision of the forces disturbing thought as what many considered to be 'the American century' approached. To some, like Gertrude Stein, the turn into the new century was laden with special promises; others came closer to despair. The American writing of the period hovered between the two, responding sometimes with a joyous sense that a new evolutionary cycle was starting, or a bleak suspicion that a new dehumanizing order was rising to transform all the circumstances and images of American life.

Indeed Adams's crucial year, 1900, saw the appearance of a work by a new American writer which seemed an instinctive response to his ironic vision. Its author was the son of German Catholic immigrants who spoke their native language at home, so he came to literature partly as a linguistic stranger. Breaking with his Catholic faith, he read Tolstoy and Herbert Spencer, and new theories in experimental psychology and physiology; his way to the novel had been through journalism, so strengthening his naturalist credentials. And his novel was about an individual trapped in the world of super-sensual forces, a world of energy and power drifting, none the less, towards entropy. Its first chapter, entitled 'The Magnet Attracting: A Waif Amid Forces', begins:

When Caroline Meeber boarded the afternoon train for Chicago her total outfit consisted of a small trunk, which was checked in the baggage car, a cheap imitation of alligator-skin satchel holding some minor details of the toilet, a small lunch in a paper box and a yellow leather snap purse, containing her ticket, a scrap of paper with her sister's address in Van Buren Street, and four dollars in money. It was in August, 1889. She was eighteen years of age, bright, timid and full of the illusions of ignorance and youth. Whatever touch of regret at parting characterized her thoughts it was certainly not for advantages now being given up. A gush of tears at her mother's farewell kiss, a touch in her throat when the cars clacked by the flour mill where her father worked by the day, a pathetic sigh as the familiar green environs of the village passed in review, and the threads which bound her so lightly to girlhood and home were irretrievably broken.[1]

The book was *Sister Carrie*, the author Theodore Dreiser, born in Terre Haute, Indiana, and the opening theme of the break with the past and the entry of Carrie Meeber into a new world of goods and forces introduced one of the most powerful of twentieth-century American novels.

Sister Carrie outraged most of its few early readers, and it lay in abeyance until it was reissued, after success in England, in 1911. Its outrage lay in Dreiser's refusal to structure his fictional world, which is heavy and dense with the substance of things, the claims of the material, according to a moral perception. In his story of Carrie's ascent through the material world, in which she uses her own body as more material, chance usurps rational decision, instinct usurps moral guidance, and will and desire operate independently of convention. The story starts in the familiar universe of realistic things, but it soon steps beyond it. Another paragraph or two on, and Carrie is moving into a new force-field, as well as into a new fictional discourse:

> When a girl leaves her home at eighteen, she does one of two things. Either she falls into saving hands and becomes better, or she rapidly assumes the cosmopolitan standard of virtue and becomes worse. Of an intermediate balance, under the circumstances, there is no possibility. The city has cunning wiles no less than the infinitely smaller and more human tempter. There are large forces which allure, with all the soulfulness of expression possible in the most cultured human. The gleam of a thousand lights is often as effective, to all moral intents and purposes, as the persuasive light in a wooing and fascinating eye. Half the undoing of the unsophisticated and natural mind is accomplished by forces wholly superhuman.

The passage begins in morality and ends in naturalist theory, where the disposition of transhuman forces makes moral questions finally irrelevant. The transhuman is humanized and becomes sensual and enveloping; the human becomes increasingly material and mechanized. Carrie is no sooner on her train to Chicago than she meets her first human seducer, Drouet, the 'drummer' or commercial traveller, the 'smaller and more human tempter' who is really no more than

---

[1] References are to the Penguin American Library edition of *Sister Carrie* (1981), based on the restored Pennsylvania edition text. See the useful introduction by Alfred Kazin to the Penguin edition for the text's complicated history.

one voice of the city. Dreiser immediately generalizes him, and makes him an emblem of the rootless, tempting city where moral order is sacrificed to larger expressionist forces. The novelist may imply a morality; he organizes a post-moral system. He talks of Carrie's 'undoing', but he sets her in a world so sensually to hand, so contemporary, alive, and restless, that her amoral viewpoint, her response to the force-field, seem inevitable.

One of the things that has often been noticed about *Sister Carrie*, and variously read as the book's strength or weakness, is that it moves on to create a world in which there are no real human attachments. Some displacement of the person is endemic in naturalism, and makes the tendency a post-liberal one; it depends on a new economy of relations between person and process. But what is noticeable in Dreiser is precisely that the force he removes from people he relocates in things. The city and the machine, goods and property, have romantic powers, and indeed the capacity to make choices for human beings. The city tempts, like a 'magnet', says Dreiser, but also like a lover, who is a human magnet. Carrie may start out as the 'waif' caught amid forces 'wholly superhuman', but she soon becomes a most effective user of them, so that her apparent 'downfall' is actually her energetic ascent. By the end of the first chapter, she is being assimilated by the 'great city', Chicago itself, with its massive mobile detail, its commercial 'power and fact', its tempting wealth and degrading poverty. And while Carrie enters at the bottom, an untrained job-hunter, an object ('"We're not exactly in need of anybody," he went on vaguely, looking her over as one would a package'), she finishes, one city further on, at the top, the actress-dancer in a world of decadent love, the bearer of its roles and masks. A 'little soldier of fortune', she not only adapts to but becomes an urban process, a moving principle of amoral energy.

In *Sister Carrie*, naturalism turns towards expressionism, and finds the means to display not just the ironies but the energies of American urban culture, or post-culture. Crane had used naturalism as a mode of aesthetic perception and a tactic of irony; Norris had seen it as a neo-philosophy generating the plots of modern romance. Dreiser takes up a position of personal implication; he is part of the naturalist world. He delights in the struggle, moves emotionally along with Carrie, shares many of her wants, and looks with her at the alluring material possibilities of the great dream theatre of city life. His characters, too, generally understand that they are *within* a naturalist world, and respond to its laws of energy; they know their own shortage of self. At the same time Dreiser stands outside, as naturalist commentator, generalizing, explaining human action in neo-scientific terms, moving from detailed specifics ('her total outfit consisted of . . .') to the large generalities ('Half the undoing of the . . . natural mind is accomplished by forces wholly superhuman'). He sees much more than Carrie, and distances her, but he takes each scene of her life as a self-justifying event and he shares her sense of living in an exciting post-moral world. The result is that *Sister Carrie* is founded on an unmasked economy of want, a sexual economics in which the self is an object, objects have selves, and the body is a none too intimate instrument in social success.

Carrie's essential psychology is located for us on her first seduction, after she loses her job at the shoe factory, and Drouet reappears and offers her money. Into her morning-after reflections, Dreiser enters with Spencerian behaviourist views: morals are social products, and if the voice of conscience ('only an average little conscience, a thing which represented the world, her past environment, habit, convention, in a confused way') complains, other, stronger voices speak in her. There is the 'voice of want', desiring not just money but that in the material world which makes it more than material ('Fine clothes to her were a vast persuasion; they spoke tenderly and Jesuitically for themselves. . . . The voice of the so-called inanimate'). And Dreiser speaks Jesuitically too, creating a version of experience in which desire metabolically wins. So Carrie soon drops Drouet for Hurstwood, his social superior, a saloon manager, 'genteel', 'respected', 'an interesting character after his kind', following desire's higher economics. In turn Hurstwood breaks his failing marriage and steals from his employers to win Carrie's energy. In front of his employer's safe, his mind functions as a machine, a 'clock', wavering between two commanding instincts, one towards convention, the other towards desire; as he holds the money, uncertain, the safe door snaps shut. By symbolic transposition, machinery becomes his mind, just as his mind becomes a machine. The two then flee to New York, a 'newer world', and follow out their appropriate spirals of motion: Carrie's upward, Hurstwood's downward. (Dreiser supports all this with semi-scientific psychological theories.) At last Carrie becomes the actress Carrie Madenda, her onstage face 'representative of all desire'; we see her at the last in her rocking chair, in perpetual but entropic motion – the none too happy hooker, the modern star, material wants satisfied, yet needing (like the author himself) something more, a realm of art and culture beyond the material. Meanwhile Hurstwood sinks into the realms of naturalist disaster, becoming a strike-breaker, a Bowery bum, finally a nameless suicide who ends in a pauper's grave. Dreiser emphasizes the ironic contrast, but he typically shares Carrie's final lack of concern – for, by the end of the novel, the laws of inevitability have become paramount.

The novel (now available in its full, unedited version) has always generated mixed critical reactions. 'It is not intended as a piece of literary craftsmanship,' Dreiser said of it, 'but as a picture of conditions done as simply and effectively as the English language will permit.' Yet the book does in fact have strong literary pretensions, and pretentiousness – one reason why the original text was edited. The author's local stylistic gestures can make us uneasy; but Dreiser's power lies in style in a larger sense – his capacity to create fictionally a vigorous world that is seen mechanically and causally, yet which overflows with vital energy. Material life becomes abundant with hieroglyphics; individuals in it toss on a 'thoughtless sea', moving either with or against force, in a total metaphoric flow encompassing success and failure, consciousness and the expressive voice of things. In these terms, *Sister Carrie* is the strongest of Dreiser's books. *Jennie Gerhardt* (1911) tells a similar story, but with more caution and Christianity. His 'trilogy of desire', *The Financier* (1912), *The Titan* (1914), and *The Stoic* (1947, posthumous), about the financier Cowperwood, who struggles upward from poverty to sexual and economic success, is an ambiguous portrait of capitalism, with some progressive doubts but with a deep admiration for Cowperwood's Nietzschean energies. *The 'Genius'* (1915) is about an energetic and sexually active artist and is in part a portrait of the novelist himself.

But Dreiser did write one other great novel, *An American Tragedy* (1925), when he revived his naturalism to explore a decade when the American dream seemed tainted with materialism. In this book he sees from the standpoint of the victim alone, as if the kinetic energies he had earlier seen as a part of American life could now work only for its destruction. The book is highly documented, based on an actual murder case, and it analyses critically a social process – Clyde Griffiths' evolution from bitter poverty to social promotion and finally to the electric chair. The naturalist crux is at the centre of the story: if man is the product of circumstances and determinants, in what sense may he be guilty of the crime, murder, for which Clyde is charged? Clyde is incompetent in his ambitions and divided in his will, torn between his pregnant mill-girl mistress and the rich girl he wants to marry so that he can win his place in the American sun. But he is a product of American expectation and of the social pressure toward ascent. Dreiser makes the novel turn on a fine naturalist irony: Clyde wants to be rid of his mistress; he takes her out on a photographic expedition in a boat on the lake; his inward conflict between murder and kindness makes him move towards her; the boat rocks, the camera strikes her, and she drowns. Clyde is charged with murder, and much of the book is given over to the complex legal arguments in the courtroom. Dreiser takes the fundamental naturalist questions – How do motive and intent arise in a world where mind merges with matter? How do we relate desire to act? How does the clock or camera of the mind function? – and applies them to a compassionate concern with injustice. *An American Tragedy*, powerful as it is, thus becomes a simpler book than *Sister Carrie*: a fiction of social protest and a challenge to the American dream, rather than a work of cosmic irony or denuded modernity. It marks an essential direction in which American naturalism moved, though, by the 1920s, it already seems dated – in fascinating contrast to that other tragedy of the American dream, Scott Fitzgerald's *The Great Gatsby*, which came out in the same year.

II

It was, in fact, the period between *Sister Carrie* and *An American Tragedy* that saw naturalism become a staple mode of American fiction. *Sister Carrie* was attacked and neglected, and Dreiser was put off novel-writing for a decade; but over the immediately following years other writers, like Upton Sinclair and Jack London, turned naturalism into the great American adventure story, populist and popular. Both were writers of extraordinary abundance, entrepreneurs of fiction; Upton Sinclair, when he died, left more than eight tons of papers to Indiana University; Jack London made over a million dollars from writing, and produced more than fifty books – novels, stories, and socialist propaganda – between 1900, when he began to write, and 1916, when he committed suicide. Fed by the rise of progressivism and the growth of muckraking journalism, naturalism turned – as Dreiser himself was to turn – towards social protest and political exposé. It voiced popular indignations, challenged the trusts, explored the shame of the cities, and found in all this a romance of liberation which consorted with the mood of the time.

Upton Sinclair wrote several romances before he turned to the radical naturalism of *The Jungle* (1906), still his most famous and most successful novel, and a book that interestingly compares with *Sister Carrie*. It too is set in the underside of Chicago, in its work places, bars, and immigrant ghettos, and it begins with the allure of the city, this time for two young immigrants, Jurgis and Ona, who have come from the Lithuanian forest and from feudal European injustice to America, 'a place of which lovers and young people dreamed'. But in the classic naturalist set-piece scene of the immigrant wedding with which the book opens the seeds of disillusion are already present; a 'subtle poison' is in the air as the great city, greed, and capitalist competition break up the old folk solidarities and leave individuals exposed. Jurgis, seeking to make a life for himself from his honesty, strength and independence, soon becomes a victim of the competitive system. As a foreign labourer he is exploited to depress the wages of others; he moves from being the virtuous worker to becoming the scab and the bum, like Dreiser's Hurstwood. Hurstwood, though, fails from within, from a want of energy; Jurgis fails from without, through the corruptions of the system. He can therefore be rescued by rescuing himself, by learning the facts of the oppressive process and discovering the philosophy of socialism.

Thus the book ends not on victimization but in hope. The old community may have gone, but can be replaced by working-class solidarity; indeed utopia seems at hand, as we see Jurgis thinking about a 'great potato-digging machine', as the pain of his destroyed family is healed by the responsive glances of a beautiful girl entrant to the party, and as the socialist vote mounts in the election. *The Jungle* starts out as a much more subtle novel than it finishes, but its switch from an artistic to a propaganda function in the end served its purpose. As a result of the book, Roosevelt initiated an enquiry into the food laws, and reforms were made in the meat-packing industry; Jack London identified the novel as 'the *Uncle Tom's Cabin* of wage slavery'. Sinclair went on to write numerous novels of indignant social documentation, heavily researched, often about money (*The Metropolis*, 1908) or business processes (*King Coal*, 1917; *Oil!*, 1927), culminating in the 11-volume *World's End* sequence, started in 1940, which takes its radical hero Lanny Budd melodramatically through the international political landscape of the western world. Sinclair's work was often coarse, but he made it apparent that populist naturalism could become the discourse of record and reform, as well as the basis of prodigious publication, and a massive commercial adventure in writing.

It was a lesson equally evident in the career of Jack London, the great writer-hero of the pre-war years. London's life itself became a popular adventure, recorded in his writings: illegitimate, he grew up in San Francisco, and was a cannery worker, sealer, hobo, and gold prospector in the Klondike before he turned to writing, which proved the greatest opportunist adventure of them all. Like Sinclair, he was filled with evolutionary, libertarian, and political ideas, culled from Darwin, Haeckel, Frazer, Nietzsche and Shaw, ideas which he deployed with a popular touch and a sense of adventurous melodrama. But where Sinclair wrote of cities and social problems, London wrote much of the outdoors, of travel, violence, adventure. His writing was popular with children as well as adult readers, and as an adventure novelist he is still read widely today. The politics were deeply and instinctively felt, however, and his social ideas rich and abundant, though it would be hard to call them other than confused. He adopted a scientific world-view towards 'this chemical ferment called Life', but it was a mixture of myths of democracy and myths of strength and superiority, including very much of his own. It came naturally to him to see life – whether outdoors or in the mills and factories – as a battle of wills, forces, and energies, mirroring the struggle in nature itself. Social protest exists in his work, but its central issue is survival, the evolutionary instinct, the law of the tribe and the pack.

That work poured out in a variety of forms: the boys' adventure story, so popular in an era of imperialism and adventurism (*White Fang*, 1906); the political fable of the future (*The Iron Heel*, 1907); the sea story (*The Sea Wolf*, 1904); the novel of racial characteristics and superiorities (*A Daughter of the Snows*, 1902); the autobiographical novel of his own idealism (*Martin Eden*, 1909). London's better work is a blend of sharp political curiosity and awareness, self-taught ideas transmitted in popular form to others, heroic self-dramatization, strong life hunger, and apocalyptic despairs alleviated by an adventurous sense of romance. Two books of 1903 suggest the mixed funds he could draw on. *The People of the Abyss* is reportage, derived from his experience in the East End of London, where he spent several months as a tramp, penetrating the unknown jungle on society's doorstep. As he exposes its horrors politically, he himself stalks through this jungle less as reformer than as Nietzschean superman, commanding the life around. The fictional *The Call of the Wild* shifts the jungle back into nature: the story of Buck, the 'aristocratic' dog forced to encounter 'the reign of primitive law' when he is stolen, taken off to the Yukon, and put into a dog team among savage beasts 'who know no law but the law of club and fang', it is about the recovery of old instincts. Buck becomes leader of this primal animal community, knows 'blood longing', and finally becomes a killer, 'surviving triumphantly in a hostile environment where only the strong survived'. It was heady lore for adventurous Rooseveltian times, part of the new century's attempt to recover the vitalism and primitivism that civilization and gentility had silenced. The intricate connection between the two books, both concerned with the collectivity of experience and the laws of struggle, with groups, packs, tribes, and classes, is not hard to see. Tribes need leaders, evolution needs individuation; in all of this we find life's true adventure.

There were, however, novelists of the new century for whom naturalism was less an ebullient mode of literary action than a philosophy for a post-religious age, a form of metaphysical pessimism and fatalism. One such was Ellen Glasgow, a writer from that historically battered and pained region, the South. She came from, and was the troubled historian of, a Virginia where the traces of feudalism and chivalric romanticism had outlasted the Civil War; and the 'expiring gesture of chivalry' is the theme of her early fiction – *The Battle-Ground* (1902), *The Deliverance* (1904). But here her treatment is sentimental, though she recognizes the need for a historical stoicism rather than false creeds of nostalgia, traditionalism, and gentility. It was as the satire grew sharper, and the unreality of the prevailing mores more apparent, in novels like *Virginia* (1913), that a naturalist sense of cosmic indifference grows in her work. The very titles of her late books – *Barren Ground* (1925), *Vein of Iron* (1935) – suggest the bleak and deprived space in which human beings attempt to find purpose, to erect culture, sustain institutions, hold ideals and illusions. Ellen Glasgow is very much a novelist of culture and social mores, in whose books comedy of manners move steadily towards a deeply tragic sense of life. Institutions contest with harsh nature, history displaces, ritual and code are built over void. Her novels were – as she said in the preface to *The Sheltered Life* (1938) – 'the prolonged study of a world that, as the sardonic insight of Henry Adams perceived, no "sensitive and timid natures could regard without a shudder"'. Yet, dark in vision, they are also formally very exact, the work of a writer of enormous culture and intelligence penetrating to the void over which that culture is built.

III

It was thus in many forms that naturalism developed, in the American fiction between 1900 and World War I, into a familiar and inclusive usage, capable of expressing attitudes as various as political radicalism and a deep sense of human irony. Yet, as Philip Rahv once observed, naturalism came along to make its inventory of a material and process-ridden world at the point when it was just beginning to dissolve.[2] It was a form of positivism, and positivism was under challenge from the new sciences, particularly psychology; a form of realism, when realism was under challenge by new arts exploring the inward and the aesthetic. Science, as Adams saw, was growing increasingly relativistic, looking into uncertainty and chaos, assuming that reality was not objectively given but subjectively apprehended through consciousness. In America, this view was shared by pragmatism, of which William James, teaching philosophy and psychology at Harvard, was an originator. In *Principles of Psychology* (1890), he explored the gap between mind and action, noting that reality was not immediately apprehensible, but required to be approached provisionally, through the empirical, or pragmatic, assumption that order is 'gradually won and always in the making'. Hence attention must fall on to the mechanisms of consciousness; and, where science had once seen an objective observer, where Crane saw a picture-taking shutter connecting inner and outer experience, Dreiser a clock of thought, James offered a more fluid and, in the

[2] Philip Rahv, 'Notes on the Decline of Naturalism', in *Documents of Modern Literary Realism*, ed. G. J. Becker (1963).

event, crucial metaphor: 'A "river" or a "stream" are the metaphors by which it [consciousness] is most naturally described.'

The metaphor was readily transmuted into literature, and particularly a new kind of literature that was just beginning to emerge. In this William James had some part; he undoubtedly influenced his brother Henry, as well as one of his own most famous pupils, Gertrude Stein. In 1897, Henry James returned, with *The Spoils of Poynton* and *What Maisie Knew*, to the novel. *What Maisie Knew*, which, said one contemporary critic, added 'a whole new concept of reality to the art of fiction', particularly marks the change in his work, a change that clearly points it towards modernism. *Maisie* is a novel of consciousness under test; its theme is the process by which the mind – that of the child Maisie, the 'light vessel of consciousness' on whose perception the book is centred – responds to or rejects impressions, experience. James explains this in his preface: he has, he says, given Maisie a vivacity of intelligence, 'perceptions easily and most infinitely quickened,' so that she can 'know' the promiscuous adult world in which she grows up. He takes up his own narrative position beside and with the little girl's understanding, at the same time substantiating round it those complexities she must intuit. It was a pragmatist method, requiring a process of apprehension both in character and author, and deriving, as William James said, from both a mental and a moral process. If reality is not to be known except by being taken in, consciousness must become the crucial question; and so, in Henry James's late work, it does.

In 1900, the year of Adams's multiverse, James put aside a book, *The Sense of the Past*, he had started to write, and sketched a different scenario: 'the picture of a certain momentous and interesting period, of some six months or so, in the history of a man no longer in the prime of life, yet still able to live with sufficient intensity to be a source of what might be called excitement to himself, not less than to the reader of the novel.' This is the plot of *The Ambassadors*, not finally to appear until 1903; a book started after it, *The Wings of the Dove*, appeared in 1902. These two books and their immediate successor, *The Golden Bowl* (1904), are the centre of James's late phase, coinciding with the artistic ferments of the new century. They return to the international theme he had earlier discarded, and its motion from innocence to experience; for now the problem is not to learn from experience but to know what experience *is* – how it is redeemed from life's contingency and order, given form by the perceiver,

perceptual shape by the novelist. The apprehensive and the compositional process become analogues; James, in *The Ambassadors*, 'sticks
close' to his centre of consciousness, Strether, and the changing
colouration of his consciousness as he grasps the 'inner' story, that of
Chad Newsome. By starting the novel with Strether's arrival in
Europe, and keeping all the material as an aspect of his consciousness, within the 'discriminated occasion' of his awareness, James
holds the whole book within an apprehensive mode of vision.

This is in striking contrast to the method of *Sister Carrie*. Both
books start with a discarding of the past, an arrival in a new place,
where a new force-field grasps the characters. But where Carrie is
engulfed, almost sexually, by the process of reality, Strether may not
outrightly know it; he works with impressions, potential, powerful,
but neither determining his conduct nor forming an implacable
reality 'out there'. Where Carrie is the waif amid forces, Strether is
the 'enquirer', and process lies not outside but within the self, from
the very first words forward. The essential concern, then, is with the
way the 'reservoir' of Strether's mind is filled with the forceful
'current' of new impressions, summed up at its most complex when
he sees the two lovers boating on the river, as in, exactly, an
impressionist painting. Now, as James says in his preface, he 'at all
events *sees*; so that the business of my tale and the march of my
action, not to say the precious moral of everything, is just my
demonstration of this process of vision.'

Related and yet different concerns run through *The Wings of the
Dove* and *The Golden Bowl*. In *The Wings of the Dove* James sacrifices
his intimate identification with a parallel consciousness, Strether's,
to a more oblique angle of attack, a complex intercourse between his
own textual position and a 'modern' character who is moved through
a harsh world of things, which refracts and interacts with her. The
book begins (the contrast with *Sister Carrie* is again sharp):

> She waited, Kate Croy, for her father to come in, but he kept her
> unconscionably, and there were moments at which she showed herself, in the
> glass over the mantel, a face positively pale with the irritation that had
> brought her to the point of going away without sight of him. It was at this
> point, however, that she remained; changing her place, moving from the
> shabby sofa to the armchair upholstered in a glazed cloth that gave at once −
> she had tried it − the sense of the slippery and the sticky. . . .

The sympathetic character gone, person and context can be related
and located only by a very oblique grammar ('She waited, Kate

Croy ...'). Again here, as in *The Golden Bowl*, the work is aesthetically and morally obsessed with consciousness; but it is concerned to reflect the harsh material surface of modern life, forcing the novelist into distancing manoeuvres. Indeed the bowl itself, the symbolic object, flawed, which stands in the shop as Prince Amerigo and Charlotte Stant negotiate their plan to sacrifice love to material need, concentrates just this. *The Golden Bowl* is a novel of hardened form, of aestheticism grown ironic. The characters may *live* as consciousnesses, but they are positioned as objects, indeed *objets d'art*, vessels of being with cash value. Maggie Verver tells Amerigo in her love speech that he is 'a rarity, an object of beauty, an object of price'. Charlotte's body is seen by the Prince as like 'some long, loose silk purse'. And the book is dominated by the collector Adam Verver, whose spirit is likened to 'a strange workshop of fortune ... one with the perfection of machinery'. It is in this novel and in *The Sacred Fount* that James moves most surely into the modern forcefield, and responds – as indeed Dreiser does – by finding a new relation between consciousness and material substance. By the end of *The Golden Bowl*, the material and weighty world of things has won, a physical world beyond feeling or consciousness that must claim its due while sustaining its unreality.

One effect of the complexity of James's late method is that he left his public, as well as his literary successors, with two ways of reading his work. To some, his essential contribution was to the extension of realism and the development of the social and moral novel, which he helped to turn into a negotiable American form; to others the signficant element was his contribution to modernism, his translation of realism into something quite other. 'Can you see that any day was no part of his life,' Gertrude Stein wrote in her portrait of James; or, as she put it in another place, 'the form was always the form of the contemporary English one, but the disembodied way of disconnecting something from anything and anything from something was the American one.' The curve of James's career in fact echoes a fundamental development from nineteenth-century to new twentieth-century practices in fiction. In the event, both his contributions – to the social novel of manners and morals, and to experimental modernism – were profitably to feed American writing.

Thus, when Percy Lubbock once defined Edith Wharton herself as 'a novel of [James's], no doubt in his earlier manner', we can see at once what he means. Mrs Wharton's fiction in fact shares much with that earlier manner: a product of the New York patriciate, born the rich, polite, and anxious Edith Jones, she grew up to a world in which social codes and customs were intensely real, the contention between classes significant, the rise of new wealth, commercialism, and corrupt politics after the American Civil War a serious anxiety. At the same time her books, her very act of writing, arose from the imprisonments of an unhappy society marriage and the containment of women by puritanical conventions. Both she and James were expatriates to Europe, their withdrawal shaped in part by a sense of decline and debasement in the America they knew. They wrote of similar milieux, similar international themes, similar feelings of dislocation towards their native land, similar agonies about the gap between cultural and aesthetic desire and material fact. But both were uneasy about the connection others saw between them. She complained saying in a letter of 1904 that 'the continued cry that I am an echo of Mr James (whose books of the last ten years I can't read, much as I delight in the man) . . . makes me feel rather hopeless'. She wrote, after all, from one generation later, with a much starker sense of the direction of historical change, and from a different sexual and a somewhat higher social standpoint, and with no appreciation at all of the later Jamesian complexities.

Yet both worried about the relation of society and consciousness, and were caught between two different models of that relation: a 'traditional' view that society is composed of people becoming more aware of their own, and others', true nature through sensitivity and introspection, and that personality is concrete and genuine behind outward appearance; a more 'realist' or 'naturalist' view that people are shaped and perhaps even created by their social conditioning and status. Hence a sense of ironic contradiction inhabits the work of both writers. As with Ellen Glasgow's novels, Edith Wharton's are battlefields in which two perceptions of the self, one voluntarist, devoted to morals and culture, the other determinist, concerned with individuals as victims of society and process, contend. Her books are about values, but also about their economic derivation. In one of her best books, *The House of Mirth* (1905), the heroine, Lily Bart, is seen in the light of both views, with consequent irony. Lily is the 'highly specialized product' of a civilization that needs specimens of beauty to exhibit, 'a rare flower grown for exhibition' in high society; but her moral scruples afford her no basis for survival in a system based on economic energy. Lily attempts gradually to bridge the two by behaving not as a social product but as a moral agent, but this threatens her position and sets her on a downward spiral, and she comes to suspect that morality has no social support, is merely 'a perpetual adjustment, a play of party politics, in which every concession had its recognized equivalent': this might be said to be the naturalist or determinist crisis. However Edith Wharton does not finally support this view, respecting also the ideal of cultured society for which in this novel Seldon speaks, a 'republic of the spirit'. But the outcome is irony, and the result tragedy, for there is no real class to enshrine morality, especially for women, who are not in control of their economic destiny. Morals and culture have place but not power, and so the moralist may desire one world and the naturalist perceive another. Mrs Wharton's writing is filled with a distinctive sense of waste, founded on emotional renunciations, willed self-confinement, and a sense of universal inhospitality.

Her books explore this in various ways. *Ethan Frome* (1911) moves towards naturalism in its story of the loveless imprisonment of an unhappily married farmer who attempts suicide with his mistress and then must live out the rest of his life with his wife and the injured lover. *The Custom of the Country* (1913), probably her best book, is the story of Undine Spragg, a frankly erotic heroine with 'the instinct of sex', a Carrie Meeber looked down on from above in her social ascent, grasping for 'something beyond', 'a more delicate kind of pleasure'. As the title suggests, the book is a social satire, an exploration of an America where cultural décor and material desires mesh strangely; the specific custom in question is divorce, which enables Undine's erotic and social mobility. Undine is a decoration who knows her 'trading capacity', her sexual rate of exchange, Mrs Wharton's most powerful image of the modern entrepreneurial woman, operating on the fringe of the utilitarian economic process to win her way. Like Carrie, she ends up with everything and nothing. On her fourth marriage, to a European aristocrat, she now possesses all the elements: American energy and money, European rank and culture. But one small thing is missing: 'She had learned that there was something she could never get, something that neither beauty nor influence nor millions could ever buy for her. She could never be an Ambassador's wife [because she is divorced]; and as she advanced to welcome her first guests she said to herself that it was the one part she was really made for.'

It is a book of extraordinary economic unpeeling, its irony made partly from patrician outrage but more largely from satirical delight in 'the chaos of indiscriminate appetites which make up [New York's] modern tendencies'. With her best late novel, *The Age of Innocence* (1920), Mrs Wharton left that modern scene for a backward glance at the 1870s, when the American patriciate was first encroached on by the new and upstart wealth of the Gilded Age. She applies her ironies equally to that patriciate, trying to live by a provincial, puritanized version of European culture, and using it as appurtenance and convenience, and to the new wealth, even more vulgar than the old, producing yet more displacement. Again, the story becomes one of enforced renunciations. Newland Archer, the sensitive married hero, cannot find his place, and his drama comes when he falls in love with the European Countess Olenska, who does not fit American mores. Politics is corrupted and action denied; the intelligent are caught in the Henry Adams syndrome of being displaced from significant action. The old rich marry their children to the new, and these follow Teddy Roosevelt into politics and materialism. At the end of the book, Newland Archer, having sustained the conventions, unlike his Jamesian namesake Isabel, is caught in the opposite version of her prison. He stands in Paris, looks up at the Countess's window, feels the city's richness, 'the incessant stir of ideas, curiosities, images and association thrown up by an intensely social race in a setting of immemorial manners,' and knows he has lost the flower of life.

IV

In subjecting the social and moral novel to the pressures of naturalism and of irony, to a world where intelligence and individual culture must compromise with process and primitivism, Edith Wharton laid one path forward from James, the earlier James rather than the later, into the modern American novel. But another crucial path was that represented by Gertrude Stein. Miss Stein represented quite the opposite kind of cosmopolitanism from Edith Wharton's. Born in Allegheny, Pennsylvania, to an upper-middle-class Jewish immigrant family of aesthetic tastes, she spent part of her childhood in Vienna and Paris. Unlike Mrs Wharton, imprisoned in class and unhappy marriage, Gertrude Stein was a new woman from the start, seizing on the radical opportunities opened by the 1890s with their note of female emancipation. She went to the Harvard Annex (now

Radcliffe College) and there studied with William James, as well as George Santayana and Josiah Royce. There she met the late-nineteenth-century crisis in American thought which pragmatism sought to resolve, responding to William James's proposal that there was not a solid but a pluralistic universe, which drove attention inward to the psychology of awareness, the means by which we find emotion, generate action, create reality.

At the same time she shared with William James a behaviourist or naturalist dimension. 'I was interested in biology and I was interested in psychology and philosophy and history, that was all natural enough, I came out of the nineteenth century and you had to be interested in evolution and biology,' Miss Stein later said. However, she did not intend to stay in the nineteenth century: 'I was there to kill what was not dead, the nineteenth century which was so sure of evolution and prayers.' At Harvard, where she worked on experiments in automatic writing, she became a kind of pre-Freudian psychologist. She took this further by beginning medical studies at Johns Hopkins University, but was not successful. Her brother Leo, a self-conscious period aesthete and an art historian, encouraged her to move beyond behaviourist science to aesthetic speculation, and she began to write, experimenting with artistic form, and with the behavioural act of writing itself, because it revealed underlying principles of mental action. She began a book, soon set aside and posthumously published as *Things As They Are* (1950), about a tense, three-cornered lesbian relationship; it reveals the influence of William James in its thought and Henry James in its technique, its method of what she called 'disembodiment' or abstraction. Now Leo and she moved to Paris, looking, as she said, for 'gloire'. But when Edith Wharton was to choose Right Bank, patrician Paris, Gertrude and Leo chose Left Bank, bohemian, atelier Paris, setting up a salon that would become a centre of artistic modernism.

For their arrival, in 1903, coincided with a period of radical developments in art in which they gradually became interested. The Steins were collecting, and became involved with the Post-Impressionists, notably Cézanne, and then with the Fauves and the movement that was to become Cubism. Meanwhile, Gertrude had begun a translation of a work of late-realist naturalism, Flaubert's *Trois Contes*, which developed into a reconstitution, with an American setting. Appearing as *Three Lives* in 1909, its three linked stories, 'The Good Anna', 'Melanctha', and 'The Gentle Lena', are psycho-portraits of three servant girls in Bridgepoint, presumably Baltimore. It draws on some of Flaubert's naturalist assumptions, but aims to render the consciousness of the girls rather than tell their stories, to create complex studies of simple persons. In what is generally recognized as the most interesting story, about the mulatto girl Melanctha, Stein concentrates on the rhythms of the girl's thought-speech, with a distinctive intonation: loose sentencing and repetition are emphasized; present participles and verb-nouns dominate the telling, creating rhythm and rhyme; the texture here becomes distinctively Steinian. 'Sometimes when they had been strong in their loving, and Jeff would have inside him some strange feeling, and Melanctha felt it in him as it would soon be coming, she would lose herself in this bad feeling that made her head act as if she never knew what it was they were doing.'

This is naturalism in process of decomposition; causality and pattern diminish, consciousness dominates, and the aim is a semi-scientific study of the rhythms of mind. As Stein explained in her later lectures and essays ('Composition as Explanation', 'Portraits and Repetition', 'Poetry and Grammar'), this method represented the breakthrough to a modern mode of composition. Its post-causal, synchronic, present tense she called 'the synchronic present', explaining: 'there was a continuous recurring and beginning there was a marked direction in the direction of being in the present although naturally I had been accustomed to the past present and future and why, because the composition around me was a prolonged present.' The repetition or recurring was memoryless, and based on a new grammar in which, as in painting, the noun or realistic object is depleted ('A noun is the name of anything, why after a thing is named write about it'), verbal and adverbial forms predominate. It was a method of abstraction, post-naturalist, post-impressionist, moving onward from Flaubert and Cézanne. And, just as Cézanne was engaged both in creating and de-creating his paintings, so that they conveyed the inner energy of subject and also the perceptual art of their creation, so in prose Gertrude Stein moved towards a verbal version of estrangement and abstraction.

These were the methods Stein tried to take further, to novel length, in her next major project, *The Making of Americans*, a work largely written over the key Cubist years of 1906–8, though not published until the 1920s, and not printed in full until the 1950s. *The Making of Americans: The Hersland Family* (1925) merges two interconnected enterprises: the composition of a cubist novel, and the composition of a novel about Americans, a Great American Novel which was to be the epic of the sensibility of a nation. Stein saw Americans as natural cubists – products, that is, of the new composition, newly positioned in history and time. Hence the title is doubly apt: this is a book about the making of the nation through immigration, settlement ('The old people in a new world, the new people made out of the old, that is the story I mean to tell') and the fictional or compositional problem of creating their story out of words and tropes. The underlying task – that of creating a national epic of foundation, which covers three generations of a German-American family, the Herslands (the implication of the name is clear; and they were based on the Steins) – is familiar, the compositional mode new. It is a tale less of individual characters or discriminated events than of repetitions and variations, an implied timeless history of mankind, distilled through Americans because they especially possessed the sense 'of the space of a time that is filled with moving'. And 'the space of a time' is exactly the subject of the novel, and the nature of its form: diverging from realism and story sequence, operating less as narrative than as a spatial disposition of words, it is indeed parallel to Cubism.

Never short of confidence (she once observed that there were three twentieth-century geniuses, Picasso, Whitehead, and herself), Miss Stein readily explained the importance of the project: 'A thing you all know is that in the three novels written in this generation that are the important things written in this generation, there is, in none of them a story. There is none in Proust in *The Making of Americans* or in *Ulysses*.' The comparison is justified; *A la recherche du temps perdu*, *Ulysses*, and her novel are all classics of the Revolution of the Word, endeavours to build a new continuum of experience based on consciousness. But where Proust draws on involuntary memory, and Joyce on myth and archetype, Stein, finding memory too much engaged with causality and chronicity, and myth not sufficiently subjective, emphasizes compositional rhythm itself. All three books display the need to violate old narrative logics; Joyce finds an element of historical crisis in this need, and Proust a sense of loss, but for Stein it is a matter of experimental joy. Prose repetition was the heart of the method, as she emphasized in her supporting essay, 'The Making of *The Making of Americans*' (1935). Here she stressed the book's relation to her work at Harvard, where she had studied the fundamental tropes of speech repetition ('I was sure that in a kind of a way the enigma of the universe could in this way be solved'). It was a way to reach the 'bottom nature' of mankind, for language rhythm mimes the deep structures of consciousness, the way every person shows aspects of every other. So a novel can move from anyone to everyone, through 'all the kind of repeating there is in them'. The method, though, raised problems of concentration; the book contains hundreds of pages of repetition systems, making it one of those books it is better to have read than to read. This challenged the relevance of the novel form itself to the modern task, as Stein indeed now said: 'I had to find out inside everyone what was in them that was intrinsically exciting and I had to find out not by what they said not by what they did not by how much or how little they resembled any other one but I had to find out by the intensity of the movement that was inside them.'

The Making of Americans is a crucial work of American innovation, a high modernist novel we are now coming to understand better; but it is important that to find that 'intensity' Miss Stein felt the need to turn away from the novel, the form that encouraged 'remembering' and narrative. Now she sought the short form, the brief piece that might offer the verbal equivalent to the concentration and instantaneousness of a painting: to the collage, the Cubist figure painting, or still life. From 1908 on her work is best understood as prose painting. Many of the paintings are portraits, 'portraits of anybody and anything . . . That started me composing anything into one thing.' They took as subjects fellow artists, like Picasso or Matisse, writers, like Apollinaire, and patrons and friends. From 1911 she turned more towards still life and collage, as in her next book, *Tender Buttons* (1914), where narrative gives way to verbal montage. Mixing cubist concentration with surrealist associationism, the pieces start by naming an object or subject, then develop systems of verbal, mental, or rhythmic association, ranging from rhymes or puns to very personal connections. Feelings of synaesthesia are drawn on; the hard is softened, or the soft made hard, as in the book's title itself. This book marks the high point of Gertrude Stein's importance as an innovator; it also established her influence in America.

But after this her own work itself began to soften, towards the indulgences of *The Autobiography of Alice B. Toklas* (1933), witty and fascinating, but a work of veneration of Miss Stein written, of course, by Miss Stein. By this time, Stein's place in modern experiment had become accepted by many younger American writers, to whom she became guru and arbiter during the expatriate, avant-garde Twenties. She became a central translator of the experiments of painting into fiction, and the experiments of Europe into America – the place she regarded as experiment's natural home. Her work was indeed an amalgam of European-influenced forms and American experiences; she rightly saw that the thought of William James, and the writing of Henry James, had already pointed in this direction. Her own writing is often read as the very antithesis of naturalism; what it rather shows is that there was a far greater connection between naturalism and modernism than is sometimes supposed. But, like Ezra Pound in poetry, Miss Stein marks an essential stage in the modernization of American fiction. And if the best work of the crucial next two generations of novelists displays a thinning of the naturalist surface, a questioning of many of the traditional premises of narrative, a changed economy of work and stance, a more emphatic commitment to exploring the process of writing, above all a sense of the world – especially the American world – as a 'new composition', then all this owes a very great deal to Gertrude Stein.

3 Artists and Philistines: 1912–1920

... our artists have been of two extremes: those who gained an almost unbelievable purity of expression by the very violence of their self-isolation, and those who, plunging into the American maelstrom, were submerged in it, lost their vision altogether, and gave forth a gross chronicle and a blind cult of the American Fact.

Waldo Frank, 'Emerging Greatness' (1916)

One's first strong impression is of the bustle and hopefulness that filled the early years from 1911–1916. ... Everywhere new institutions were being founded – magazines, clubs, little theatres, art or free-love or single tax colonies, experimental schools, picture galleries. Everywhere was a sense of secret companionship and immense potentialities for change.

Malcolm Cowley, *Exile's Return* (1934)

I

In 1913, Americans were disturbed and affected by an exhibition that was very different in kind and spirit from those grand expositions of modern technological and cultural marvels which had so troubled the spirit of Henry Adams. In this year, under the sponsorship of the Association of American Painters and Sculptors, a notable exhibition of paintings was put on display in New York City, and then moved on to Chicago and Boston. The Armory Show brought the American public face to face, for the first time, with the experimental movements in painting that had been developing in Europe in the century's first decade, since Impressionism: movements like Fauvism, Cubism, and Expressionism, painters like Van Gogh, Cézanne, Picasso, Brancusi, Duchamp. These were set alongside another tradition of the modern, the work of American painters of the naturalist 'Ashcan school'. The two strands of modern art seemed in contention: the new naturalism, strong in America, was factual, reportorial, socially aware; the new post-impressionism from Europe represented a challenge to realism, an anarchic vitalism, an image of the modern as displacement in perception, a breaking up of forms. As happened with its London counterpart, the show organized by Roger Fry at the Grafton Galleries in 1910, much of the response to the Armory Show was ribald: art students in Chicago burned a copy of Matisse's *Blue Nude*; Marcel Duchamp's *Nude Descending a Staircase* provoked widespread parody. Among the 30,000 Americans who saw the 'sensational' show, there were those ready to affirm naturalism as the true American impulse, aligned with the nation's rising progressive principles; others sensed that the new European forms were a genuine expression of contemporary experience, and touched on the complexities and possibilities of American life.

The Armory Show arrived at a notable turning point, to an America excited by progressivism and radicalism – it had had a choice among three Presidential candidates running on versions of the progressive ticket, when Woodrow Wilson won the office in 1912, and the Socialist candidate, Eugene V. Debs, amazingly polled a million votes. The new radical spectrum now emerging ranged from confident new versions of the progressive impulse to new left-wing radicalism, expressed by Big Bill Heywood, John Reed, the anarchist Emma Goldman; it also extended into new experimental artistic movements, coalescing with the political groups around the common desire for a radical emotion. This spirit was fed by a generation consciously in transit from an old to a new America, moving from small town to big city, from old 'puritan' containments to new emotional and social liberation. Bohemia was growing, new political and artistic groups were springing up everywhere, little magazines were flourishing. In 1911 the politically radical magazine *The Masses* (later *The Liberator*, suppressed for its pacifism after America entered the war), a mixture of socialism, anarchism, and feminism, began in New York's Greenwich Village, shortly followed by *The New Republic*, an organ of Europeanized liberalism that offered itself as Wilson's wartime conscience. In 1912 the literary avant-garde made its strike in Chicago with one of the first of the new 'little magazines', *Poetry (Chicago)*, shortly to be followed by *The Little Review*. Many of the new feelings and changes had come out of the 1890s; but they reflected an age which saw around it a new landscape and cityscape, a new separation from the past, and a new hunger for radical expression and action.

In *A Preface to Politics* (1914), Walter Lippmann sought to define the new mood, as one where 'the goal of action in its final analysis is aesthetic and not moral – a quality of feeling instead of conformity to rule'. Older progressivism had drawn intellectually on scientific positivism and naturalism, but now a new spirit of thought, emphasizing intuition, feeling, life-force, and creative evolution, seemed evident in the ideas of Bergson, Sorel, and Freud, Nietzsche, Wells, and Shaw. In 1909 Freud lectured in America, and his ideas of the unconscious, of repressed forces, of sexual revolution spread as far as the popular press (Mabel Dodge serialized an account of her psychoanalysis in the Hearst papers); Bergson's romantic ideas of creative evolution and intuition acquired influence, their acceptance being, said the liberal magazine *The Nation*, 'the expression of a revolt from the dreary materialistic determinism of the closing years of the last century'. A new romanticism thus seemed to underlie the modern movement, though many criticized it – the expatriate T. S. Eliot, seeking a new 'classicism', the 'New Humanist' Irving Babbitt, reading it as a force 'allied with all that is violent and extreme in contemporary life from syndicalism to "futurist" painting'. Indeed the new tendencies sought their revolt not just in politics but in art and in consciousness itself, producing an alliance between political radicals and the artistic avant-garde. And when progressive radicalism grew disillusioned, by the entry into world war, by doubts surrounding the Bolshevik revolution in 1917, by the Versailles peace talks of 1919, and when the America of the 1920s turned to a rampant new commercialism and social conservatism, it was in the arts rather than politics that radical challenge was expressed. Progressivism weakened, but the experimental avant-garde enlarged, generating a modernist art which also challenged the age's materialism, the nostalgic return to old American values, the revival of Puritanism.

The message of vitalism, abstraction, and modernism was therefore not lost on the generation of 1913. 'Looking back on it now,' Mabel Dodge (Luhan) wrote in her autobiography *Movers and Shakers* (4 vols., 1933–7), 'it seems as though everywhere, in that year of 1913, barriers went down and people reached each other who had never been in touch before; there were all sorts of new ways to communicate as well as new communications. The new spirit was abroad and swept us all together.' Moreover the new infusion from Europe, which the Armory Show represented, was helped by the fact that Americans had been involved in it already – expatriates like Ezra

Pound and Gertrude Stein, who now became crucial mediators. When Harriet Monroe started *Poetry (Chicago)*, her 'foreign correspondent' was Ezra Pound, who introduced not only expatriate American poets like T. S. Eliot, 'H.D.', and Robert Frost, but the newest French tendencies. Indeed *Poetry* became a magazine in contention, between Pound's cosmopolitan modernism and 'Imagisme' and Harriet Monroe's American progressivism, which promoted the presence of many significant new Midwestern poets, like Carl Sandburg and Vachel Lindsay. It was a version of the same contention apparent in the Armory Show, where Matisse and Duchamp appeared beside the native naturalists. 'Mr Lindsay did not go to France for *The Congo* or *General William Booth Enters Into Heaven* . . .,' wrote Miss Monroe in an attack on Pound. 'He is revealing himself in relation to direct experience, and he is not adapting to his work a twilight zone which is quite foreign to him, as it is, generally speaking, to the temperament of the nation.' Yet, in the event, the lessons of modernism were adapted, and with a remarkable speed. Amy Lowell was soon crossing the Atlantic to wrest the Imagist movement in poetry from Pound, to bring it back to America; Gertrude Stein came to be seen and valued as both the literary and the American wing of the Armory Show. Or as Mabel Dodge, who having 'sat' for one of Gertrude Stein's prose poems had good reason to promote her, put it: 'Gertrude Stein was born at the Armory Show.'

But the main reason for this adaptation was the emergence in America of a new generation of writers who responded to and in varying degrees were influenced by the rising modernist spirit. At first it was the poets who were most notable: Robert Frost, William Carlos Williams, Wallace Stevens, Marianne Moore, Edgar Lee Masters, Vachel Lindsay, Carl Sandburg. New experimental theatre groups, like the Provincetown Players, also emerged; Eugene O'Neill was a product. Social criticism intensified, in the work of Randolph Bourne, H. L. Mencken, Walter Lippmann, and Van Wyck Brooks, who saw these ferments as 'America's coming of age'. Fiction was slower to respond, and the corresponding movement did not really flower until the 1920s, one of the most remarkable ages of the American novel. But the advance signs were there, above all in the work of two notable precursors, Sherwood Anderson and Sinclair Lewis, writers who, like many of the new wave, came out of the Middle West, retained strong qualities of native feeling, yet expressed a spirit of revolt and formal change which was to spread through the novel of the Twenties.

II

Sherwood Anderson was indeed to become an ideal embodiment of the change of 1913, for he dramatized his revolt against commerce and into writing to coincide almost exactly with it. Born in 1876 (and hence of the same generation as Crane, Norris, Dreiser, and Gertrude Stein), he came to writing late, having worked as labourer, soldier, farm hand, and paint salesman, before – as he liked to explain – he walked out, in the key year of 1912, on wife, family, and the paint factory he now owned in Elyria, Ohio, to go to Chicago and enter its opening world of art and bohemianism. Anderson exaggerated the story: he was already writing before the break, the break was a breakdown, the marriage lasted some while longer, and he continued in advertising in Chicago. But, as he saw, the tale had a symbolic truth; Anderson was enacting the period's shift from confining countryside to bohemian city, from puritan commercialism to unrepressed creativity, from material to organic values. Art was protest, and that protest became an essential motive of his fiction, everywhere imbued with his desire to release psychic energy and find new forms for art, new shapes for existence. The painful personal movement towards the discovery of spirit, involving both an unfolding awareness of possibility and a reaction against the material limitations that everywhere stifle it, was to be his central subject. His early novels tried to do this through methods and perceptions close to those of naturalism. *Windy McPherson's Son* (1916) enacts his own break from commercial servitude, and turns into an assault on the cultureless void of contemporary mechanical America, which generates the frustration of the central character, and the psychology of distorted desire that shapes him. *Marching Men* (1917) tells the reverse story, of a man moving up the ladder of success to a material advancement that proves meaningless; it aspires to a political solution, looking for an answer in the collective desires and energies of the proletariat. But neither naturalistic methods nor political solutions would quite serve; Anderson's concern was really with subjective and solitary renewal. This pressed his work beyond naturalism into new forms. Waldo Frank, Anderson's Chicago friend and fellow novelist, saw the point; reviewing *Marching Men* under the headline 'Emerging Greatness', he already sensed that the book took the 'elemental movement' of factual naturalism forward towards 'form and direction, the force that causes it being borne into the air'.

Anderson's hunger for new forms was indeed evident. He had read Stein's *Three Lives* and, after mocking it at first, come to feel that it 'contained some of the best work done by an American'. Then, following the Armory Show, he looked at *Tender Buttons* and found there a bareness of composition, and a sense of priority of form over content, which he found vital 'for the artist who happens to work with words as his material'. As a result, he said, 'I became a little conscious where before I had been unconscious', and the increasing need to distil an aesthetic response, to make writing a formal enquiry, began to reshape his work. While publishing the early novels he had been writing a number of short stories with a common setting, a small Ohio town like the one from which he had come. These he now began to link together, rather in the manner of the great modernist short-story cycle of these years, Joyce's *Dubliners* (1914). Like Joyce, Anderson was concerned to press naturalist materials towards revelation, epiphany – the crystallization of experience, the disclosure of form. The 26 stories of *Winesburg, Ohio* (1919) are a cycle not simply because their characters together make up the life of one small Middle Western town, nor even because they share a common modern loneliness. The fundamental link is artistic: the stories explore two kinds of creativity driving towards experience and disclosure, that of the characters at the centre of each separate story, that of the author himself, seeking a formal deliverance from his writing. Like *Dubliners*, *Winesburg* can be read naturalistically, as an account of individuals trapped by social confinement and paralysis, narrow human experience, and the puritanical burdens and guilts of American small-town life. So, in the story 'Godliness', Jesse Bentley, driven by puritan religious zeal into increasing the potential of his land, becomes a dour, selfish figure, a product of 'the most materialistic age in the history of the world', who discovers that his own nostalgic desire for individualism is curiously meshed with a coarse new commercialism. Jesse becomes malformed by the forces within him and the forces that surround him, grows narrow and distorted in changing history; this expresses Anderson's essential theme in the volume, which is the ways in which external and internal limitations on freedom produce psychic distortion, a containment of human creativity, a clutching at a single narrowed truth.

In this way, Anderson's characters, in different fashions, become what he liked to call 'grotesques'; indeed, his original title for the collection was to have been *The Book of the Grotesque*. He retained that title for the first and prefatory story, a small credo for the volume, depicting a writer like himself who recognizes that individuals become grotesque when they seize one truth from the many, make it their own, 'try to live . . . life by it'. In fact Anderson's use of the term is perplexing, because he meant two things by it. On the one hand, the grotesque was his subject; like his friend Edgar Lee Masters, whose poem cycle *Spoon River Anthology* (1916) was also an influence on him, Anderson wanted to portray a gallery of damaged small-town figures, caught in moments of distortion and loneliness, the conditions of their distortion, the moments of their self-discovery. But he also wanted to make the grotesque his *method*, a modern technique of writing, for, as he said, 'in *Winesburg* I made my own form.' The grotesque was his modernist means of depicting an estranged world in order to distil its nature and concentrate on the forms by which distortion might disclose underlying creativity. The stories are modern experiments, avoiding traditional plotting and self-explaining methods of causality. Anderson declared that there were 'no plot stories ever lived in any life I knew about'; he said his aim was to give the feel of 'a story grasped whole as one would pick up an apple in the orchard', that he was seeking 'a new looseness', to show 'lives flowing past each other, the whole, however, to leave a definite impression'. One essential way to perceive modernism is to see it as an art that insists on its internal frame, on the active presence of the medium used, on the 'foregrounding' of the artistic activity, so that the achievement of the story's form becomes part of the story. This was how Anderson's work now developed, in an endeavour to render the intuitive, the unspoken, the unconscious as essential realms of experience, manifest both *within* the story and in the *making* of the story.

Anderson's stories were thus both psychological and aesthetic – one reason why they are readily open to Freudian readings. Anderson claimed he knew Freud only at second hand, but he wrote at a time when Freudianism was being widely assimilated in America. The stories of *Winesburg* certainly have an intense psychological content, a serious concern with sexual repression, and with the intimate relation of sexuality to creativity; they are also, however, concerned with the possibilities of creative recovery, above all through the creative act of the stories themselves. Hence, in 'Hands', Wing Biddlebaum's nervously moving hands may indicate his suppressed homosexuality, but they also are an image of the hunger for expression, and call for an artistic elucidation. The restless activity of these hands, 'like unto the beatings of the wings of an imprisoned bird, had given [Wing] his name. Some obscure poet of the town had thought of it. . . .' The 'obscure poet' is linked with the task of discovering 'many strange, beautiful qualities in obscure men'; the imprisoned motion calls for elaborate tactics of artistic surrogation. Other poets and potential writers are here, above all the young reporter, George Willard, a classic period portrait of the artist as a young man. He is the one who will make the journey out, to whatever success or failure; he becomes the partial but not complete confidant of the silent, imprisoned citizens, whose desires can only be expressed obliquely, wordlessly, in corners, in the dark, creating the beginnings of the appropriate images which can then be transfigured, not by Willard but by the author beyond him, into oblique but revealing form. Wing is thus a typical citizen of a town that is alive with half-hidden creativity; he is one of many 'twisted apples' transmitting incomplete messages of need, messages like the always crumpled notes, the 'paper pills', of Doc Reefy. And, hungering for an artist to speak for them, these characters call by implication for an art of a new kind that can manifest, can newly signify, their unfinished utterance.

It is the notion of unspoken depths beneath its surfaces that unifies *Winesburg*, and indicates the nature of its task. Its characters are repositories of the untold, trapped in voyeuristic pain; but direct utterance cannot reveal the truth, the truths being too many. Hence Ray Pearson, married to a nagging wife in 'The Untold Lie', wants to utter his truth, to warn a friend not to marry, but finally accepts the value of silence: '"It's just as well. Whatever I told him would have been a lie," he said softly, and then his form also disappeared into the darkness of the fields.' Like his form itself, speech is illusory, and statement will not serve to give the meaning of a statement, or a story. Hence Anderson must find a symbolic form which self-consciously enquires into the capacity of language and art to reach towards revelation. Completeness may not come in life itself, and George Willard cannot amend the lives of others or greatly help himself; but it may come in form, in artistic coherence. Like Ray Pearson, Wing Biddlebaum, at the end of 'Hands', retreats into darkness. He is now the town victim, but beyond the damaged life there remains the transcendent power of the image that has dominated his story. So the tale ends as it began with Wing's hands, which 'flashing in and out of the light, might have been mistaken for the fingers of the devotee going swiftly through decade after decade of his rosary'. The social plot contains; the verbal plot, always urgently there in these storyless stories, reveals. George Willard, the potential artist, the one character who can leave the tight puritanical world of Winesburg to follow his 'dreams', points a way; but even he remains within the stories, and his understandings are never more than limited. He links the separate stories by being in them; but it is only the work itself, made coherent through its own poetic existence, that can achieve timeless completion.

Winesburg was Anderson's one outright triumph, though remarkable volumes of short stories – *The Triumph of the Egg* (1922), *Horses and Men* (1923), and *Death in the Woods* (1933) – followed it. His aim to take the modernist methods he had developed in short fiction into the novel, exploring 'the new American life, . . . the whirl and roar of modern machines', proved somewhat less successful. His novels of the 1920s were an assault on the deadliness of material American life, an attack on modern commercialism and industrialism, which were eroding the organic centres of American life and generating sexual aridity; but, at novel length, Anderson struggled to relate social issues to aesthetic redemptions. *Poor White* (1920) is a powerful story about a poor young man, Hugh McVey, from the Mississippi Valley, who is drawn from this Twainian world by a New England woman who points him towards a puritanic industriousness. Moving to Ohio, he invents machines to supplant painful toil, only to find that they also suppress creativity; men and machines become alike grotesque. The fable is explicit: 'It was time for art and beauty to awake in the land,' Anderson writes; 'Instead, the giant, Industry, awoke.' What is missing can, it seems, be replaced only by the aesthetic sense, and by poetic style and technique. His work moved towards an experimental rhetoric, and his next two novels – *Many Marriages* (1923), about modern sexual aridity, and *Dark Laughter* (1925), about the paralysis of the white industrial mind, undercut by the dark laughter of the black servants – are comparable with 'poetic' avant-garde works like E. E. Cummings's

The Enormous Room (1922), or William Carlos Williams's *The Great American Novel* (1923), with its cry of 'Break the word . . . If I make a word I make myself into a word.' Both Anderson's books deal with the period theme, of mind severed from body, rational thought from vital flux, of contemporary emptiness and sterility, through methods of impression, monologue, rhythmic poetic flow. 'There is an idea of a new novel form floating in me, something looser, more real, more true,' he said of *Many Marriages*, 'I want to go after that.' In *Dark Laughter*, the debt to Joyce and Stein and the experimental text is explicit. Yet Anderson's lyric discourse seemed never to become more than discourse; for the next generation of experimental writers, he was to be an important precursor, but not an entire success.

By now he had moved to the bohemia of New Orleans, and met and helped William Faulkner, whose early work was influenced by him, but who also saw the problem: 'He worked so hard at this [exactitude] that it finally became just style,' Faulkner said; 'an end instead of a means: so that he presently came to believe that, provided he kept the style pure and intact and unchanged and inviolate, what the style contained would have to be first rate.' Faulkner parodied him briefly, Hemingway, whom he also helped, at length in *The Torrents of Spring* (1926). The doubts were understandable, but Anderson's role in opening up the fiction of the Twenties to modernist possibilities was crucial. As Waldo Frank said, he had led the way out of the naturalistic devotion to 'the blind cult of the American fact', and brought home the recognition that works of art are aesthetic objects with their own value and values. Faulkner, who praised as well as parodied, was helped to his own sense of regionalism, his own challenge to industrialism, his own sense of dark laughter; Hemingway mocked, yet that portrait of the young artist adrift in a world of the pain of others that starts in George Willard becomes, in his Nick Adams, a figure pushed to new pressure when death becomes commonplace and the landscape loses all reassurance. Stein praised him: 'really except Sherwood there was no one in America who could write a clear and passionate sentence,' she said. For Anderson art was the antithesis to puritanism, and puritanism was increasingly the American mode of mind and being. And if many writers of the next generation found the space between style and life, or between the bohemian present and the rooted organic past, the troubled space they must cross, they found these divisions and compositions very considerably under Anderson's tutelage.

III

Sherwood Anderson and Sinclair Lewis are often compared, and it is
not hard to see why: not only did they share similar Middle Western
populist origins, the main subject of both was American small-town
life, its power in American culture, and the Twenties revolt against
it – a revolt that led them both towards the city and the idea of the
transcendence of art. Both developed beyond naturalism, but in two
quite different directions: Anderson's primary quest was towards
form: Lewis was always drawn towards the cult of the American fact,
but turned naturalism into a mechanism of satire. Born in 1885 in
Sauk Centre, Minnesota (which would become 'Gopher Prairie' in
Main Street, the book that established his reputation), Lewis left his
small-town background for an Eastern education, initially at Oberlin
College, then at Yale. In the East he was socially unhappy, but he
turned away from his fundamentalist religious background to
become an atheistic socialist. He then moved in pre-war progressive
circles, working with Upton Sinclair on his Helicon Hall settlement
project, then in a communitarian experiment in California, through
which he met Jack London and began selling him plots. Back in New
York in 1910, Lewis moved on the fringes of radical circles, met
Emma Goldman, read Shaw and Wells, and moved from hack writing to larger literary ambitions. H. G. Wells clearly influenced his
earlier novels – like *Our Mr Wrenn* (1914), about the preoccupying
theme of the times, the little ordinary man trapped in dull routines
but hungering for an adventurous release, a land of romance beyond
the real. But it was when the war ended, and America turned away
from progressivism towards commercialism and 'normalcy', that
Lewis found the subject that made him a major writer.

That subject, as for Anderson, was the small town and the Middle
West he had left behind him; for Lewis, it was a potent expression of
the prevalent mood of ruralism, isolationism, and national nostalgia,
of the uneasy politics of red scare, Prohibition, the reviving Ku Klux
Klan. He observed an America that had 'gone through the revolutionary change from rustic colony to world-empire without having in
the least altered the bucolic and Puritanic simplicity of Uncle Sam',
and he turned to look back at his own origins: at 'Gopher Prairie',
the typical American small town, whose Main Street is 'the continu-
ation of Main Streets everywhere', and at 'Zenith', the Midwestern
commercial city of middle America. This was the heartland where

the composing of an advertisement was considered an act of artistic creation, and the Ford car standing outside the Main Street garage stood for 'poetry and tragedy, love and heroism'. Lewis was never quite to know what the higher culture he desired for America was, but he knew that what defused it was what he came to call 'the village virus', the small-town celebration of 'dullness made God'. And he did know this small-town material, and seized on it in an excited mixture of love and hate, celebration and satire. His two key books, *Main Street* (1920) and *Babbitt* (1922), were remarkably toned – lingering, even loving satires that none the less gave the intellectual unease and despair of the Twenties an essential mythology. As H. L. Mencken, who shared Lewis's mixture of disappointed radicalism and obsession with the follies of what he called the American 'booboisie', put it, they were the work of 'the one real anatomist of American Kultur'.

Lewis's success came from his full and intimate knowledge of the world about which he wrote. He populated it, amassed its detail, reproduced its material décor, its institutions, its operative sociology, so that the reader could draw from his books about the imaginary Western state of Winnemac both a loving recreation and an angle of critical distance. The technique is neo-documentary or sociological: Lewis works like a researcher in displaying the institutions and rites, the goods and chattels, the ideologies and sexual mores. Sociology was indeed one of the instrumentalities of the Twenties, one of the ways of encompassing the deep sense of change that came in the decade; *Main Street* fascinatingly compares with Robert and Helen Lynd's book *Middletown* (1929), which anatomized a middle-American, middle-way American town. Lewis had the sociologist's capacity to identify, document, and recognize the weight and the function of contemporary American *kitsch*, to penetrate an entire cultural process and iconography, and to show Main Street not just as a place but a state of mind, Babbitt not just as an individual but as a fundamental American type, an instance of 'Babbittry'. At the same time he had a satirical distance, a tone that mocks and deflates, if not quite totally. His satire, never quite poised, reveals him as a materialist with romantic longings, a man with one foot firmly in the world he satirizes. His books have the power often possessed by middle art, that of re-creating without entirely interpreting a fundamental cultural situation.

So *Main Street* assaults 'the contentment of the quiet dead', and fundamentalism, strict moralism, self-justifying commercialism; but the deadness comes alive in Lewis's hands as a kind of dreaming innocence from 'good little people, comfortable, industrious, credulous', and above all limited, accepting, even being excited by, the fundamental change that Lewis observes – the change from an old pioneer world to a new world of business and commerce, from an American idealism to a bland and patriotic materialism. We see all this through the eyes of Carole Kennicott, a modern American girl with 'a quality of suspended freedom', whose marriage to the doctor in Gopher Prairie ties her to the town. She rebels, in *bovaryste* fashion, against 'dullness made God', and hopes either to restore this 'smug in-between town, which had changed "Money Musk" for phonographs grinding out ragtime' to simplicity, or to bring it into touch with modern artistic culture. Carole's romanticism is itself unsophisticated, and her sentimentalism ('I just love common workmen') is based on the dreaming illusions shared in one way or another by nearly all Lewis's characters. He clearly half admires Carole, perhaps more than the modern reader might; but he does see round her, recognizes her patronizing ways, and displays her inevitable defeat, since her desires contain an element of the absurd. She does escape briefly, to the big city of Washington; but he has her come back to Gopher Prairie and lapse into 'the humdrum inevitable tragedy of the struggle against inertia'. However, Gopher Prairie has itself changed, and perhaps the essential story of *Main Street* lies in the town's transformation from the world of the buggy to the world of the Ford and the Buick, from market village to modern commerce. The book ends as Gopher Prairie attempts to meet the Twenties world by trying to become a centre for industry and state institutions, employing a booster, Mr Blausser, a man of Punch, Pep, and Go, the personification of a self-vaunting new America (the America of Bruce Barton, who wrote a life of Jesus as the most successful businessman of all time) hiding empty materialism under proud and optimistic rhetoric.

It was that new America, the America whose business is business, that led Lewis forward to his next book, *Babbitt*. Surely his best novel, *Babbitt* is set firmly in the world of the early Twenties, in the bustling commercial, stoutly Republican, Middle Western city of Zenith, where beneath the modern skyline of office buildings – 'austere towers of steel and cement and limestone, sturdy as cliffs and delicate as silver rods' – the spirit of small-time business and suburbia rules, and all-American mores flourish, confident that they represent the best the nation stands for. The loving touch with which Lewis draws his cityscape suggests the book's tone; there is indeed wonder in this modernizing world. What he needs is a wondering innocent suited to enjoy it; Lewis admirably creates him in the realtor George F. Babbitt, Lewis's Pooter, the small man who is made by and marvellously loves the commercial life and technological goods that surround him. Babbitt is a joiner and a community man who attaches himself to every lodge, church, business group, or social institution that might give him confidence, status, amusement, or identity ('Nothing gave Babbitt more purification and publicity than his labors for the Sunday School'); all this Lewis watches with satirical pleasure, for Babbitt allows him access to all the social groupings and community activities which his sociological method needs. Babbitt thus becomes exemplary, the boyish *naïf* obsessed by goods and uneasy in his family life, who none the less sees himself as the all-American male, 'a God-fearing, hustling, successful, two-fisted Regular Guy, who belongs to some church with pep and piety in it, who belongs to the Boosters or the Rotarians or the Kiwanis. . . .' He loves the touch, feel, and substance of material American reality. Mechanical devices are 'symbols of truth and beauty', and give him 'a delightful feeling of being technical and initiated'. He knows himself both the beneficiary of prosperity and the agent of the commercialism that is bringing bustle and growth to America, and as long as these things remain real for him his loyalty and faith manage to persist. At the same time, Lewis gives him the little man's boyish innocence that moves towards revolt. He described the book as a GAN about a TBM – a Great American Novel about a Tired Business Man – and Babbitt does grow tired of worshipping at the tower of 'the religion of business'. He mildly comes to question the anti-intellectual, class-conscious, and racist opinions he learns from his newspapers; he comes to rage against 'mechanical business', 'mechanical religion', 'mechanical golf'. But, if mildly tragic, his revolt, like Carole Kennicott's, goes nowhere; even his great escape into the more 'natural' American past is defeated by attacking mosquitoes. Beaten both in the mechanical war and the sex war, he becomes that familiar Twenties figure, the little anti-hero, caught between conventionality and restless longing.

Babbitt has its sentimentalities and *longueurs*, like all Lewis's work; but it strikes a remarkable balance between naturalism and satire, and stands even now as a classic version of middle American values. It was a triumph Lewis was not really destined to repeat. By 1930, when he won the Nobel Prize as an embodiment of the critical spirit of the Twenties, his powers already seemed to be in decline. *Arrowsmith* (1925) was an attempt to create a positive and reforming American hero in the figure of a crusading doctor surrounded by corruption and misunderstanding; more successfully, *Elmer Gantry* (1927) had portrayed a revivalist religious charlatan with considerable satirical power; with *Dodsworth* (1929), he had returned to 'Zenith', but, again attempting to portray a character who distils some of the virtues and strengths of Middle Western simplicity, had softened his tone. His romantic fight with materialism and provincialism had lost its bite, and his novels became commonplace, slipping towards banality. For the younger writers now appearing, it was Anderson, not Lewis, who represented the stronger potential for American fiction. Anderson himself pointed up the difference between them when he said that Lewis had 'an amazing attention to the details of lives', but no instinct at all for the inward forces that drive them. Lewis's world, solid and amassed, was no longer the world the new writers, fascinated by the impact of change, and war, perceived; and it was Anderson's path of consciousness and form that seemed to count the more.

4 Art-style and Life-style: The 1920s

The uncertainties of 1919 were over – there seemed little doubt about what was going to happen – America was going on the greatest, gaudiest spree in history and there was going to be plenty to tell about it. The whole golden boom was in the air – its splendid generosities, its outrageous corruptions and the tortuous death struggle of the old America in Prohibition. All the stories that came into my head had a touch of disaster in them. ...

F. Scott Fitzgerald, 'Early Success' (1937)

Whole departments of [the puritan's] psychic life must be repressed. Categories of desire must be inhibited. Reaches of consciousness must be lopped off. Old, half-forgotten intuitions must be called out from the buried depths of his mind, and made the governors of his life.

Waldo Frank, *Our America* (1919)

I

'As I figure it:', Henry Adams had written in an apocalyptic equation at the turn of the century, ' – 1830 : 1860 :: 1890 : x, and x always comes out, not 1920, but infinity.' Adams, of course, was offering another of his laws of proliferating energy, but it might well have been a prophecy of the sense of change, disorientation, and uncertainty that affected America after 1920. Undoubtedly one of the reasons for this new sense of dislocation was the First World War, the first major foreign conflict in which the United States participated. The war the United States entered in 1917, to make the world 'safe for democracy', as President Woodrow Wilson put it, had a deep impact on American thought and development. In Europe its consequences were clear: more than six million dead, old empires disestablished, the geopolitical map transformed, political and economic chaos, the coming, in Russia, of the century's first major revolutionary state, and widespread apocalyptic despair about the end of civilization. Its soil untouched, the United States seemed less directly affected; indeed it emerged from the war an economic beneficiary, now a creditor rather than a debtor nation. It also emerged more deeply convinced of 'basic' American values, suspicious of foreign entanglements, uneasy about the direction of world affairs, distrustful of the progressive politics of the pre-war years. Looking to itself, the nation concentrated on business, economic expansion, the advancing of technology, the spread of consumerism. The new developments seemed simple extensions of traditional American principles of individualism, self-advancement, and the pursuit of abundance for all. Yet change was everywhere visible as the economy boomed. Wealth spread, mores altered, the texture of life changed, the new technologies appeared in every home and street; a consciousness of change and generational difference became widespread. The sense of cultural disorder and collapse apparent in Europe affected Americans too; so Amory Blaine, hero of Scott Fitzgerald's first novel *This Side of Paradise* (1920), knows he belongs to 'a new generation dedicated more than the last to the fear of poverty and the worship of success; grown up to find all gods dead, all wars fought, all faiths in man shaken.'

For Americans as well as Europeans, then, the war was felt as a point of crucial translation, demarcating the beginning of a new era, the Twenties, as clearly as the Great Crash marked its end. One did not need to have gone to Europe or fought in battle to feel the sense of change and generational separation; it became part of the American culture of the decade. In fact, many American writers *did* go, as if to some necessary educational and literary experience. A significant number served as soldiers or members of the ambulance corps in Europe, and came to link their first post-adolescent encounter with 'life' with that experience. John Dos Passos, Ernest Hemingway, E. E. Cummings, and Edmund Wilson, all central novelists of the Twenties, were in the ambulance corps; Hemingway, famously, was wounded on the Italian front, and turned that wound into an essential metaphor for the pain of life in a new troubled age. Scott Fitzgerald had just finished officer training and was about to embark for Europe when the Armistice was signed; William Faulkner trained with the Royal Canadian Air Force, and was to encourage the myth that he had served as a pilot in France. For many of these writers, the war was the subject of their first literary utterances. It was an image of fundamental transition, a challenge to the small-town values among which many of them had grown up, to old heroic ideas of battle, to ideas of 'culture' as a body of established values, modes, languages. 'Culture' had also meant Europe; but now Europe, tearing itself to pieces on the battlefields, meant experience not as art and tradition but as horror, extremity, historical exposure. Language itself seemed to shrink, to become inoperative in the face of what was happening, and those who had been to war seemed fundamentally cut off from those who had not – Krebs, in Hemingway's story 'A Soldier's Home', comes back to his Middle Western background to find old values, meanings, and modes of speech useless to him. In the apocalyptic new history, now begun, men needed new perceptions, new modes of existential self-knowledge, new styles of living and expression to survive.

So the war produced the war novel: John Dos Passos's two works of growing disillusion, *One Man's Initiation: 1917* (1920) and *Three Soldiers* (1921); E. E. Cummings's experimental *The Enormous Room* (1922), about his confinement in a French prison camp after he had expressed pacifist views; realistic battlefield works like Thomas Boyd's *Through the Wheat* (1925); novels about the 'separate peace' of the disenchanted modern hero like, above all, Hemingway's *A Farewell to Arms* (1930). These were books in which the experience of war enforced a new style, expressing a transformed set of relations between man, nature, culture, and history. But what dominated the American Twenties was the *post*-war novel – the novel penetrated by war, making of it an apocalyptic metaphor, the sign of a world severed from its past, changed, darkened, modernized. 'I was certain that all the young people were going to be killed in the war,' Fitzgerald said, explaining the genesis of *This Side of Paradise*, written in his leaves from military service, 'and I wanted to put on paper a record of the strange life they had lived in their time.' Hemingway's *The Sun Also Rises* (1926) is – like D. H. Lawrence's apocalyptic *Lady Chatterley's Lover* (1928) – dominated by the castrating, modernizing war wound, present not just in his hero but in the surrounding 'herd' of his generation, hunting for a new life-style and a sense of value in an emptied world. Images of waste and sterility prevail in the writing of the Twenties: famously in Ezra Pound's *Hugh Selwyn Mauberley* (1920) and T. S. Eliot's *The Waste Land* (1922), but also in the 'Valley of Ashes' of Fitzgerald's *The Great Gatsby* (1925) or in the circling emptinesses of *The Sun Also Rises*. Likewise William Faulkner's *Soldier's Pay* (1926) focuses on the central image of the wounded soldier returning wasted from the battlefield to a new world where sexual relations have grown oblique, traditional heroic values dislocated. The war spoke to the sense of a bleak modern invitation, a new fissure between old versions of life and present fact. And one answer was a recovery of decadence itself, the attempt to make style transfigure history, give shape to personal life, generate aesthetic substance from contingency.

The decadent sense was, however, prompted not just by war, but by post-war American development. The compromises of Wilson's Versailles Treaty, the failure of the U.S. Senate to ratify his proposals for a League of Nations, the red scare, the extending of Prohibition through the Volstead Act, the reversion to what the Republican President Harding, Wilson's successor, called 'normalcy' – all helped to intensify the feelings of political failure, purposelessness, and cultural emptiness that mark so much of the writing of the Twenties. In his Thirties novel that looks back on the Twenties, *U.S.A.*, John Dos Passos was to make 1919 – the year of Versailles and the red scare, which marked the defeat of progressive expectations – the fulcrum year, and, from the standpoint of the Depression, it was not hard for him to see the Twenties as what it became for many afterwards – the decade of illusions, political ignorance, flaunted capitalism, materialism, isolationism, intolerance. Yet the paradox of the Twenties was that this conservative decade set in motion some of the most profound changes in modern American history – changes less political than behavioural, psychological, and structural, which swept away many of the values Americans thought they were holding fast to. For, as the economy moved its centre from production to consumption, as credit ran free and personal spending boomed, as the middle class expanded and the nation became linked through new technologies in media and transportation, modernity seemed to move at an accelerated pace. Lifestyles shifted, the generations divided, sexual mores altered. The age of puritanism and Prohibition was also the age of psychoanalysis, jazz, and flappers; the age that challenged innovation and looked nostalgically back to the rural past was also the time of massive new technical and commercial developments – the automobile, the aeroplane, the movie, the radio, the high-rise excitement of the modern city. The mixture of reaction and innovation was exemplified in the key conflicts of the period – the Scopes trial, the Sacco–Vanzetti case. It was also apparent in the arts, which were haunted by images of a simpler rural past even as they responded to and incorporated the new modernity.

But if the American fiction of the Twenties was a fiction of experiment, decadence, and dissent, it was not a fiction of total despair. Turning away from naturalism and progressivism towards the avant-garde, the experimental, the bohemian, it expressed a disillusionment with and displacement from American life, nowhere more evident than in the mass exodus of American writers to Paris. Elements of once-progressive disappointment and anger at the social order of the Twenties lay behind many of these expatriations – manifest in Harold Stearns's essay anthology of 1922, *Civilization in the United States*, in which many other ex-progressives concluded that, under the new order, there was none; Stearns himself recommended that American writers get out. Paris offered a cheap bohemia at favourable rates of exchange, but behind the dissent an the desire for the new there often lay a nostalgia for an older and more pastoral America; writing in the experimental ateliers of Paris, many of the expatriates wrote, at a formal distance, of a rural, often a Middle Western, American world left behind. Taking instruction from Stein, Pound, and Joyce in the already established tradition of European modernism, they none the less infused that modernism with American myths. Drawing on the modernist lore of cultural collapse, adapting the post-realist conventions of the dissipation of chronology and linear narrative, of discontinuity between history and form, they groped towards a new mythology that expressed not just the discontinuities and defeats but also the excitements of the energetic modernity of contemporary America. As Gertrude Stein had said, modernism seemed peculiarly American, a natural expression of the new 'space-time continuum' that was a fact of American life. The techniques of modernist style – spatial form, rapid cutting, the need for newer and harder modes of expression, mechanization or abstraction of the human figure, a sense of historical dislocation, psychic lesion, the void anonymity of nature and landscape – seemed to offer a discourse appropriate to American experience. It expressed the tempo of change, the sense of movement, the evanescence and dislocation of city life, but perhaps especially the feeling that America was itself the centre of modernity.

The adaptation of modernism in the American fiction of the Twenties newly linked that fiction with much of the most important experimental work now happening in Europe; but it was also a way of responding to the forces of change at work in American experience. Modernism was, in a sense, reportorial, a new style of art responding to new styles of life. One part of its aim was to capture new consciousness and new structures in literature: hence John Dos Passos's attempt to render the changed city through expressionist techniques in *Manhattan Transfer* (1925), Faulkner's to examine the temporal and historical disorders of modern Southern consciousness in *The Sound and the Fury* (1929). But another was not so much to depict the collapse of order and structure as to attempt to recover it through the discontinuous construct, which could explore the parts of a culture in the attempt to discover a new coherent form. Thus an important endeavour running through the American modernism of the 1920s is the attempt to overcome the sense of historical fracture and Spenglerian cultural despair through a spatial modern epic, a new version of the Great American Novel. Fitzgerald both dissipates and creates the American dream in *The Great Gatsby*; Stein, in *The Making of Americans* (1925), attempts to invest America with a modernist myth; Thomas Wolfe's grandiose autobiographical experiments may teach him that the past is lost, and one can't go home again, but also that one might dream the myth of the reconstituted nation ('So soon the morning, soon the morning, O America'). Modernist epical ambitions underlie William Faulkner's entire Yoknapatawpha saga, as they do Dos Passos's critical yet yearning *U.S.A.*, which fragments in order both to expose and redeem fragmentation.

It is this that gives American modernist writing both its reportorial quality and a sense of hope and promise that is not present in many of the disjunctive epics of European modernism – in which the awareness of the modern as a state of psychic, historical, and political extremity goes deeper. The American novel of the Twenties is extremely attentive to the feel of the modern, and to its unease. It is haunted by apocalyptic anxieties, troubled with a deep cultural unease, and displays a decadent dismay in the face of the material world and the political order. It none the less hungers to make the world re-cohere, either by reaching behind the present to a recovered pastoral world, or to some timeless moment set beyond the contingency of modern time, or by attempting to make form itself an expression of culture as possibility. Underlying the decade was, in fact, an excitement in experiment which gave to American fiction a whole new impulse. Major new forms and talents appeared;

Malcolm Cowley rightly calls this time a 'second flowering', to be compared with the first great American flowering in the 1840s and 1850s, the age of Hawthorne, Emerson, Melville, and Whitman. The writers who now appeared gave the American novel a new version of the modern and a new version of modernism. 'Something subtle seemed to pass to America, the style of man,' said Fitzgerald, that extraordinary close recorder of the decade, in an essay; to a considerable degree, this was true of the style of modern fiction also.

II

The writer of the Twenties who most obviously felt the intensity of modern American experience in all its specified and evolving detail was indeed Scott Fitzgerald. To many of his critics he has seemed little more than a chronicler, a man so immersed in the social life of his times, its money, amusements, behaviour, fashions, the unwinding daily detail of history, that he could not stand back and consider it. Fitzgerald was, more than most, a novelist of immersion; and this, the heart of his literary tactic, was paid for at high cost. It involved a competition for public fame and attention that cut deep into his psychic life, his marriage, his writing. His essay 'The Crack-Up' draws a close analogy between the historical development of America in the Twenties and his own psychic curve, euphoria turning to trauma and disturbance; the Slump itself becomes the public analogue for his own personal crack-up. Such identifications were functional exactly because Fitzgerald lived them as such, tying himself to the glossy cosmopolitan life-style that was part of the decade's experimentalism, and drawing from this his sense of personal and artistic style. His age ran roughly parallel to the century's decades; born, in Saint Paul, Minnesota, in 1896, his twenties were the American Twenties. In 1913 he went east to Princeton, entering the world of the East Coast patriciate, a world of promise, wealth, and dream, which would always allure him, in which he would always be a parvenu, about which the stories he now began to write would tell.

His first book, *This Side of Paradise*, came out as the new decade started, and was an instant best-seller, rivalling in the lists a novel by a fellow Minnesotan, Sinclair Lewis's *Main Street*. Fitzgerald offered a quite different view of the modern, attempting to catch the mood of his distinctive troubled generation, those just too young for war.

Like another fashionable contemporary novel, James Branch Cabell's *Jurgen* (1919), it is a consciously decadent book, about the 'golden boy', 'hallowed by his own youth', who makes his own life the object of social and aesthetic experiment. Amory Blaine is the 'romantic egoist', drawn on the one hand by narcissistic investment in his own youth and beauty, on the other by the fragile promises of society: Princeton's 'glittering caste-system', and the beautiful woman who embodies it but stands just out of reach. Beauty and money become transposed versions of each other; style is all, a kind of desperate self-expenditure, history being internalized as fashion, self-presentation, daring conduct. More energetic than good, the book lays down, if in unresolved form, many of Fitzgerald's primary themes: the evanescence of wealth and beauty, knowledge of the damnation of self-love, a consciousness of history's fragility, a neo-religious idealism transposed on to society.

The book's remarkable success encouraged Fitzgerald to take on the stance of style-setter for his times, the filter and promoter of its moods and fashions. He married his remote woman, Zelda Sayre, and together they began to perform the Twenties as a dance of romance and cynicism – chasing conspicuous wealth, but consuming, too, the underlying moral and economic fragility. Zelda was the new woman, the flapper displaying toughness, maleness, moral provisionality; Scott was the new man, flamboyantly consuming style, writing for 'my own personal public – that is, the countless flappers and college kids who think I am a sort of oracle'. The titles of his next books of stories – *Flappers and Philosophers* (1921), *Tales of the Jazz Age* (1922) – suggest his determined relation to period style. His next novel, *The Beautiful and Damned* (1922), displays the 'touch of disaster' that he saw as another essential theme: Gloria and Anthony Patch want to make their marriage a 'live, lovely, glamorous performance', trusting that 'something is going to happen'. But moral inconsequentiality and the pressure of time take their toll: 'I don't want to live without my pretty face,' cries Gloria.

But now, this early, uneven work over, Fitzgerald's fiction took on a new seriousness. This is sometimes explained as the result of his learning the capacity to stand back; yet if anything his immersion in the times increased. Like his character Dick Diver in *Tender Is the Night* (1934), compelled to risk ordinariness and sanity to understand the consciousness of others, Fitzgerald believed the writer must be a 'performing self', an agent in the places where the times are most fully enacted. Both his personal and fictional styles were modes of involvement; but now, in his better work, he began increasingly to understand the compelling forces behind this psychic overextension. With *The Great Gatsby* (1925), one of the most notable of American twentieth-century novels, this mixture of involvement and understanding reaches an extraordinary balance. The book is a classic of formal control (Fitzgerald had learned it in part from Conrad); it is also a book that seeks exactly to enter its own time and place while reaching beyond it – just as its central character, Jay Gatsby, aims to do. It is the story of a gross, materialistic, careless society of coarse wealth spread on top of a sterile world; on to it is cast an extraordinary illusion, that of the ex-Jay Gatz, the self-created Gatsby. A man whose poor past and corrupt economic supports are hidden in his own glow, Gatsby like-wise decorates his entire world through his love for Daisy Buchanan. Society is decadent in one way, Gatsby in another: he is a dandy of desire, a desire that has been redirected from its human or material object into a fantasy, one which seeks to retain a past moment in an endless instant of contemplation. His aim, in effect, is to transfigure money into love – a symbolist dream, an assault on reality, the system, the clock of time itself. The clock still ticks, and Fitzgerald hears it; Gatsby is a corrupt dreamer, Daisy a corrupt object of love, married to a violent, damaging husband, surrounded by 'careless-ness' and social indifference, her voice full of money. But he grants the grandeur of the invented self and the gaudy worth of its passions: 'The most grotesque and fantastic conceits haunted [Gatsby] in his bed at night. A universe of ineffable gaudiness spun itself out in his brain while the clock ticked on the wash-stand and the moon soaked with wet light his tangled clothes upon the floor. . . .' Gatsby embodies the symbolic aim of the book itself, a figure floating on the American dream while beneath him a confusing record of economic and social facts unravels.

Gatsby is a coarse Platonist, devoted to the pursuit of a 'vast, vulgar and meretricious beauty', but his dream sustains its force, partly because the book allows him to invest naturalist fact with his personal intention, and recognizes the symbolist necessity, partly because it is mediated through a narrator, Nick Carraway, who consciously stills the voice of judgement. Carraway's peculiar tolerance comes because he is himself involved in a fantastic life in which he is something of a parvenu, but also because he is the instrument of Fitzgerald's oblique method of interpreting the tale. *Gatsby* is a novel of modern dream life; its means call for something more than naturalism or direct moral assessment. It is itself a semi-symbolist text, set in the surreal world of the modern city, New York and its environs, its startling detail thrown up in instants and images – in the shifting fashions in clothes and music, the décor of hotel rooms, the movements of traffic, the ash heaps and the hearses that catch Carraway's eye on his mobile, hyperactive way through the populous landscape. As narrator, Carraway becomes a voice of what Fitzgerald called 'selective delicacy', filtering impression and sensation in an order appropriate to his growing understanding of Gatsby's nature, distributing about him a landscape of generative images, so that Gatsby, who might be thought of as a corrupt product of this world, is gradually distinguished from it, set against it, finally made a victim of its contingency and carelessness. The novel's theme is the suffusion of the material with the ideal, of raw stuff becoming enchanted object; this is so not just because of Gatsby's peculiar powers and qualities, but because it is the basis of the mode of writing itself, as it invests Gatsby's actions, parties, and clothes with a distinctive, symbolic glow.

Two alternative worlds, one of careless wealth and the other of ashen poverty, are hence set in contrast in the novel – watched over by the absent god, the sightless eyes of Dr Eckleberg. But the real contrast is between the contingency of both these worlds and Gatsby's search for a transfiguring vision, for a world beyond the clock of historical time, for a life meaningless unless invested with meaning. Fitzgerald's aim is surreal, the making bright of certain evanescent things so that they have the quality of dream; but at the novel's end that dream is withdrawn, and another surreality, the nightmare of an unmitigated mass of material objects, takes its place. Gatsby's death is the product of carelessness and contingency. Nick imagines it:

I have an idea that Gatsby didn't himself believe that it [the phone call from Daisy] would come, and perhaps he no longer cared. If that was true he must have felt that he had lost the old warm world, paid a high price for living so long with a single dream. He must have looked up at an unfamiliar sky through frightening leaves and shivered as he found what a grotesque thing a rose is and how raw the sunlight was upon scarcely created grass. A new world, material without being real, where poor ghosts, breathing dreams like air, drifted fortuitously about ... like the ashen, fantastic figure gliding toward him through the amorphous trees.

On the one hand there is the world of time arrested, the past held suspended, of love and dream; on the other there is a modern world of dislocated, rootless, and grotesque images; from the mixture Fitzgerald distils two essential components of modernist writing. The book made him the extraordinary historian of those two inter-locking worlds – the world of modern history invested with a timeless myth, where the clock is tilted back like the clock on Gatsby's mantelpiece as he kisses Daisy, and the world of history disinvested, reduced to fragments without manifest order, a modern wasteland. This tension and ambiguity persist into the famous ending, where Fitzgerald both recreates 'the American dream', the dream of an innocent, pastoral America created by man's capacity for wonder, and sees it as a nostalgic desire for that which time itself defeats. As Gatsby is an artistic surrogate, chasing with his 'creative passion' a symbol that is both transcendent and corrupted, *The Great Gatsby* is a symbolist tragedy – about the struggle of the symbolic imagination to exist in lowered historical time, and about that symbol's inherent ambiguity, its wonder and its meretriciousness.

Gatsby is probably Fitzgerald's best, and certainly his most finished book: a realization of his talents in the Twenties, a sign of his power to enter a world that was both gaudy and destructive and to distil a meaning from it. He had succeeded not just in internal-izing the times – the spirit of a 'whole race going hedonistic, deciding on pleasure' – but in realizing them as form. But, as Twenties unease grew, Fitzgerald internalized that too, sensing the economic cost to be charged, the moral interest due. A formal success, *Gatsby* was not a financial one; Fitzgerald now had to undertake the production of countless popular magazine short stories to maintain his life-style, delaying his next novel, in any case going through many drafts. Behind the public façade, the marriage to Zelda was now strained, as each fought for self-preservation and survival. The Crash of 1929 destroyed the symbolic base of their existence, and by 1930 what was latent in the inner politics of that marriage – Zelda's schizophrenia, Scott's alcoholism – was evident. 'No ground under our feet,' he noted in his ledger, as the life-style they had both promoted began to tear to pieces. He now began to read Spengler, Henry Adams, Freud, and Marx, and sensed the need for a 'Great Change'. He grew aware of the historical displacement of the rich, looked towards the roots of his own wealth, began to grant the reality of the historical process and to probe the sexual disorder of the times.

All this went into the plan for his next novel, *Tender Is the Night*, a troubled and troublesome book of which we have two versions, and which Fitzgerald described as follows: 'Show a man who is a natural idealist, a spoiled priest, giving in for various causes to the ideas of the haute Burgeoise [*sic*], and in his rise to the top of the social world losing his idealism, his talent and turning to drink and dissipation. Background is one in which the liesure [*sic*] class is at their truly most brilliant & glamorous. . . .'[1] The background is the expatriate, socialite French Riviera where Americans gather, art and wealth converge, the great gaudy spree goes on past its due season, and a post-war generation attempts to reconstruct an existence after the war has shelled the old society to death. But cause is divorced from effect, and on the map of modern disturbed geography amusement lies next to *Angst*, the French Riviera close to the Swiss psychiatric clinics in which the price is paid. *Tender Is the Night* is a novel of psychic disorientation, in which that disorientation is seen not only within itself, but in relation to the processes of history – thus, says Fitzgerald, 'At that moment, the Divers [his central couple] represented externally the exact furthermost evolution of a class.' The book is set in a world of chance, violence, unexplained deaths, with echoes of the war sounding constantly in the background. The method is panoramic and expository, but historical scope is related to an inner violence and despair – above all to the insanity of Nicole Diver and the way this implicates her husband, the psychiatrist Dick Diver, the modern saviour who seeks to heal the pains and bear the burdens of these rich disintegrating psyches in a disintegrating, sexually confused and perverse world. Like Gatsby, Dick attempts to unify the chaos and give a meaning to the disorder; like Gatsby, he is an idealized hero, a man with a 'fine glowing surface' who distils bright moments of transcendence, makes life into a successful and ever-moving party. He is the master stylist – 'there was a pleasingness about him that simply had to be used' – and much of the early part of the novel is about his powers of unification, the capacity he has to make the world fall into place for others. His powers are more

[1] Fitzgerald's 'General Plan' for the book, reprinted as 'Appendix B' in Arthur Mizener, *The Far Side of Paradise* (1951; rev. ed., 1965). A revised edition of *Tender Is the Night*, edited by Malcolm Cowley and incorporating some of Fitzgerald's own ideas for the book's rearrangement, appeared in 1951. The complicated history of the text is analysed in Matthew J. Bruccoli, *The Composition of 'Tender Is the Night'* (1963).

than psychiatric, they are sacral; he blesses the world he enters, and is indeed its 'spoiled priest'.

But to do this Diver must indeed dive into this collapsing historical world, must risk his initial integrity – 'He knew ... that the price of his intactness was incompleteness' – and his illusions – 'they were the illusions of a nation, the lies of generations of frontier mothers who had to croon falsely that there were no wolves outside the cabin door' – in the chaotic, war-shattered life of his times. Marrying Nicole, one of his patients, wealthy and corrupt, he assimilates her mixture of amusement and pain; his humanism becomes tarnished, his disintegration slowly begins. A redemptive figure at the start, at the end he is broken by drink, violence, and emotional strain; no longer able to perform the symbolic trick – once done with elegant ease – of lifting a man on his back while surfing, he fades from the significant history of the book in its last pages. Like Fitzgerald, he becomes the implicated man; the implication draws him into the heart of the disaster, the psychic overextension, that is now Fitzgerald's essential theme. The book's awareness is psychological, social, and economic all at once; what we see is a top surface, a world of individuals propelled by underlying processes into expressive action which reveals what those processes imply. *Tender Is the Night* differs from *Gatsby* in having two methods extensively evolved: one is spatial–symbolic, a method appropriate to the priestly artist-figure at the book's centre who is seeking to hold on to romantic integrity and wholeness amid destructive time; the other is historical–evolutionary, the story of that time as system, a developing history with which Fitzgerald was not attentively concerned. Process and symbol struggle to give the novel an oblique chronology, and Fitzgerald was never sure of its true order of construction; he began to amend it even after publication, which is why the contemporary reader now has the original and a reconstructed text to choose between.

The novel's incompleteness has a certain appropriateness; for incompleteness and exposure were now Fitzgerald's theme. In the notable essays of 1936 and 1937, 'The Crack-Up' and 'Early Success', he looked at the disintegration of his earlier style in life and art, playing his own thirties against his twenties, and the Thirties against the Twenties, distilling his concern with exterior and inward dissolution. By now the alcoholism was serious, Zelda was in a mental hospital, and Fitzgerald turned towards Hollywood, for a job as screenwriter. His last novel *The Last Tycoon* (1941), set there, is yet more incomplete; the book was left unfinished at his early death, in 1940. But evidently it was to tell a story similar to that of *Tender Is the Night*, the story of another master stylist and integrative man, destroyed by disintegrative forces in the external world and in his own emotional life. But where *Tender Is the Night* had been expository and extended, *The Last Tycoon* was to reach back towards some of the methods of *Gatsby*: surrealistic concentration on scene, and use of the first-person narrator, so that the action is seen through Cecilia Brady, the Bennington junior with an ironic view of Hollywood but in love with Monroe Stahr, the 'last tycoon'. Again there would be a bonding of image and age, consciousness and economics. Hollywood, the setting, is the great dream factory of American illusions – Nathanael West was also distilling its surrealist significance in *The Day of the Locust* (1939). Stahr, the last of the great producers, living among these distorted and manufactured images, attempting to retain command, is a man who 'had just managed to climb out of a thousand years of Jewry into the late eighteenth century', and who cherishes 'the parvenu's passionate loyalty to an imaginary past'. He is at the end of his period of possible existence; unionization, modern complexity, contemporary disintegration threaten him, and he is the now failing hero: 'There was no world so but had its heroes, and Stahr was the hero. . . . The old loyalties were trembling now, and there were clay feet everywhere; but still he was their man, the last of the princes.'

Like *The Day of the Locust*, *The Last Tycoon* is a classic novel of cultural images caught at a point of extreme distortion. History has itself become distorted; Stahr is compared to past American Presidents, the princes who must relate their inner lives to public needs and fantasies, but Andrew Jackson's home is closed, and a man dies on its steps, while Abraham Lincoln appears in the commissary, 'his kindly face fixed on a forty-cent dinner, including dessert, his shawl wrapped around him as if to protect himself from the erratic air-cooling. . . .' An absurdist, half-finished landscape of plasticated dreams and desires surrounds Stahr, and is part of him, outward history and inward psychic world. Apocalyptic disturbances overtake him; at the beginning of the book is a grotesque scene where an earthquake sends a flood sweeping through the studio lot, carrying a floating head of Siva on which two 'survivors' ride. From the head descends a woman who bears the face of Stahr's dead wife

– a woman he now pursues through a sequence of transitory, fragmented scenes, as one might decadently pursue both survival and death itself. The book is made of such concentrated images, and predicts Stahr's downfall – tragedy set in waning history. The tragedy was in a sense Fitzgerald's own. A writer who had struggled intensely with the problem of unifying form and time, art and process, hoping always to find a romantic and a moral value, he had watched the old dream of wealth and wonder redeemed pushed to its extremity. Moreover his career was declining, his sensitivities were raw, and he had intimations of his own coming death. *The Last Tycoon* as we have it, unfinished, ends with a work note he had written to himself: 'ACTION IS CHARACTER' – a fair epitaph for a writer who had struggled through living to generate an experimental form for modern experience.

III

It was a phrase that, if in a different way, equally well fitted Fitzgerald's friend and rival throughout the Twenties, Ernest Hemingway. As his fellow expatriate in Paris, Fitzgerald had helped Hemingway with the end of *The Sun Also Rises* and encouraged his publication; by the Thirties, Hemingway, disliking 'The Crack-Up' essay and Fitzgerald's frank exposure of weakness, was emphasizing the distance between them. Like Fitzgerald, Hemingway was a writer firmly engaged in his time – he called his first real book *In Our Time* (1925) – and felt bonded to his own generation, those who had to cope with the unreasonable wound of war. Like Fitzgerald, he saw the task as relating a life-style to an art-style; the writer was a performing self who assimilated and distanced areas of self so that they provided an economy of form. But where for Fitzgerald this had meant taking open risks with himself and with experience, and where, in the event, this proved true for Hemingway as well, the important issue for Hemingway was, exactly, economy – a controlled self-expenditure, a stylistic and bodily toughness, a controlled use of words. Technique, in life and writing, was precision – the precision that, Hemingway came to feel, Fitzgerald lacked. Hemingway's fictional construct was always to be a clean, well-lighted place, a world of the hard, well-registered minimum. Fitzgerald loosely amassed material, wasted it and himself; Hemingway's was always to be a world where romantic feelings and pains were hidden causes, never quite stated, a specified, exact, exclusive world, with its own type of terrain, its *paysage moralisé*, its own geography of sanctified places, special drinks, guns, and rods, its own distinctive ways of speech. Over that terrain, moving with the same toughened and selected economy, as its appropriate tenant, passes the specified Hemingway hero, crossing the dangerous troubled estate with a certain air of ease and comfort which cloaks but does not fully conceal what lies behind: the tension, the insomnia, the wounds, the pain, the modern nightmare.

It was this capacity to produce a style of pure limitation that made Hemingway seem to his readers and critics both an experimenter with modern experience and modern form. His hard objectivist technique was, as critics have pointed out, analogous to modernist poetic doctrines of 'impersonality' and the 'objective correlative'; at the same time it is conditioned by personal experience. Hemingway was born in 1899 in Oak Park, Illinois, and grew up in a family divided, with a powerful, genteel, evangelical and repressive mother, and a weaker, finally a suicidal, father. Male roles and functions were driven from the house and into a world of nature both initiatory and meaninglessly cruel – the world of the Michigan woods, where the family spent their summers, and which Hemingway would evoke in many of his stories. In 1917 Hemingway went to work as a journalist in the *Kansas City Star* newsroom; he then extended his encounter with 'reality' when he joined the American Field service as an ambulance man and served on the Italian front, where he was wounded in 1918. The episode became the key existential encounter and he sought, in a sense, to repeat it thereafter in stylized situations of sporting danger, as the bullfighter, the boxer, the big-game hunter, the fisherman. Returning home to an America that now seemed bland and sterilized, he worked as a journalist and returned, in 1921, to Paris as a special correspondent, with letters from Sherwood Anderson introducing him to several of the expatriate gurus. Though he later played down the episode, he sat with profit at Gertrude Stein's feet and assimilated much of her modernist lore. Bohemian decadence was not, on the face of it, Hemingway's style; he preferred to model himself on the journalist, the soldier of fortune, the sportsman, those who functioned through skill, professional competence, above all in the presence of a centralized event, a 'real thing', which must be precisely confronted under rituals of formal control. 'Begin over again – and concentrate,' Stein told Hemingway, looking at his early stories; and concentration now became his fictional aim. He moved towards a formalized, anti-adjectival prose style which looked less like an aesthetic mannerism than an elimination of all loose or evocative references. 'All you have to do', he has told us he told himself, 'is to write one true sentence. Write the truest sentence that you know.' Style was, then, a merging of the act of writing with an act of being, a setting of limits on false experience or false verbal action. Language marks the point of inter-course between the realized self and the outward and knowable event; it is a self-authenticating act of address which purges the world of contingency or association, concentrates it down to a linguistic essence. Language thus intensely contains the self, becomes the hard, firm intermediary between consciousness and object or event, displays the struggle of the encounter in an economic, taut authenticity.

Hemingway's extraordinary new linguistic economy was first dis-played within the tightness of the short story, in two short volumes published by an expatriate press in Paris – *Three Stories and Ten Poems* (1923) and *in our time* (1924) – but above all in the enlarged *In Our Time*, published in the U.S.A. in 1925. Containing 15 stories and many untitled vignettes, it presents in 7 of the stories Nick Adams, a character who is clearly a surrogate for the author, and who appears again in the volumes *Men Without Women* (1927) and *Winner Take Nothing* (1933). Initiation is the theme of these auto-biographical stories, some about Nick as a child growing up in a Midwestern family with a genteel mother and a defeated doctor father, experiencing the pains of acquaintance with death and violence, and some about the violence of war itself, seen as a naturalistic horror where the corpses of the dead appear worth no more than the dead animals in the Chicago stockyards. In both worlds, nature consumes its own creations, appears only as a field of external exposure. The mind and emotions, limited in their response, enforce a tragic stoicism, a dependence only on those things that one cannot lose; desire rashly expended leads to a tragic outcome. Words themselves, potentially a form of emotion, must likewise be contained, to convey the precise thing, the disturbing centre of experience, without romanticization. Adjectives are cut to a considered few, causal connectives and metaphors are reduced, objects function as subdued symbols, hard, energetic instances. The outward violence and inward exposure thus demand a controlled limitation of feeling, an ironic materiality in which a small number of details live starkly, carefully juxtaposed one to another. The aim of the language is double – to force attention to the economy of the gesture, the cleanness of the line, and to convey with integrity and stoicism the larger outline of the experience. Hemingway's writing is not psychological in the familiar sense; it does not get inside, but projects action outward, which is why the terrain is exactly mapped, the place and season crucial. But the outward world is a total metaphor for a psychic condition, that connection being gained by the reader's filling of the empty spaces and occupying the area of implicit pain and hysteria.

Hemingway's search for a controlled modern style explains his parody of his mentor Sherwood Anderson in *Torrents of Spring* (1926); it is also the theme of his first novel, *The Sun Also Rises* (published in England as *Fiesta*), a book explicitly about the commanding pressures of modernity, about the Twenties seen both as historical condition and as fashion, a new era of style. The novel remains one of Hemingway's very best precisely because it does give a historical location for his vision, a psycho-history for his prototypical hero, a pathology for his romantic existentialism. Here that hero, and the book's narrator, is Jake Barnes, a writer who, genitally wounded in the war, experiencing the compulsory stoicism of his sexlessness, is compelled to hunt for a new manner of living, a style for his situation: 'I did not care what it was all about. All I wanted to know was how to live in it. Maybe if you found out how to live in it you learned from that what it was all about.' 'Learning to live in it' is the collective activity of the book, Hemingway's most explicitly 'fashionable', set as it is in the expatriate Paris and Spain of the Twenties, among American and European artists and cosmopolites and their attachments and hangers-on. The book is a Baedeker of social and moral knowledge, a suitable education in the right drinks, the right places, and the right sensibility; it turns on knowingness, that initiate's access Hemingway's work would always provide. But fashion, the attempt to realize the instant of history, is a condition; and the achievement of *The Sun Also Rises* is its penetration into what that condition is; by acquiring a style of living we may indeed learn 'what it was all about'. The novel is a portrait of a modern elect, the 'herd' of initiates who seek the territorial, social, and emotional map appropriate to their troubled selves, for whom fashion and cynicism have replaced traditional morality, religion, and idealism. A new romanticism prevails, but it is the romanticism of managed and stoic pain, arising from the capacity to display strength and exactitude, to discover in the world of potentially false experience occasions of pleasure and joy, without forgoing the sense of modern trauma or crossing the line beyond justly expended emotion. In the clean tight performance of Romero's bullfighting in Spain, the clear momentary natural joy of the fishing trip, the images of exactitude come, the small essences of chaotic existence.

The Sun Also Rises is prefaced by two epigraphs, one from Ecclesiastes about the endurance of the earth, the other from Gertrude Stein: 'You are all a lost generation.' Hemingway clearly meant them to be read together, and wanted the 'lost generation' tag removed when it became a cliché; Gertrude Stein doubted whether she had ever said it. None the less the book does turn firmly on the idea of the coming of a distinct new generation, functioning in a new nature and a new history, transfigured by war and its aftermath, tested and reduced in expectation by it, bearing certain kinds of psychic trauma and certain kinds of knowledge unknown to their predecessors – or for that matter to innocent contemporaries like Robert Cohn, who uses the wrong language, reads the wrong books, likes the wrong countries for the wrong reasons, feels the wrong feelings. Of that new awareness the most resonant symbol is the wound, actual or symbolic – that intolerable intrusion into the self which is also the ultimate realism, initiating, pointing to modern exposure, the assault from nothingness, the vacancy of present history. It leads to a world of trauma, sleeplessness, loss, consciousness of *nada*, the void in the universe; it also creates common consciousness in those who – like, above all, Jake Barnes and Lady Brett Ashley, the British aristocrat man–woman whose nymphomania is the counterpart to Jake's enforced sterility – share the insight of the modern, mixing romantic desire with a sense of its displacement. Beyond nothingness and sterility there are glimpses of renewal: Jake's wound is in fact an ambiguous symbol, affording him strange protection against sexual disorder and the new, androgynous world of sexual relations. In this world decadent indirections are necessary; Jake's impotence, Brett's nymphomania, are complex interlocking images of sterility turned to heroism. The book's final image, of the policeman's upraised baton, suggests the entire condition of its world; direct emotion is obstructed, but redeployed indirectly, either as a wasteful using up of experience or as contained lonely purity. The need is to find the clean line; Jake's impotence keeps him within a world of tight male comradeship, of men without women, the things one cannot lose; though it is 'pretty to think' that things might be otherwise, prettiness is not to be had. But contained survival *is* possible, in the right places, beyond the social world, in the primitive pastoral life glimpsed in Spain and on the fishing trip. Indurant nature, the abiding earth with its muted hostility, can be encountered, if finesse and craft are present, in a ritual, managed expenditure of self.

Much of Hemingway's later fiction concentrates on versions of that encounter, with nature and the separate self. *A Farewell to Arms* (1929), his next novel, confronts the war directly, to see it as a grotesque manifestation of nature. Set on the Italian front, amid disease, slaughter, and retreat, the book's careful topography enfolds and limits the bleak, nihilistic events, the records of corpses and of the empty movements of men. Mountains, lakes, and rain are both context and condition; metonyms in Hemingway's disconnected prose, they become metaphors, like the rain that washes over the deaths that haunt the book. Lieutenant Frederic Henry, the narrator, is the flat recorder, another modern stylist cut off from the discourse of the past: 'I was always embarrassed by the words sacred, glorious and sacrifice and the expression in vain. Abstract words such as glory, honor, courage, or hallow were obscene beside the concrete names of villages, the numbers of roads, the names of rivers, the numbers of regiments and the dates.' Yet the feeling suppressed by Henry's controlled method of nominalization leaks out as tragic symbolism. Similarly his controlled response to the horrors of war is put at risk when he falls in love with Catherine Barkley, the British nurse, and, making his 'separate peace' by deserting from the Italian army, hopes to make it a peace for two. The feeling suppressed in *The Sun Also Rises* is released, and the two attempt to construct a collective solitude from love: 'We could be alone when we were together, alone against the others.' But the images of threatened death in the rain accumulate; nature and war alike contend against any such attempts at domestication. The ironic landscape generates a tragic outcome: Catherine dies in childbirth, sacrificed to the inexorable process of pain: 'That was what you did. You died.' Naturalism now reveals itself as a lasting tragedy for the human individual within the indifferent landscape:

Once in camp I put a log on top of the fire and it was full of ants. As it commenced to burn, the ants swarmed out and went first toward the center where the fire was, then turned back and ran toward the end. When there were enough on the end they fell off into the fire. Some got out, the bodies burnt and flattened, and went off not knowing where they were going. But most of them went toward the fire and then backward toward the end and warmed on the cool end and finally fell off into the fire. I remember thinking at the time that it was the end of the world and a splendid chance to be a messiah. ... But I did not do anything. ...

Indifferent or mutely hostile nature generates its own controlled reaction: as the book ends Lieutenant Henry, returned to a condition of stoic isolation covering tragic pain, walks back to his hotel in the overwhelming rain.

In Hemingway's novels and stories of the Twenties verbal and emotional economy unite to form an existential, central modern style, a complex formal attenuation comparable to period tendencies in painting. In his next book, the reportage study *Death in the Afternoon* (1932) – mainly about Spanish bullfighting, but above all about the style-making process and the exactitude it required – Hemingway was to reflect: '... the real thing, the sequence of motion and fact which made the emotion and which would be as valid in a year or in ten years or, with luck and if you stated it purely enough, always, was beyond me and I was working very hard to try to get it.' But at the same time both *Death in the Afternoon* and *Green Hills of Africa* (1935), also reportage, involve considerable personal display; the style, which depends exactly on the rhythm of expression and containment, was beginning to harden into mannerism, and Hemingway himself to harden into a tough-guy hero performing publicly. And there was another change; like so many American writers in the Thirties, Hemingway was moving away from the ethic of solitude into a communal or social ethic. *To Have and Have Not* (1937), the story of Harry Morgan, the liquor smuggler who has shipped contraband from Cuba to Florida during Prohibition, and then during the Depression tries to secure his survival as an independent entrepreneur by increasing acts of corruption, deals with economic carelessness and injustice. The buccaneer Harry, who says 'I don't know who made the laws but I know there ain't no law that you got to go hungry', shows courage and skill in the decadent and collapsing world. But as he dies he offers the new Hemingway lesson: '"No matter how a man alone ain't got no bloody chance."' It is the reverse lesson from the Twenties novels, and it seems superimposed on an uneasy, lesser book.

For Whom the Bell Tolls (1940), with its Donnean principle that

'No man is an Ilande', also embodies Hemingway's new sense of social engagement. About the Spanish Civil War, it involves its growingly committed hero, Robert Jordan, in a Republican sabotage operation behind the Fascist lines, and in a love affair with the Spanish girl Maria, raped by the Falangists who have murdered her father. Jordan begins as the old provisional Hemingway hero ('if he were going to form judgments he would form them afterwards'), but he acquires a belief in the value of sacrifice, that once absurd abstraction; and love, once the main area of risk and betrayal, here becomes a complex mystical union, not only with the other ('one and one is one') but with nature and the earth itself. Like the dying Harry Morgan, Jordan, having accomplished his mission, lying wounded and waiting for death at the book's end, amid a nature that has now become tolerant and receptive, finds he has learned a lesson from life: 'I wish there was some way to pass on what I've learned, though. Christ, I was learning fast there at the end.' As Jordan moves from an existential to a transcendental world, so Hemingway moves from an existentialist to a transcendentalist mode of fiction, in which the old tragic naturalism and nihilism yield to a new humanism; the tense modern self at last finds a mode of satisfyingly heroic action, and becomes not stoic victim but active agent. The novel is as notable a record as any we have of the crucial Spanish conflict, but in encompassing this change Hemingway's tight prose was already losing something of its precision. The result is a striking release of much that, it would seem, Hemingway's previous style and perception had striven to contain: his work now turned towards a ripe modern romanticism.

Life indeed now seemed to conspire to let that romanticism grow; he increasingly conducted himself as his own best hero. After having been a war correspondent in Spain, and running a decoy ship off Cuba hunting German submarines, he became a correspondent in Europe in the Second World War, flew missions with the RAF, formed an irregular army in France, and liberated the Ritz in Paris ahead of the French army. His wound became the most famous since Philoctetes', his sleepless nights the most famous since Lady Macbeth's. He became an image of modern endurance, an heroic stylist even to himself; at the same time the underlying unease was increasing. *Across the River and Into the Trees* (1950), appearing after a ten-year interval, is the story of such a legendary man, Colonel Robert Cantwell, as much a version of the later Hemingway as hero as were his previous heroes of his earlier self. He is heroic but also wounded and damaged, as Hemingway now was; he feels an instinctive comradeship for 'those who had fought or been mutilated'; his terrain is that of sport, war, and élite society, of Venice, gun emplacements, and shooting platforms. He is a universal insider and a deeply ritualized man, a man of ultimate codes; human experience is brought to a sequence of personal acts and graces, from fishing to eating to love-making, and these rituals must have the same precision of style as Hemingway earlier gave to language. Indeed the complex idea of an exclusive language points to a social Elect, and now Cantwell is the leader of one. What justifies his election is his wound and what he makes of it; and a main theme of the book is his return to, and his ordering of, the place where it happened. In one sense this is a summative book, the realization of Hemingway's principles of a lifetime. But, though it starts brilliantly, it acquires a curious absurdity, becoming a pastiche or parody of the earlier and more tentative Hemingway style. Cantwell reaches 'accurately and well for the champagne bucket', he 'stands straight and kisses true', and in peacetime restaurants has a table in the corner to keep his flank covered. In this hardened form, the Hemingway code and the Hemingway sentence become clichés – much as Anderson's codes and sentences had when Hemingway parodied them some twenty years before.

But it is of course the purity of its limitation that links Hemingway's work so deeply with modern experience and style. The linguistic economy becomes a purified universe and a purified morality, a distinctive world brought down to a given terrain, a given version of history, a given use of the self in all things. That self, made authentic by one's risk-taking human performance, is a romantic derivative of the quest to know truly, and is forged outside society from fragile inward resources, which then acquire the capacity for truthful discovery. As in decadence, the morality of right sensations becomes central. Yet acts of authentic violence can become just violence, physical self-celebration a losing cause as age takes away what strength and endurance have given, and the underlying desperation therefore increases again. And now what in Hemingway's life had seemed secure and morally justified was indeed being taken away, as, after a series of major accidents, his battered body began to lose the strength for the key male rituals he had celebrated: drinking, hunting, fighting, making love. His next book, *The Old Man and the Sea* (1952), with its essential message of endurance, its assertion that a man may be destroyed but not defeated if he secures his own humanity, responds to this; it is a naturalistic novel with a humanistic outcome, a tale of ritual encounter between the old Cuban fisherman and the forces of erosion itself, as he battles first with a giant marlin, which he tames and catches, then with the predatory sharks that reduce the prize to a skeleton he nevertheless brings home to port. The mode is simple and epical, a method of symbolic allegory with powerful Christian allusions; its lesson seems far away from Hemingway's early note of nihilism, but was implicit in it; its myth of heroism, humility, and the moral virtues of endurance undoubtedly helped Hemingway to win, in 1954, the Nobel Prize for literature.

Yet the novel had its dark underside, made apparent when some of the other sea stories with which it was to have been linked appeared, posthumously and not fully completed, as *Islands in the Stream* (1970). The three tales of the book are about Thomas Hudson, a painter living in Cuba, whose personal life mirrors Hemingway's own. Hudson is a broken stoic, who keeps passing beyond the limits of his own control, as he loses his dependence on strength, sexuality, comradeship, and fatherhood. The stories are about wear and tear, and the familiar tragic dimension is extended now into a realm of total loss, of extreme pain and sexual regret and deprivation, after two wrecked marriages. The stoic spirit is pushed to its limits; the Hemingway hero, the hero of experience and expertise, is now plagued by the conflict between the remains of romantic hope and a rising despair. And, physically weakened and so deprived of many of the essential 'realities' of the to-the-hilt physical living both his human performance and his writing had celebrated, Hemingway himself now grew fearful of himself and doubtful of the motives of others; when the writing that ultimately justified all the action no longer came, the shadow of nothingness that had underlain even his most optimistic and humanistic novels from the 1930s to the 1950s became everything. Life-style and art-style were together collapsing, coming to the end of a complex heroic enterprise. On 2 July 1961, he drew that, his largest story, to a tragic conclusion, killing himself with a shotgun, as his father had many years before.

IV

Hemingway's vision of a world that had been brought by war to the end of its innocence, requiring new styles alike of life and art, was shared by many of his generation. The First World War seemed a turning-point for many Americans, if for various reasons: as a failed moral crusade, as an entry into European corruption, as a capitalist plot to protect investment and stave off western revolution. It was in the last guise that John Dos Passos saw this war, and the surprise is that he should have gone to it at all. The illegitimate son of a self-made lawyer of Portuguese stock, he was a lonely, weak, withdrawn child who once noted of himself: 'was ever creature more dependent on literature for life and stimulus.' Moreover, by 1916, when he left Harvard, he had been moving towards radical, anarchist, and pacifist principles, under the influence of Emma Goldman. Yet the war attracted him, as an essential reality, and he went to France and Spain to be nearer to it, trying to persuade his father to let him join the ambulance corps. And this, on his father's death, he did, explaining meanwhile to his friends that he had not 'gone militarist' but 'merely wanted to see a little of the war personally' and face 'the senseless agony of destruction'. In letters, diaries, poems, and a novel he began to write collaboratively with Robert Hillyer, he condemned 'the mountain of lies', the 'merry parade that is stifling in brutishness all the fair things of the world'. But though war was 'suicidal madness', it was also the ultimate experience, calling for immersion and expression: 'I want to be able to express, later – all of this – all the tragedy and hideous excitement of it. I have seen so little I must experience more of it, & more. The gray crooked fingers of the dead, the dark look of dirty mangled bodies . . .'

Dos Passos now began on a stylistic quest that took him through various forms and manners of the novel, as he tried to establish the right tones and the right historiography for the experience he felt he must render. The initial report comes, quickly, in *One Man's Initiation: 1917*, first published in England in 1919. Like Barbusse's *Le Feu*, it is an immediate, confused book, a subjective response, as the title suggests. It is centred on one individual and sensitive soldier, Martin Howe, who has origins very like Dos Passos's own, and who sees the war primarily as a violation of his cultural values and his sense of form. Dos Passos is clearly guilty about this aestheticism, which seems like a mode of withdrawal. Larger historical issues lie behind the book – the mountain of lies issued by the government, the brutal effects of the army machine, the potential of the rising revolutionary fervour which Dos Passos sees in the army and to which he came to attach a cleansing hope – but these are present only impressionistically.; the true concern is with Howe's own uneasy personal awarenesses and his aesthetic pain. That Dos Passos wanted to take a less personal, a broader, a more historical and explanatory view is evident in his second war novel, *Three Soldiers*, the very title of which suggests a broader span, the sense of war as a collective experience.

Three Soldiers has an elaborate structure, a design intended to display war as a massive machine, crushing individualism – a machine that spreads outward into general life. The three soldiers are Andrews, a sensitive composer who begins to assimilate mechanical military rhythms, until he revolts romantically against regimentation; Chrisfield, the farm boy from Indiana, unthinkingly brave and instinctive, pushed towards the murder of those who now organize and limit his manhood; Fuselli, the city clerk who hopes for the great adventure and ascends the military hierarchy, until he catches venereal disease. Dos Passos strives for a modernized, expressionistic style in which the rhythmic mechanization of life and the reduction of men to functionaries in an antlike collectivity are caught and enacted. But he cannot quite forgo the subjective mode and assert an objective historical significance for the story; the war becomes simply an 'unbearable agony' and a choice between self-abnegation and desertion. By suppressing, with his harder style, those flares of romantic and aesthetic subjectivity which are the reason for opposing war, Dos Passos appears to move away from his own needs. The papers that blow around Andrews's room at the end of the novel, as, in full self-knowledge, he silences himself and waits for the military police, appear like an image of Dos Passos's personal self-abnegation.

Dos Passos's real breakthrough to modern style came in *Manhattan Transfer*, a remarkable novel set not in war but in that other key metaphor of both naturalist and expressionist writing: the great modern city. A book consonant with the developing principles of European modernism, it belongs among the great urban classics – James's *The Princess Casamassima*, Conrad's *The Secret Agent*, Joyce's *Ulysses*, Doblin's *Berlin Alexanderplatz*, Biely's *Petersburg* – where the city is seen less as a vast system or warring jungle of forces than a synchronic environment of multiple consciousnesses, flickering impressions, contingency and variety. *Manhattan Transfer* adds to the old naturalist city of determining and destructive mass the new expressionist city, of energy, strange selfhoods in remarkable juxtaposition, a modern Eros. The methods relate to those of the massive urban novel like Biely's, where experience falls into strange luminous units, as well as to the collage and montage techniques of modern film-makers like Eisenstein and Griffith. The debt to Joyce is apparent (Dos Passos bought *Ulysses* in Paris in 1922), but where Joyce presents his paralysed Dublin as a city from which form can arise only through the revelation of art, Dos Passos, in more constructivist fashion, sees his Manhattan as a vast collective motion, a mechanical womb, a machine both for giving and suppressing life. We may see in his Jimmy Herf a figure of the sensitive individual defeated; but what is displaced from the individual life is reinvested in the operational city itself. Mechanism and destructiveness are dominant, and characters become like the impersonal environment through which they move; but the environment has its own vast motion and vigour. As Jean-Paul Sartre said in an admiring essay, what Dos Passos had invented was an 'authorless novel' with 'characterless characters': 'acts, emotions and ideas suddenly settle within a character, make themselves at home and then disappear without his having much to say about the matter. You cannot say he submits to them. He experiences them.'[2] Dos Passos's Manhattan is a dynamo filled with motion, an endless contention between the vitalistic and the mechanistic where – as in Hart Crane's long poem *The Bridge* (1930) – the mechanical takes on romantic powers in the world's most modern and most futuristic city.

But as the Twenties ended, and the direction of fiction markedly changed, Dos Passos's techniques changed too. *Manhattan Transfer* is spatial and synchronic, portraying a cyclical and purposeless history. But Dos Passos had been steadily moving towards communism and anarchism, ahead of most of his contemporaries. In the three-volume sequence of novels consisting of *The 42nd Parallel* (1930), *Nineteen Nineteen* (1932), and *The Big Money* (1936), collected together as *U.S.A.* (1937), he sought to use his spatial techniques in a historical continuum, and to treat history as process. *U.S.A.* is really a very Thirties history, which reads backwards into American life to cover the nation's evolution from 1900 through to the late 1920s. Seen from a Thirties radical viewpoint, the Twenties were the nadir, the discredited decade, dominated by commercialism and materialism, the suppression of Radicals

---

[2] Jean-Paul Sartre, *Literary and Philosophical Essays* (1955).

(culminating in the executions of Sacco and Vanzetti) and of rising bull-market absurdities pointing towards economic crash. *U.S.A.* is therefore a negative history, a process towards integration (with progressivism) and then disintegration. Dos Passos draws on the techniques he had evolved in *Manhattan Transfer*, using pluralized narration, large ranges of characters, intersections between documentary matter and naturalistic materials, to create a massive modernist epic. Spreading over a large historical curve and a vast geographical span, the work's concern is not just with the interior but the international life of the United States in its evolution from power to superpower, and from simple to complex modern capitalism.

U.S.A. distils all Dos Passos's personal as well as his formal concerns. It is not only a large vision of America corrupting itself over his own lifetime, distorting the psychology of its citizens, running deeper into the capitalist morass and the profitmongers' war and then into a gross commercial peace, so losing touch with community and with language itself; it is also a great technical enterprise in which the attempt is made through presentational techniques to relate the subjective aesthetic life of the author to historical process. The book has four basic structural levels – the extended life stories of the many fictional characters; the factual biographies of actual public figures; the 'Newsreel' collage of documentary data, headlines, songs, speeches, reports; and the 'Camera Eye' sections, a stream-of-consciousness flow of perception from the novelist's own position. These technical levels interfuse, but each has its own implicit historiography. Thus the individual stories, of Margo Dowling, Dick Savage, J. Ward Moorhouse, and so on, are tales of types. Some of them intersect, others simply run parallel, some continue for the entire sequence, others drop from sight; but they make up a compound narrative of disappointment and failure, especially of progressive failure, or of corrupting commercial success. The portraits of actual historical individuals make up a radical hagiography of heroes (Big Bill Heywood, La Follette, Veblen, Randolph Bourne, Frank Lloyd Wright, protesters, artists, or dreamers) and of villains (Woodrow Wilson, J. P. Morgan, Insull, politicians and capitalists). The Newsreels, collected from documentary sources, function sometimes as a contingent collage, sometimes as a source of ironic juxtaposition, illustrating the conflict between rhetoric and reality. And the 'Camera Eye' sections follow a helpless narrator, existing in a pained isolation of images, self-dwarfing and self-abnegating, a man hungry for speech and clarity but unable to do more than register impressions until the Sacco–Vanzetti case provokes him into verbal outrage.

The work oscillates between two possibilities: a collectivist and expressionist epic of American life, and a modernist anti-epic – where the sum of the parts indicates not collective meaning but loss of meaning. Underlying the book is an ideal of America, based on past myths, collective hopes and desires, and the possibility of a great reformed technological civilization. The young man in the prologue who walks through the emptying urban streets sees disjunctive lines, but finds himself greedy for speech, hungry in Whitman-like fashion to master contradictions: 'U.S.A. is the world's greatest rivervalley fringed with mountains and hills, U.S.A. is a set of bigmouthed officials with too many bank-accounts. . . . But mostly U.S.A. is the speech of the people.' But by the end language cannot emerge from the growth of the nation, for it is run by other systems; hence it can only be turned against its process ('America our nation has been beaten by strangers who have turned our language inside out...,' 'We have only words against'). The multiplication and division of consciousness are the technical processes of the book, and the damaged nature of modern experience; they change in function, from being the expression of at first a collective and then a contingent history. For in all the main lines of narrative there is at work a historical sequence of growing mechanization, dehumanization, a suppression of aesthetic hopes and radical possibilities, a defeat of organic potential and ideals of culture that underlie the book and make epic ambitions possible. But (much as in Ezra Pound's *Cantos*) juxtaposition turns to disjunction, connection to disconnection, and the attempt to celebrate the nation turns into awareness of the space between its real and ideal meanings.

The three volumes of *U.S.A.* thus explore three phases of a declining history. *The 42nd Parallel*, dealing with the years from 1900 to American entry into the war in 1917, presents twentieth-century hopes for the new nation, and moves rhythmically towards the rise of the progressive impulse and radical challenges to the capitalist system; it then takes us towards the European battlefields, ending with the enforced silence of the character Charlie as his ship approaches wartime France. In *Nineteen Nineteen*, the fulcrum volume, the war is seen as the 'plot of the big interests', as a place of horror, debasement, new sexual opportunity, and rising revolutionary momentum, culminating in the Russian Revolution. But no western parallel comes, and even 'separate peace' is not really possible; everything ends in the corrupted idealism of the Versailles conference, while, back home, the general strike of 1 May 1919, which may be 'the first morning of the first day of the new year', collapses into the red scare, leaving open the path towards commercialism and superpower capitalism. *The Big Money*, set in the Twenties, follows this through, portraying a society economically cohesive, socially divisive, and emotionally and personally destructive. The emotional collapse of the main characters and the economic wasting of the system run parallel; the deaths of Sacco and Vanzetti mark the end of direct social hope. But Dos Passos is writing out of what comes after, and the growing myth behind the book, of a true idealism hidden in the people and in the timeless history of the continent, which is set against 'history the billiondollar speedup', is a Thirties myth; it attends to economic laws and processes, but believes in something else – the endurance of the land, the speech of the people.

Dos Passos uses modernist techniques as a form of modern historicism: *U.S.A.* is not intended simply as an external history of a crisis, but the expressive *form* of a crisis within the writer's own aesthetics, his own capacity to generate myth or create language. He had written throughout of the man who seeks for reality and wholeness, but cannot quite succeed in finding it. His dealings with the American Communist party were analogous; he got in deep but always retained his independence, and he was, in the leftward swing of the 1930s, early in deciding that communism was not the answer: rather the despotism of Henry Ford than that of Mike Gold. 'I think there's more life in the débris of democracy than the comrades do,' he noted, and grew into an American Firster. His later novels, some of large ambition, like *Mid-Century* (1961), attempted to construct the myth that, in *U.S.A.*, history had been working to destroy; paradoxically, they lack the power and invested technical complexity of his earlier, major fiction.

V

Dos Passos was an important contributor to American fictional modernism, but perhaps the most crucial and exemplary figure of all was William Faulkner. Not all critics have shared that view of him. To many, he is pre-eminently a novelist of that distinct region of the United States, the South: a complex late product of its romance tradition, its celebrations of heroism and chivalry, its idealisms, its semi-feudal social institutions, its rooted struggle against industrialism, its defeats, pains, and anxieties. To others he is, rather, one of the great figures of international modernist experiment – a writer with the range, capacities, and formal preoccupations we associate with Joyce, Proust, or Virginia Woolf, an experimenter, a symbolist, a witness to modern exile. His own view of himself was as a private man and a farmer, a man of his region, a writer writing of enduring human values, honour, endurance, compassion, sacrifice, in a rhetoric bred, as he put it, 'by Oratory out of Solitude'. He did have a bohemian phase, but in the Southern capital of New Orleans, and never attended the expatriate feasts of Paris; he did fly in the war, but only as a trainee pilot in Canada. Though his writings draw on the primary methods of modernism – stream of consciousness, collage presentation, time shifts and achronicity – he never fully explained, in his own aesthetic statements, the impulses that drove him to use those techniques. And, where many modernists probed ever further into experiment, Faulkner's most experimental writing occurs as a 'phase' in the middle of his career.

But these two views of Faulkner are not incompatible; indeed they attest to his extraordinary complexity. It is largely when his work grows most Southern and, in that sense, most provincial or localized that his technical experiment emerges in its full force. Certainly Faulkner was very much a writer of the South; born in 1897, he grew up in Oxford, Mississippi, and spent most of his life there. Going early to New Orleans to pursue his ambition to write, he found there Sherwood Anderson, and a bohemian climate; his early work, much influenced by all this, was mostly in poetry, and its debts to the Romantics, especially Keats, but above all to the *fin de siècle* decadent poets, are notable. These early writings are packed with avaricious borrowings, the accumulation of a self-educated provincial catching at certain romantic and new modern texts (like *The Waste Land*) to define his aesthetic preoccupations and find his way. Like Fitzgerald, Faulkner saw himself as a romantic egoist, and knew that beautiful was damned; he saw the world of art hunger crossed with the wasteland of modern life. And he too saw the need for redemptive style, in the new decadent fashion. So, as he moved towards fiction, notions of the failure of history, the decline of the west, the degenerations of modernity, the narcissism of modern existence, the displacement of sexuality, the need to refine sensation, and the claims of bohemia were all part of his push towards a modern definition of art and the discovery of a modern style.

His first two novels, *Soldier's Pay* and *Mosquitoes* (1927), were thus works of the new decadence. The motif is clad in its modern garb, in figures like the death-hungry airman, the epicene new woman, the artist hunting stasis out of time. In *Soldier's Pay* the central figure is the scarred, blinded veteran, Donald Mahon, who comes home to find the malaise of post-war society in the sterility of the people around him, unable to connect desire and fulfilment. In this voided world symbolist spaces and enclosures abound. The virginal and unchaste are ever in contention, while time rots and wastes. *Mosquitoes* is set directly among artists in New Orleans; the Keatsian search in the book is for a timeless beauty that will both capture and transcend present reality, and for a mode of realization that is more than words or euphony, that is wrapped in life. In both these novels, Faulkner seems to adopt the modes of the sophisticated and cosmopolitan writer, though there is much inner unease. But with *Sartoris* (1929), a great change came. Faulkner returned home, discovering that his essential materials were not simply contemporary, but had an extended historical and social dimension, emerging from his familiar Mississippi environment, and its past. This is a far less arch, much more deeply textured novel, fairly conventionally presented; it is a novel of deep social investment, exploring a community at many levels. Out of the book comes Yoknapatawpha County, Faulkner's local, Mississippi version of Hardy's Wessex, a complex invented society overlaying a real one which he was to rearrange, alter, and complicate through most of the rest of his novels. With Jefferson as its county seat, and with its distinctive world of displaced aristocrats, carpet-baggers, sharecroppers and entrepreneurs, its blacks and its standing chorus of town gossips, with its woods, pine-winey afternoons, bear hunts and its own historical 'curse', coming from the possession of Indian lands, the history of slavery, and the deep lesion of the Civil War, Yoknapatawpha becomes a totally functional society, a community with its quite distinct class and racial structure, its own inward agonies, its own processes of historical transformation towards commercialism and industrialism.

Faulkner sets the present of *Sartoris* in the post-World War I world, in the uneasy and changing South to which the ex-flyer the young Bayard Sartoris returns, uneasy about his manhood and his place, seeking his masculine death recklessly in modern machines. But one world evokes another: Bayard's is a latter-day version of the reckless courage of his Southern aristocrat ancestors. And one story evokes another; the present, in debased form, both releases and re-enacts the past. Two essential contrasts dominate: one between the masculine chivalric cult of the Sartorises, and the feminized world of the Benbows, delicate, intellectual, and finally narcissistic, at odds with action and time; the other between those who have an invested historical and social sense, like the Sartorises, De Spains, and Compsons, and those who act according to entrepreneurial and commercial self-interest, above all the Snopeses. Out of these contrasts arises a third, between past and present, a past of action, a present of sterility, a world of men, a world of women. For class barriers now fade, aristocratic manners are superimposed on a commercial world, slaves have been replaced by sharecroppers, the women have learned to turn inward and the men towards inner tragedy, and above all the machine begins to dominate. Thus a special postage stamp of soil, haunted with its own history, institutions, and sense of modern tragedy, now began to be populated, and 'I discovered', said Faulkner, 'that writing was a mighty fine thing. You could make people stand on their hind legs and cast a shadow. I felt that I had all these people, and as soon as I discovered it I wanted to bring them all back.'

But bringing them back seemed to involve a complex aesthetic introversion, as if the very fact of making his own characters part of a larger history and hence part of a pluralized narrative forced this on him. But so did other things: a deep sense of temporal disjunction, an apocalyptic sense of time; and a desire to penetrate the psychic myths underlying the needs and rituals of this society. It is in the work of the end of the Twenties and the Thirties that we can feel Faulkner's experimental power at full force: in *The Sound and the Fury* (1929), *As I Lay Dying* (1930), *Light in August* (1932), and *Absalom, Absalom!* (1936). These are works which involve a sense of history, but they are not necessarily historical novels; and they reach, most of them, segmentally, in small selective units, into the Yoknapatawpha experience, yielding it up not as expository narrative but as units of perception. The underlying history – reaching from the point of settlement in the new land to the contemporary, dislocated instant – is itself an imaginative fiction, a process where moments of concentration and dissipation occur both collectively and personally, where psychic time strangely crosses historical time, where chiliastic moments in the world and frozen instants of personal perception interweave, where the chance of human innocence is newly offered to the American, but where taint, corruption, and rape re-enact their historical and hereditary cycles. Faulkner's writing contains some of the most powerful moments of modernizing unease in contemporary literature. The intensity arises partly from the facts of Southern history: the South concentrated in a single event, the Civil War, a hundred years of western history, facing a modern exposure, a cultural defeat and deprivation, and the process of industrialization all at once. Hence Faulkner's history is apocalyptic: it exists in the context of a fallen Eden, though its degenerating sequence – as land as spirit yields to land as property, woods to axes, gardens to machines, South to North – none the less contains moments of promise, renewed outside time and process and put into play the contingencies of a careless historical development.

In the books that Faulkner now undertook, modernist pluralization begins to occur, arising from temporal disjunction and the broken relation between 'social' and 'subjective' consciousness. He displays a remarkable compendium of fictional strategies, structuring his work not through chronological or historical ordering but through alternative radical sequences challenging such orders and generating symbolic resonance. His tactics have very different rationales than do, say, those of Joyce or Proust. One of these is the historical interlocking of the stories; his characters have, so to speak, a reality outside the stories in which they occur. As Faulkner said of them: 'These people I figure belong to me and I have the right to move them about in time when I need them.' The same applies to the larger history of Yoknapatawpha: Faulkner does not give it to us as really 'there', but manifests the conditions under which he is inventing it on this occasion. 'Time', the interlocking of present and past, personal and public histories, is actually an essential mystery in Faulkner's work. In these central novels and the related stories, there is a recurrent structure of a continuous present behind which are stacked up different layers of time, validated in the story by a variety of justifications. Thus, in the long story 'The Bear', in *Go Down,*

Moses (1942), there are layers belonging specifically to the evolution of Ike McCaslin, the central figure, dealing with his life at sixteen, eighteen, and so on; and others having to do with a broad apocalyptic historical conspectus (*'Jun 1833 yr stars fell'*). In *The Sound and the Fury*, we have a noncausative or continuous present given us for mimetic reasons, because we are dealing with the perceptions of Benjy, an idiot with the mental age of five; but we also have complicated strata of consciousness relating to the reasons for Quentin Compson's suicide. In *Light in August*, there is a stream of consciousness appropriate to Joe Christmas's present position as it relates to the crises of his childhood, which are there in his consciousness without their actually being 'known' to be there, and this helps us comprehend his confused psychic and racial identity. Yet beyond all this there is an experimental author extremely and self-consciously interested in his own rhetoric and structure, his own power to generate form.

These novels of the late Twenties and early Thirties are classics of spatial form, each very different, and generating its own rationale. There are, though, two recurrent paradigms: one is historical or exterior temporal intrusion into personal life; the other is the instant of wonder or personal renewal, or of delocalized vision, of Adamic self-discovery (as experienced, say, by Ike McCaslin in 'The Bear'), converted into an eternal moment within time. It is the conversion of this – the flow and the arrest, the process and the transcendence – into art that constitutes the distinct basis of Faulkner's history and his experimentalism. These key novels are modes of penetrating the symbol, the psyche, and the historical continuum. In *The Sound and the Fury*, the central story concerns Quentin's attempt to arrest both historical and subjective time and maintain Candace's virginity from psychic corruption and time's flow; the novel started, Faulkner has told us, from the single image of Caddy's dirty drawers. There are four layers of interlocking response: Benjy's tale told by an idiot in the continuous present holds the story and its images in the form of a timeless memory; Quentin transliterates the image into psychic and historical tragedy, in one form of cause-and-effect; Jason sees it all causally and empirically; and Dilsey offers an enduring continuity. Associative links, like the coincidence between Caddy's name and the caddie at the golf course, generate the process of multiplication. These inward psychic connectives permit Faulkner's primary concern with consciousness to develop; at the same time the story links outward to the larger 'objective' history of Yoknapatawpha, in which Quentin's suicide is a key event. *As I Lay Dying* shows a different experimental tactic. About the six-day funeral journey of the Bundren family, it is told through 59 interior monologues, reflections on movement and stasis, living and death, the moving wagon 'with an outward semblance of form and purpose, but with no inference of motion, progress or retrograde', and the complicated and grotesque panorama of life surrounding it.

The early Thirties saw a change in Faulkner's preoccupations – a darkening of his themes, an increased concern with a sterile modern evil, with the destruction of men by either the corrupt and dirty sexuality of women, or their fecundity, with the dark outcome of the South's history of puritanism and miscegenation. *Sanctuary* (1932) creates a figure of modern evil in Popeye, the emptied man who has 'the vicious depthless quality of stamped tin', and who revenges his impotence with his corncob rape of Temple Drake, the whore-woman whose decadent sexuality in turn defeats the sentimental sanctuary of innocence sought by Horace Benbow. *Sanctuary* is sensational, and was written largely with commercial intent; *Light in August* draws on similar themes for probably Faulkner's finest novel, a work of extraordinary experiment written through extreme narrative indirections. Here three essential stories interlock. The central narrative is about the black wandering orphan Joe Christmas, whose sexual dislocation brings about the murder of the woman who protects and taunts him, and so his final self-sacrifice to racial lynching. The story of the Revd Gail Hightower shows sterility in another form, as Hightower attempts to lock himself into one time-less Civil War moment when life had meaning, and, unable to relate either to love or violence, now seeks, like Christmas, his own cruci-fixion. And both these dark stories are enfolded in a third, that of the fertile and abundant Lena Grove, the country woman come to town to find the father of her child, who lives in a natural timelessness and endurance, a lasting autumn of natural sexuality, opposite to the rigidly puritanic world of the town. Faulkner produced in this period one more extraordinary experimental novel, *Absalom, Absalom!*, a work that locks in more directly to his continuous history of Yoknapatawpha. It is the massive, historical, gothic story of Thomas Sutpen's 'design', of cursed land, old tragedies and crimes, of the interlocking of history and psychic disorientation and perversion. It is his last truly 'modernist' book, but it opens yet another phase of Faulkner's writing.

For by now, Yoknapatawpha County − 'William Faulkner, sole owner and proprietor', 2,400 square miles of crossing histories, a web of dynasties and genealogies, taints and crimes, stories and storytellers − was becoming infinitely populous. Much of Faulkner's later work extends that populousness, as in, for example, the extraordinary stories of *Go Down, Moses,* with their complex exploration of the transformation of the virgin American land through taint, crime, and racial exploitation into emptiness and void, but their images of redemptive timelessness. Faulkner found many tones of voice for this − from the bleak tragedy of *Absalom, Absalom!* to the comedy of his late Snopes trilogy (*The Hamlet*, 1940, *The Town*, 1957, and *The Mansion*, 1959) or the spirited note of his last novel *The Reivers* (1962). In his later books, some of his complexity of manner went, or moved towards convention. But that complexity had always come from two visions. One was Faulkner's quarrel with history; his multiples of consciousness seem, like Eliot's fragments, to be of a piece with the loss of meaning and order that he saw in the lapsed Eden of the American South. The other was opposite: Faulkner was interested not just in the disorders of the psyche, but in its plenitude, its sentience and lyricism, its structures and myths. And because consciousness is creative, as indeed it is in the lyrical flow of prose within the author's own mind, then time need not destroy; rather it can be re-lived, passed on from one human being to another. The past is perpetuated, and so renewable; through consciousness itself history may become timeless.

So the artist is central, and style his business. Faulkner came to create a language that worked not through cause and effect, but through processes of imagistic distillation, through symbolist suspensions that work between motion and stillness, coalescing past and present, between the advancing movement and the static centre, perception and the thing perceived. Such moments form the heart of his style, as in this from *Light in August*:

Though the mules plod on in a steady and unflagging hypnosis, the vehicle does not seem to progress. It seems to hang suspended in the middle distance forever and forever, so infinitesimal is its progress, like a shabby bead upon the mild red string of road. So much is this so that in the watching of it the eye loses it as sight and sense drowsily merge and blend, like the road itself, with all the peaceful and monotonous changes between darkness and day, like already measured thread being rewound on a spool.

Faulkner's sentences repeatedly work like this, producing not the 'scrupulous meanness' of modern style that Joyce advocated and Hemingway realized, nor that 'fear of abstractions' advanced by imagism, but a complex, prolix, lyrical modern rhetoric. That rhetoric is of a piece with Faulkner's conviction that the modern lapse is temporary, that in human lives there are transcendent powers of endurance, that the curse may be lifted, that history, past or present, retains the potential for becoming timeless myth.

In 1950 Faulkner won the Nobel Prize for Literature, and spoke of his belief in 'courage and honor and hope and pride and compassion and pity and sacrifice', the human material of the timelessness in his work. That work originates amid the anxieties of the Twenties, in its decadent despair, its attempt to create the novel as a modern and a modernist genre, a form for encompassing our understanding of the disorientations of, but also the possible artistic recoveries in, twentieth-century experience. Faulkner portrays a world in which history goes awry, and his central figures experience extreme disorientation or psychic damage, in which both time and person are grotesque. But, changing through striking switches of genre, from tragedy to comedy, from tales of sound and fury to stories of amused narrative loquacity, his work moves towards formal and mythic recovery. Both the regionalism and the modernism of his enterprise made him a central modern influence. The extraordinary line of modern Southern gothic fiction would surely not have been realized without him; he creates the landscape and the historical and moral anxiety that feed the work of major successors like Robert Penn Warren, Eudora Welty, Carson McCullers, and Flannery O'Connor. But his activation of the possibilities of modern form as a new discourse for coping with temporal and psychic disturbance, for the existential dislocation of the modern mind, has made him an international influence, as powerful a force in, for example, modern French fiction as in the Southern tradition. Faulkner's was a major contribution to the key enterprise of the Twenties, the attempt to perceive the modern alike as a historical situation and a new aesthetic condition.

In its hunger for new styles, new mores, new forms, new modes of personal self-realization in time and history, the American Twenties supported one of the most notable generations of modern writers of fiction. Yet, in a repeated fable, their new formal intensity was based on an artistic withdrawal *from* the American Twenties, a reaction against puritanism and materialism, an avant-garde displacement. In fact, these writers shared their age's mixture of progress and nostalgia. They looked on America through the long lens offered by bohemia or Paris or decadent irony, but they also returned to catch the notes of acceleration that made the decade one of modernization and change. It was one of the ironies of the decade that many writers who had thus expatriated themselves, convinced that America would never understand its advanced artists, found themselves, by the decade's end, famous and commercially successful. It was a bigger irony still that the boundless commercialism and possibility that had fed the decade and displaced its writers itself exploded, in the Great Crash of 1929. It was, Fitzgerald saw, not just an economic but a psychic crisis, as a fragile, illusory time laid bare many of its underlying tensions and disorders. This theme had, however, been present in the new novel throughout the decade, as writers explored two histories, one that of what Fitzgerald called 'the great gaudy spree' of the modern, the other that of underlying economic, psychic, and formal disorder which, if understood, might lead to national rediscovery.

5 Realism and Surrealism: The 1930s

Where are the modern streets of New York, Chicago and New Orleans in these little novels? Where are the cotton mills, and the murder of Ella May and her songs? Where are the child slaves of the beet fields? Where are the stockbroker suicides, the labor racketeers or passion and death of the coal miners?

Michael Gold, 'Thornton Wilder: Prophet of the Genteel Christ' (1930)

I believe we are lost here in America, but I believe we shall be found. And this belief, which mounts now to the catharsis of knowledge and conviction, is for me – and I think for all of us – not our only hope, but America's everlasting, living dream. I think the life which we have fashioned in America, and which has fashioned us – the forms we have made, the cells that grew, the honeycomb that was created – was self-destructive in its nature, and must be destroyed. I think these forms are dying, and must die, just as I know that America, and the people in it, are deathless, undiscovered, and immortal, and must live.

Thomas Wolfe, *You Can't Go Home Again* (1939)

I

As the Great Crash of 1929 developed, over the next years, into a deep-seated national and world Depression, it grew quickly apparent that the social and cultural mood which dominated the Twenties was over for good. By 1931, as the banks and factories closed, farming collapsed, industrial plant worked to 12 per cent of capacity, millions of unemployed walked the streets, and destitution, poverty, and pain were widespread, Fitzgerald signalled the closure of his own 'Jazz Age': 'It ended two years ago, because the utter confidence which was its essential prop received an enormous jolt, and it didn't take long for the flimsy structure to settle earthward. . . . It was borrowed time anyhow.' In the same year, in his remarkable work of instant history *Only Yesterday*, the social recorder Frederick Lewis Allen looked back to see the Twenties as 'a distinct era in American history', its styles and attitudes already past and remote. It was a change quickly written into the novel. In Paris, the cheques had ceased to arrive, and Europe was also moving into economic and political turmoil; those expatriate writers who had remained through the surrealist 'Revolution of the Word' now made what Malcolm Cowley has called an 'exile's return' to the revolution of the world. They came back to an America turned in on itself and its economic and social problems. Progressive values and political passions had not been entirely submerged in the Twenties. The argument for 'proletarian literature' had penetrated from post-revolutionary Russia, and was taken up as early as 1921 by Michael Gold. Radical voices had been sounding in Jewish immigrant fiction, starting with Abraham Cahan's *The Rise of David Levinsky* in 1917, and in the Black fiction of the Harlem Renaissance, like Jean Toomer's *Cane* (1923). In 1927 intellectuals found a clear political cause protesting the execution of the anarchists Sacco and Vanzetti. But it was not really until the stock market frenzy of 1928 was followed by the collapse of a financial system built on over-spending, over-capitalizing, and over-borrowing that the need for a new accounting seemed evident.

Now progressive attitudes renewed themselves, the languages of naturalism, documentary, and muckraking were called back, writers engaged or re-engaged themselves politically, and well-known figures like Sherwood Anderson, Upton Sinclair, Theodore Dreiser, and John Dos Passos took up radical causes or wrote in the rising new radical journals of depression, unemployment, urban despair, rural deprivation. The rhetoric of social identification now became important: 'There is one thing about being a writer,' wrote Anderson, reporting a unionization struggle in a Southern mill town. 'You can go everywhere. . . . I am accepted by working people everywhere as one of themselves and am proud of that fact.' So, while castigating an economic system, one could identify with the 'real' America; while challenging the political order, one could celebrate the nation. A mood of nationalist celebration replaced cosmopolitan distance, taking on an epic note: 'America' was in all the titles, and the desire to embrace the disordered American totality drove writers like Dos Passos and Thomas Wolfe. But this did not end the problem of the writer's obligation; attachment to the cause of the 'toiling masses', usually no longer toiling, might help generate an epic naturalism, but beyond was the classic problem of literary 'commitment' – a problem made sharper by the fact that, however much the writer might agonize in bourgeois guilt, the American masses remained remarkably unpoliticized. Clear answers were on offer. Mike Gold, editor of the Communist paper *The New Masses*, which had risen again from the débris of radicalism in 1926, had throughout the Twenties attacked the political 'imbecility' of American writing. Now he urged authors to 'go left', become workers identified with the workers, experience and record and radicalize the proletarian world which provided a writer with 'all the primitive material he needs'. A violent attack by Gold in the *New Republic* in 1930 on the 'genteel' experimentalism of Thornton Wilder's bourgeois and aesthetic fiction struck home; to Edmund Wilson, it represented the start of a new literary mood.

The year 1930 was certainly one for novels of social concern and committed naturalism. Gold's own radical East Side ghetto novel, *Jews Without Money*, appeared; so did Dos Passos's *The 42nd Parallel* (the opening volume of *U.S.A.*), and books with strong, telling titles – Edward Dahlberg's *Bottom Dogs*, Mary Heaton Vorse's *Strike!*. In 1928 the *New Masses* had called for worker–correspondents and author–fighters; writers of working-class background, like Jack Conroy, or from immigrant or Black stock, like Gold himself or Richard Wright, now came to notice. Right after the Crash, in November 1929, the *New Masses* sponsored in New York the foundation of a John Reed Club for younger writers, its slogan 'Art Is a Class Weapon'; by 1934 30 such clubs existed across the nation with a total membership of over 1,200. Not all writers found the Marxist analysis convincing, but the leftward drift was powerful; it also quickly developed its own schisms. In 1934 the John Reed Clubs sponsored what would be the major intellectual magazine of the decade, *Partisan Review*, edited and largely written by the radical New York Jewish intelligentsia, and intended to challenge debilitating liberalism in writing, re-politicize writers, and engage intellectuals in modern historical argument and above all in the class struggle. Like that of the first American Writers' Congress in 1935, the magazine's position was Stalinist; but, by 1937, in the wake of the Moscow Trials, its editors were reacting against the 'totalitarian trend' inherent in the Marxist attitude to culture, questioning the preference for proletarian over modernist writing, and adopting increasingly sophisticated critical theories, recognizing, as William

Phillips, one of the editors, later explained, that 'the imagination could not be contained within any orthodoxy'.

The dissolution of the radical synthesis towards a 'new liberalism' was to be a crucial development in American intellectual life. The debates over the Spanish Civil War, the impact of the Moscow Trials, the relative success of Roosevelt's New Deal, and above all the signing of the Nazi-Soviet Pact in 1939 fractured the Marxist standpoint. In a spectacular defection from the Party after the signing of the pact, that great promoter of proletarian writing Granville Hicks noted: 'However much strength and influence the [American] Communist Party has lost remains to be seen, but it is my belief that the events of the last few weeks have largely destroyed its effectiveness.' By the time the Thirties in turn ended in the spectacular collapse of American isolationism following the Japanese attack on Pearl Harbor in 1941, which plunged America into a new world war against the Axis, most of the writers who had been on the Left during the decade had rescinded their old politics; turning now against pacificism, they often used the documentary skills developed in the Depression to report the battlefields – Dos Passos in the Pacific, Hemingway and Steinbeck in Europe – in the interests of American democracy.

It is sometimes argued that the return to realism and naturalism, and above all the move towards 'proletarian literature', was the essential direction of Thirties American writing. But this is too simple. For one thing, many of the best writers of the Thirties had begun their careers in the Twenties, and new social emphases did not fully displace their modernism. Hemingway and Fitzgerald indeed changed direction and expressed new social and historical concerns, but did not cease to be aesthetically experimental; if Faulkner's work in the Thirties grows more despairing, gothic, and historically anxious, the decade sees his most complex and modernist novels. Dos Passos's remarkable *U.S.A.*, perhaps the decade's key work, employs a latter-day radical expressionism that remarkably links the period's documentary passion with the desire for formal experiment. Many younger writers, certainly, turned to proletarian themes, entered the places of poverty, social displacement, and ghetto alienation; they sought immediacy and engagement, a language that assaulted and violated, an account that was also an attitude, but in so doing they often found themselves in a complex quest for new forms. For some, like James T. Farrell, a massive objective documentary was the answer; for others, like Thomas Wolfe, the need was for a comprehensive subjectivity. Some, like John Steinbeck, tried to recover epic myth as a language of commitment; for others, like Djuna Barnes and Nathanael West, the quest for rational and orderly myth was illusory, and what was needed was not epical realism but grotesque surrealism. The Thirties began, for novelists, as a pressing subject-matter – a world of bread-lines and ghettoes, working-class anger, bourgeois self-doubt – that was a challenge to existing ideas of form. But, as the quest for new form became more complex, as the need grew for a new language to deal with the displacement, alienation, and deep unease generated by urban, technological, capitalist American life, a new aesthetic portrait of American fiction developed which would shape the novel not just in the age of the bread-line but in that of wartime economic recovery and subsequent cold war affluence.

II

At the start of the Thirties, the dominant literary debate was about 'Proletcult', and its great proponent was Michael Gold, who described himself in 1930 as 'the first writer in America to herald the advent of a world proletarian literature as a concomitant to the rise of the world proletariat'. Assuming that modernism was discredited, an irrelevant deposit from the aesthetic, subjectivized, apolitical Twenties, he offered, in another article of 1930, his model of Proletarian Realism'. Its works should, he said, display not pessimism but revolutionary *élan*; they would deal with working-class life, and real conflicts and sufferings rather than private bourgeois agonies; they would have social themes, and go for swift action, clear form, a direct line; they would express the new poetry of materials and the spirit of the worker moulding his own world. Gold wrote with confidence, for there were a growing number of books that expressed the spirit he sought to define – not least his own *Jews Without Money*, which had come out earlier in this crucial year of 1930.

Like a number of the newer writers, including Waldo Frank and Ludwig Lewisohn, Gold was Jewish and came from recent urban immigrant stock; *Jews Without Money* is a ghetto novel, set among Romanian-Jewish immigrants on New York's Lower East Side around the turn of the century, when the Eastern European influx was at its highest. It may be 'proletarian realism'; its more obvious place is in the lineage of the developing Jewish-American novel, with its basic theme of the conflict between Old World values and new, ethnic and religious identity and secular assimilation. Abraham Cahan's *The Rise of David Levinsky*, published in 1917, the year of the Bolshevik Revolution, can be read as the starting point of such a line; his classic tale of the Diaspora Jew hungering for the promised land and seeking it in its modern mythical location, America, is a fable of economic success and moral catastrophe. Levinsky leaves the old land, Lithuania, and the *shtetl* life, already doubting his faith and sensing the appeal of the new, hoping for 'marvelous transformations' in America's 'distant, weird world'; arriving in New York with four cents in his pocket, shaving off his beard and his earlocks, he follows the path from rags to riches and becomes doubly a millionaire. The Columbus myth becomes a Jewish rite of passage, a shift from one state of history to another, from a rooted and religious life to a new world of secularism, alienation, complex sexuality; yet Levinsky's sense of 'reality' remains in the old world, and he never succeeds in connecting desire and fulfilment. Cahan's success was not just to record an essential Jewish experience, the move from Old World to new, but to find a striking fictional form and language for dealing with the consequent alienation.

Jews Without Money is a political version of this fable, the story of the intelligent Jew who stays poor and finds Marx. A highly autobiographical, indeed confessional work, it is a series of sharp thematic sketches about Gold's own upbringing and coming to consciousness. It has naturalist themes, picturing the gangsters and prostitutes, the sweatshops, rotting tenements and bedbugs, the newcomers arriving straight from Ellis Island into urban chaos and religious inertia, the political despair and the disappointed dreams going to waste in street violence, political corruption, Tammany Hall exploitation. The city is a 'jungle' and a 'prison' and defeats all wonder, all desire to make it a 'circus' of joy and pleasure; it is 'a devil's dream, the most urbanized city in the world. It is all geometry angles and stone. It is mythical, a city buried by a volcano.' In the promised land of beginning again the utopian promises fail, and the old communal and traditional life collapses under pressure of greed and selfishness, generated by competitive and individualist principles. In such a city, its wonder corrupted by harsh working conditions, disease, depravity, sexual distortion, apocalyptic messages are in order; politics must come in to restore the dream and replace the wasted faith. The old religion is tainted, and a new secular one is necessary: the narrator, identifying with the true Jews, the 'Jews without money', becomes a Communist. In most of the book, the method is imagistic, depicting a life suspended between memories of the Old World and the facts of the new one in the 'Land of Hurry Up'; to such scenes political comment provides no more than a rhetorical aside. But in the final lines the writer undergoes his revelation and conversion, to Marxism, the new transcendent religion ('O workers' Revolution, you brought hope to me, a lonely suicidal boy. You are the true Messiah'). Cahan's story of alienation is redeemed; the utopian future is given back in new form.

Gold's committed and autobiographical naturalism links his book with works like Edward Dahlberg's also very poetic *Bottom Dogs* (1930), the story of Dahlberg's own young life in orphanages and as a wandering hobo in the pre-war years. And it is a tale from the underside – like, again, Jack Conroy's *The Disinherited* (1933), about a young Missouri worker who leaves the coal mines for the auto lines of the boom, and then in the Depression discovers his class allegiance and hopes for a violent upheaval that will apocalyptically renew the city and the American dream. Apocalyptic renewal was indeed the decade's great preoccupation, and it turned writers away from the cause of a pure raw realism. But, as *Jews Without Money*, which is far better as a group of sharp vignettes than it is as an act of ideological structuring, suggested, this left writers looking for a new redemptive language appropriate to the times – a theme very exactly realized when, five years after Gold's novel, Henry Roth published *Call It Sleep* (1935), which might almost be read as a subtle commentary on Gold's book and his cause. Like *Jews Without Money*, it is the story of a boy's growing up on New York's Lower East Side amid Eastern European immigrants before the First World War, and it also deals with the collapse of the myth of the American promised land. Roth had Marxist sympathies, and he draws on the techniques of urban naturalism to present the bleak, violent streets, the debased sexuality, the embittered father, the life-giving mother, the corrupted rabbis that Gold had drawn. But Roth's subject is finally not the loss of a faith nor the need for a secular religion, but the loss of a language and the need for a sign, a new gift of tongues. His book encounters the polyglot destiny of the immigrant and sees in it the need for new creative form; the result is a major novel.

Not surprisingly, the *New Masses* reviewer attacked it: 'It is a pity that so many young writers from the proletariat can make no better use of their working-class experience than as material for intro-spective and febrile novels,' he complained. In fact *Call It Sleep* is a work of complex urban expressionism that bridged the space between social and political naturalism and fictional rediscovery. Roth concentrates on three years of David Schearl's childhood and tells his story from the perspective of his consciousness, that of a child growing up in a 'world that had been created without thought of him'. But this world is eminently a world of speech, of an endless pidgin street talk which expresses the chaos and fragmentation of the outer world and permits no adequate inner language of desire and awareness. What David seeks is a language of the self that will give him psychic and emotional wholeness in a fragmented world; the book's climax comes when he seeks his gift of tongues by plunging a milk ladle into the electrified crack in the streetcar tracks, hunting a revelation that will defeat the babel of politics and obscenity filling the street world around him. Shocked into unconsciousness, sliding towards sleep as the book ends, he is left in a new silence which has pentecostal promises, because it relates to a new inner awareness, a sense of triumphant acquiescence. And just as David's quest is for a linguistic revelation, so the writer's task is to press through the barrage of discourse that surrounds him with a chaotic multiplicity of messages, towards symbolic form. *Call It Sleep* is in consequence a work of great experimental force; undoubtedly the best Jewish-American novel of the decade, it also led the way towards the Jewish-American fiction of the 1940s and 1950s.

Roth conducts a quiet formal revolution of the radical Jewish-American novel; Richard Wright was to do much the same for Black fiction. Born in rural Mississippi, moving to Chicago on the eve of the Depression, Wright was unprepared, he said, like so many fellow Blacks, for the modern city. He entered the Chicago John Reed Club, became its organizer, and joined the Communist Party in 1934. His first book, *Uncle Tom's Children* (1938), five indignant novellas about life in the brutal racist South, goes back to his Mississippi origins. But the encounter with the city was the theme of a documentary novel, *Lawd Today,* he began next; this was finally suppressed because it did not meet party criteria, and not published until 1965, after Wright's death. The material, however, opened the way to his one major novel, *Native Son* (1940), the story of Bigger Thomas, who grows up in the Chicago slums, kills a white woman,

flees, murders again, is tried, defended as a political victim, and
executed. The situation resembles that of Dreiser's *An American
Tragedy*: Bigger is the murderer as victim, the product, as the lawyer
Max argues at his trial, of social forces, and, as James Baldwin was
later to say, the book uses the form of 'everybody's protest novel'. Its
naturalist credentials are clear; Wright explained later that he wrote
it from a scientific standpoint, inventing test-tube situations in
which to place Bigger Thomas. Yet the book's remarkable power
stems more from Wright's success in making Bigger not so much the
sacrificial victim as the figure of modern identityless man. He is a
man without essence; his condition is fear, his situation confinement,
his reaction violence. He is the outsider, who feels he lives on 'the
outside of the world peeping in through a knot-hole in the fence'.
His essential experiences are of flight, capture, and trial; he finally
identifies himself as one of 'suffering humanity'. But what we follow
is his attempt to realize an existence, discover an ego, create a self.
He makes the attempt at first through diabolic action, murder, but
also in his endeavour to resist the role of social victim; it is others,
and not Bigger himself, who see external forces as the rulers of his
existence. For Bigger this is another form of invisibility; his primary
need is to become visible to, real to, himself.

The theme, in short, is existential; and indeed Wright himself
pursued that connection by moving to Paris and associating with the
French existentialists. His novel *The Outsider* (1953) has not only a
Camusian title but a directly philosophical intention. In it Wright
displays some unease of tone, but its story of the Black rebel hero,
Cross Damon, contesting a meaningless world, is clearly an
endeavour to make the Black into a modern metaphor, the essential
type of contemporary man, 'the twentieth century writ large'. Cross
Damon is a Bigger Thomas vastly more conscious of himself. He
elects his own invisibility, pretending to be killed in a subway
accident when he is threatened with blackmail and jail. Reborn
without an identity, he is rebelliously free to invent himself. He too
commits murder, and the story presses to the limits of his demoniac
personality, pursuing the question of moral responsibility in a world
of eliminated identities. The two novels Wright published in his
lifetime may start close to naturalism, and their existential spirit is
to some degree contained and qualified by it. But their essential
theme, of a man's will to move from non-being to being, and at the
same time to see an exposed modern emptiness within such self-

hunger, was to pass on to the best Black fiction of the 1950s. The spirit of proletarian realism helped bring such books into being, but in time that spirit came to seem too narrow to contain them; Roth and Wright represent the transliteration of the kind of novel Gold celebrated into a new fictional possibility, and a decade later Jewish-American and Black fiction had evolved into central forms for the expression of American modernity.

III

But naturalist intentions and the aspiration towards a documentary inclusiveness did mean much to the writers of the Thirties, as was apparent in the work of James T. Farrell, another Chicago writer of Marxist sympathies whose subject was also to be working-class immigrant life. Farrell's background was Irish Catholic, and he had much personal experience of the Chicago streets, working in shoe stores, cigar stores, and filling stations before he began, at the University of Chicago, a sketch – about the wake for a young man who has died suddenly of drink – which was to become his most famous work, the 'Studs Lonigan' trilogy. *Young Lonigan* (1932), *The Young Manhood of Studs Lonigan* (1934), and *Judgment Day* (1935) began from a small seed, but they grew into a massive construct through what Farrell later explained in an essay as the 'objective' principles of naturalist composition. Studs, 'a normal young American of his time and his class', growing up 'several steps removed from the slums and dire economic want', was carefully chosen 'not only as a character for imaginative fiction, but also as a social manifestation'. What he manifests is not so much economic as spiritual poverty, and in this respect the Lonigan books share with the work of Gold, Roth, and many other writers of the period the conviction that the immigrant dream has failed not only through economic depression but through the corrupt and deadening pursuit of material wealth. Farrell's books are an indictment of the empty culture of Irish Catholic family, community, and religious life, and their main story deals not with the Depression years but what precedes them, before Stud's brutalized life ends with his death in August 1931, at the age of 29.

Studs is a figure at the centre of a large map of sociological and historical insufficiencies, and his story is told against a drab historical backcloth. He sneeringly leaves a school which has scarcely affected him just as Woodrow Wilson, who has promised to keep the nation out of war, is again nominated for President; he enters the jungle of the streets just as war erupts; he becomes a drunkard in the lawless era of the Twenties, and dies as the revived radicalism of the Thirties hints at the possibility of change. In every area of his life, home, school, church, and work, cultural enfeeblement exists. Farrell explained that he was opposed to a theory of total environmental determinism, such as Dreiser's work seemed to express; social causation had, he said, always to be translated into individual motivation, or 'character', so that the reader had a centre in experience with which he might identify. And what surrounds Studs is less a pressing body of conditioning and determining forces than a massive and senseless contingency, a cultureless culture invested with no weight or meaning. He lives in a naturalist world because there is nothing better, deeper purposes and intentions in cultural life having all become debased. In the absence of substantial culture, he falls back upon and exploits brutal aggressiveness and physical and sexual prowess. His main qualities in Farrell's mode of characterization are those of movement, desire, and embittered vitality; this characterization makes him the natural centre of a heavily mapped world of events and random detail, to which he responds in primal ways. Studs may be an exemplary social type, but he is also the sensory receiver of Farrell's large documentary ambitions, the reference point of a vast reportorial task.

Farrell's writing is Depression writing in more than one sense. It is a writing that untangles the crude social ambitions and expectations, and the betrayed historical promises, that have pointed the way to an economic which is also a spiritual collapse; it also responds to failing times with a sense of failure, and sees the essential choice in life as between living out an enfeebled social existence in a mis-made world and a self-destructive vitalism. Yet in this enclosure Studs's is an unconscious and primitive rebellion, and it is inevitable that attention must fall upon the accumulated power of event and experience, on the unremitting expression of the realness of real life but also on its emptiness. As a result, his landscape of raw fact seems curiously style-less; such claim as this fiction makes on our attention is through the writer's detailed acquaintance with a milieu. Farrell seemed conscious of this problem when he moved on to a new and yet longer sequence of semi-autobiographical novels devoted to Danny O'Neill, the more intelligent and creative hero of *A World I Never Made*

(1936), *No Star Is Lost* (1938), *Father and Son* (1940), *My Days of Anger* (1943), and *The Face Of Time* (1953). These are books of obsessive self-accounting, displaying O'Neill's urgent need to record and report the world he has left behind him; and they suggest that, for Farrell as for many Thirties writers, his main possession was a subject calling endlessly for recording. He made that subject, the brutalized immigrant city, into one of the convincing settings of modern American life; but, because he treated it as subject rather than as form, we turn back to his work now mostly for its documentary rather than creative interest.

If there was James T. Farrell to create, for the Thirties, the brutalized city, there was equally Erskine Caldwell to create the brutalized countryside. A Southerner from Georgia, Caldwell offered the base underside to the Southern Agrarianism that developed as a cultural and literary tendency during the 1930s. *I'll Take My Stand*, a collection of essays expressing a strong social faith in the South's distinctiveness and traditionalism, appeared in 1930; and a new Southern Renaissance displayed itself during the following years as a whole group of writers, younger than Faulkner, explored with careful formality of style a complex landscape of social and psychic extremity. Novelists like Caroline Gordon (*Alex Maury, Sportsman*, 1934), Allen Tate (*The Fathers*, 1938), and Robert Penn Warren (*Night Rider*, 1939) linked modernist concerns with a sense of an ancient and traditional history whose heritage of blood and pain needed a mannered recording. There is no such formal or social elegance in Caldwell's work, which functioned by reversing this image. A radical who had published documentary works on social problems, and some working-class fiction, Caldwell made his reputation with two novels that dealt with sharecropping life in Georgia in a mode close to grotesque comedy. *Tobacco Road* (1932) and *God's Little Acre* (1933) mixed Depression documentary with sensational sexual themes; as Kenneth Burke once said, Caldwell's naturalism comes from the way he 'puts people into complex social situations while making them act with the scant, crude tropisms of an insect'. Social seriousness is present; these are tales of worn-out land, exploited farmers, a culture of deprivation, and Caldwell said his aim was 'describing to the best of my ability the aspirations and despair of the people I wrote about'. But the realistic mode is cut across with the tradition of Southwestern humour; the life of the poor is treated as a culture of degeneracy, primitivism, and cunning. The realism turns to melodrama. Lust, avarice, and hope – Jeeter Lester's dream in *Tobacco Road* of winning a good tobacco crop from neglected land, Ty Ty Walden's in *God's Little Acre* of finding gold under useless soil – are the main subjects; Caldwell's primitive naturalism became sensationalism, striking less because of its social report than its shock value.

The naturalistic reporting of working-class life was one urgent literary task of the Thirties; another was realistic exploration of the disorders of the bourgeois world. These found their best chronicler in John O'Hara, a novelist of, as Lionel Trilling said, 'exacerbated social awareness', who converted the traditional mode of bourgeois realism into a powerful discourse for Depression times. O'Hara's fiction is built, with an exacting precision, on the patent solidity of society – the weight of things, the detailed appurtenances of possession, the symbolic value of goods, the problems of rank, class, wealth, and religion. But, like Fitzgerald, whom he recognized as a fellow parvenu for whom social advancement offered the magical subject of fiction, O'Hara wrote when there was rot at the centre, when that solidity was no longer solid. His main setting, 'Gibbsville, Pennsylvania' and the surrounding 'Region', was his own background, an area of exact social knowledge where elaborate social demarcations and discriminations had to be comprehended; O'Hara caught it as its substance collapsed under historical pressure. His novels – among the best are *Appointment in Samarra* (1934) and *BUtterfield 8* (1935) – form an essential chronicle of Thirties America, probing the gap between the social and the private self. *Appointment in Samarra* is exemplary: in it Julian English, convinced his social position is secure, fails to respond to the pressure of a changed time in which no one owns the road he travels on, and so encounters tragedy. O'Hara's tragedies come in many ways, but they turn on the perception that individuals both rest in and rebel against their social being, imperilling themselves as a result. Sexuality, above all, threatens social cohesion; O'Hara's typical hero is the respectable reprobate fleeing unsatisfactory monogamy, who then crashes tragically through the ice of social stability. It was a theme that caught exactly at Depression anxiety, though O'Hara was to sustain it onward into his novels of the 1950s and 1960s.

IV

During the Thirties, realism and naturalism seemed the 'natural' ways to record a deeply changing society. But only rarely did the realism become as precise as O'Hara's, or the naturalism grow systematically concerned with a deterministic or biological account of the human state. The one writer who made a large-scale attempt at this kind of serious naturalism was John Steinbeck, born in 1902 in the Salinas Valley of California, where so many of his books would be set. An autodidact with a measure of formal education at Stanford, a 'real poor kid' whose parents were a flour-mill manager and a teacher, he emphasized his working origins: he had been carpenter, surveyor, department-store clerk, chemist, clerk in a sugar factory, a ranch hand. Behind him was an earlier tradition of California naturalism, in the work of Frank Norris and Jack London, and he came to share their desire for a biological explanation of man's true and primitive nature. He met his appropriate guru in the marine biologist Edward F. Ricketts, with whom he was to collaborate and who offered Steinbeck a 'scientific' account of human and animal nature which led towards an idealized philosophy that was to underlie his books. (Versions of Ricketts, as the sage-like medical figure whose reflections on life guide or activate the story, appear in many of the novels.) Steinbeck's ambitions were both scientific and prophetic: to explain the corporate biology of human action, and to affirm a spiritual nature and need in human existence. And from this much of his great popularity stemmed, once he moved from the early exotic writings of the Twenties (his first published novel, *Cup of Gold*, 1929, is a ripe historical romance about the buccaneer Sir Henry Morgan) to more familiar and popular subject-matter found in the life around him.

The subjects were popular, but Steinbeck invested them with mythical concerns. His next two books, *The Pastures of Heaven* (1932) and *To A God Unknown* (1933), follow a collective motion and myth, the 'westering' movement of Americans across the continent from the settled past towards the paradise of the California valleys, where men seek their primitive roots. Increasingly he wanted to show that those roots lay not in individual satisfactions, possession of property, or regard for conventional morality. 'The fascinating thing to me', he wrote in a letter of 1933, 'is the way the group has a soul, a drive, an intent, an end, a method, a reaction and a set of tropisms which in no way resembles the same things possessed by the men who make up the group.' The 'phalanx of human emotions' was now, he said, the essential subject of his fiction. The notion arose for him from biological and to some extent political naturalism, but emerged as primitive mysticism in his central work: in his California novel *Tortilla Flat* (1935), his 'strike' novel *In Dubious Battle* (1936), the powerful novella *Of Mice and Men* (1937), stories like *The Red Pony* (1937), the tales of *Cannery Row* (1945), and above all, in *The Grapes of Wrath* (1939). This last, a book that for many sums up the Thirties, was his classic tale of 'Okie' migration in the Depression Thirties from the Oklahoma Dust Bowl to the California valleys, following that same 'westering motion' and its underlying myth through a world of natural and economic disaster. All these works are sometimes read as social realism, though this is not what they are. 'I never had much ability for nor faith nor belief in realism,' Steinbeck once explained. 'It is just a form of fantasy as nearly as I can figure.' His concern, he said, was with the 'streams in man more profound and dark and strong than the libido of Freud', the biological and sociological determinants of being, the emotions below consciousness or control, which made life into a collective mystery touching primitive and pagan powers.

Steinbeck thus also belongs to the line of American transcendentalism – the Emersonian idealism of those who saw a unified soul in man and nature, and who sought that soul's deliverance in a new America seen as paradisial Eden, where life returns to innocence and primal sources. Steinbeck's are novels of man's participation in society and nature; moral crimes occur when human needs are blocked by institutions. Natural comradeship is the theme of his first successful novel, *Tortilla Flat*; based on the myth of the chivalric comradeship of the Arthurian round table, it lushly celebrates the spontaneous, moneyless, propertyless lives of the Paisanos (Mexican-Americans) of Monterey. *Of Mice and Men* is a tragedy about the collapse of just such another 'natural' community, brought on when Lennie, the idiot 'unfinished child', commits an 'innocent' act of murder. *In Dubious Battle* (1936) takes its title and myth from Milton; the 'dubious battle' is the conflict between capitalism and communism in the heavenly California valleys, during a strike among fruit-pickers in the Torgas Valley. The novel contains some of the bitter social indignation of Norris's *The Octopus*, with which it can be interestingly compared. Steinbeck's political sympathies are clearly with the radicals, but they too are attempting to impose a system on nature: 'I don't believe in the cause, but I believe in men,' says Steinbeck's sagacious Doc Burton, expressing the spirit of the book.

And this, too, is the spirit of *The Grapes of Wrath*, the book Steinbeck wrote after travelling westward with Okie migrants from Dust Bowl and foreclosure. A work expressing social despair and political indignation at the way failure and decay breed a harvest of wrath, it is also one of the most optimistic of modern American novels – an epic narrative mural, its figures expressionistic and larger than life, the momentum mythical, and the foundation a biological evolutionism expressing Steinbeck's theories of instinctive collective existence. Two myths govern the book: one of hopeful American westering, seen as the journey from bondage to the promised land; one of heroic evolution, man's vital journey from solitude to selfhood in community. The Joad family's progress is from the aridity of the Oklahoma Dust Bowl, caused as much by the bank as by the tractor, to the Californian Eden where, despite the Hoovervilles and social opposition, old signs of promise remain, not least in the Joads' own motion from nuclear family to participation in a vaster 'we'. At times the two journeys seem to conflict or contradict. Sometimes this motion appears a rational, moral voyage towards a utopian form of human collectivity; sometimes it is a blind, amoral, instinctive process revealing not individual will and choice but an animal-like endurance. Sometimes Steinbeck is the political writer, celebrating in large rhetorical sweeps the need of men to transcend selfishness, form the human family, become one; at other times he becomes the observant scientist, indifferently watching the biologically blind actions of living systems pursuing survival. So the key scene, in which Rose of Sharon suckles the starving man after she has lost her own child, may be read as symbolic of political love and action, or (as Steinbeck himself stressed in a letter) of biological survival, life ensuring its own continuity.

As the political ferment of the Thirties died, it was the latter vein, of mythic naturalism, that Steinbeck carried on into the work for which he was awarded the Nobel Prize for Literature in 1962. His late epic novel *East of Eden* (1952) reverts to his old theme, of the American West as Eden, the virgin land where the classic dreams and struggles of man are re-experienced. The central character, Adam Trask, travels west from Connecticut to the Salinas Valley, where his sons repeat the Biblical Cain and Abel conflict that brings death into nature. By now Steinbeck's politics had changed, and his theme points not towards the making of an ideal human collective but to ideas of Jeffersonian independence cursed by man's fallen nature. Some of his more obvious weaknesses grew more apparent: his sentimentalism now cannot quite register the complexity of the evil he senses in man, nor his ruralism quite grasp the nature of industrialism. Steinbeck strains towards pure wonder, and to mythic scale and grandeur. Yet the signs were still there of the power and the transcendent hope that had made *The Grapes of Wrath* not only a work of social protest but a work of modern epic proportions seeking, and expressing, through a vitality of writing, a distilling, Emersonian oneness.

That epic and transcendental note is an important counterbalance to the social critique that ran through the Thirties. It might point to a lost unity, to a desire to incorporate all of experience, to a sense of naturalism as waste which spiritual purposes might overcome. Or the task might be seen more subjectively, as it was conceived by Thomas Wolfe – another novelist of the Thirties whose ambitions were epic, but who concentrated them firmly on himself. From the Appalachian South, and a Scots-American background, Wolfe was born in 1900, the son of a stone-cutter in Asheville, North Carolina, a place that was to become the 'Altamont' and the 'Libya Hill' of his novels when he became, as he long meant to be, a Great Writer. But the intention meant leaving home; he went to the University of North Carolina, then to attend writing classes at Harvard, then to New York and the disturbed Europe of the interwar years. On these travels he set out to catch the spirit of the times, places, people, to write, he said, of 'night and darkness in America, and the faces of sleepers in ten thousand towns; and of the tides of sleep and how the rivers flowed forever in the darkness. . . . I wrote about death and sleep, and of that enfabled rock of life we call the city.' The novels he now wrote were large epics of selfhood spread across a disorienting social and historical world of boom and slump, a vast landscape of nature and force, which he tried to bring into transcendental unity, to make 'enfabled'. The aim was to grasp at life's ebb and flow, making a myth at the centre of which was the author's own romantic self. The project was remarkably successful; Wolfe became one of the period's most celebrated writers before his early death from a brain infection following pneumonia in 1938. Though not, in my view, a Great Writer, Wolfe pursued the largest and grandest of intentions: 'The writer's task', he noted, 'is rather for us to write "why?" across the scroll of our being, and there to answer the question we have raised.' If the question was innocent, so was the answer: it lay in some fashion, as indeed for other Thirties American writers, in the grandeur of oneself.

This meant that the story the writer had to tell was essentially that of his own being and becoming, and Wolfe did this in his first novel, *Look Homeward, Angel*, which appeared in 1929, six days before the Wall Street Crash. 'All serious work is autobiographical. . .,' he said in the preface. 'The book was written in simpleness and nakedness of soul. . . . It is a book made out of my life, and it represents my vision of my life to my twentieth year.' In 1935 came a second volume, *Of Time and the River*, taking the story onward. It is a story rather like that of Sherwood Anderson's George Willard; Wolfe's surrogate, Eugene Gant, grows up in a provincial, sterilizing, yet also rooted Southern world, then breaks its confines, setting out for deeper waters of experience. Gant is an artist, leaving home to encounter new places, make new discoveries, probe the Northern cities and the foreign world; and his artist is an isolated person, by virtue of his sensitivity and special powers – his appetites must be, as Wolfe liked to say, 'gargantuan', a register of all that can be suffered, known, and felt. Art is a compact between the hungering artist and the object of his hunger, 'life'; the hero of life is the artist himself. 'There are few heroic lives,' Wolfe said in a letter, 'about the only one I know a great deal about is my own. This is boastful, perhaps, but as it is true, I see no cause to deny it.' The whole point of his work is that he never did.

Wolfe's novels thus became a confessional epic, a huge outpouring of personal experience. Organizing his writing into publishable form was more or less beyond him: Maxwell Perkins, the Scribner's editor who stayed at home while his protégés, who also included Fitzgerald and Hemingway, took on life and Europe, completed the writing process for Wolfe, cutting down the record and shaping it into book-sized units. Wolfe's role was that of the experiencer, the man who passes through life, attaching to everything – happiness and unhappiness, physical activity and solitude and reverie – those large meanings of which Eugene Gant becomes the focus:

It seemed to him that all this incredible miracle of his own life and fate had ordered all these accidental facts into coherent and related meanings. He felt that everything – the powerful movement of the train, the infinite mystery and lonely wildness of the earth, the feeling of luxury, abundance and un-limited wealth that was stimulated by the rich furnishings of the Pullman, and the general air of affluence of these prosperous men – belonged to him, had come out of his own life, and were ready to serve him at his own behest and command.

With such feelings, of course, any experience will serve both for self-enlargement and as fictional material; even things not directly experienced by Gant may be freely added to increase the general portentousness ('At just this moment the train had entered the State of Virginia, although, of course, none of the men who sat there talking knew that'). It is, in fact, classic bad writing, always enlarging itself into significance through rhetoric; Wolfe's gift was to find a logic to justify the patent extravagance. For the Eugene Gant novels are about just this sort of acquisitiveness: about Gant's sensory, emotional, and imaginative upbringing, about the 'cyclic curve of a family's life – genesis, union, decay, and dissolution' which surrounds him, about the growing sense of isolation from others, and about sterility and paralysis, which drive the artist ever onward.

Look Homeward, Angel, subtitled 'A Story of a Buried Life', explores the life of the family and of the Southern town that provides the rooted world behind Gant, offering him both the ancestral, natural setting he must have and the prison from which, as an artist, he must escape. Archetypal conflicts of this kind – stasis and motion, web and rock – generated the Wolfean myth, further enlarged in *Of Time and the River*, which takes Gant to the Northern world of change and urbanity, to Boston, New York City, Oxford, France. The city is seen as a place of wonder, confusion, contingencies, but is also 'life'; Gant's quest is to reach 'the city of myself, the continent of my soul'. The novels are novels of search – the search, Wolfe said, for a father, certainly for an organizing principle, an idea of art. This theme becomes manifest when, in the city, Gant begins a love affair with an older woman who offers to shape his life, and it is the key to his endless pursuit of something that will turn chance experience into transcendence, transform pure time into form. The problem is that of the modern artist; life starts in tradition, in the 'realism' of home life, but cannot be contained there, for, as the artist in man grows, so must the world with which he acquaints himself. Likewise in writing, Wolfe starts in the traditional novel of community, the world in which men have ancestors, live densely in families, and take the past as the guide to the present; he moves onward into the modern novel of naked quest, a quest for self-exposure within a disorderly urban world that yields up endless experience but cannot quite make it into knowledge. Emotionally and technically, Wolfe sets himself the task of fusing the two. His books then become the answer, their danger being that frequently the space in between is filled with a hungry selfhood expressed as a tireless rhetoric of wanting and desire – a rhetoric sometimes splendid, sometimes uneasily loaded with empty resonances and vague, hyper-literary echoes.

The two Gant novels made Wolfe famous; the problem was what might follow. Like Farrell, he went back to the beginnings by inventing a new surrogate self, George Webber, his history very close to Gant's, who becomes rich and famous. In *The Web and the Rock* (1939), we find him in the middle of the love affair with the older woman, but this collapses as he discovers the corruptions of the artistic life they live, and he moves on to larger historical corruptions in Germany; in *You Can't Go Home Again* (1940), he does go home again, returning to a Depression America of despair, failure, and 'the ruin of the human conscience', but finds a new social hope that the nation will lead the way from decadence to fresh humanity. From pain, corruption, decadence, and solitude, innocence is recovered, epic hope re-won. These books do differ somewhat from the earlier sequence, not alone because, posthumously, they were cut and put together by a different editor, Edward C. Aswell, with a different view of Wolfe's intentions. Wolfe himself emphasized the change, partly derived from the longer distance taken up from his North Carolina past, and a deepened sense of historical change, partly from a stronger political vision, partly by his desire to give more symbolic or mythic weight to autobiographical material, so producing a much more complex time scheme. In some ways more documentary, the works are also more 'modernist', in that the juxtaposition of elements – past life and present, large symbolic entities like the web (of traditional society) and the rock (of the city) – grows more oblique. For earlier and often clumsy narrative techniques, Wolfe substitutes far more complex modes. The logic of memory alters, the tonalities of symbolism are stronger, and there is a greater satiric and parodic distance from his material. But the autobiographical element firmly persists – these novels are epics of self, life, and America, three vast enterprises – and so does Wolfe's very American hunger for an affirmative, transcendental confession that, through his claim to have passed through crucifying experience, would make all things epical. He writes of the defeat of the Depression, the world dominance of Satanic greed, but, given his instinct for abstract rhetoric, there was little doubt what his discovery would be, a grand prophecy: 'I believe that we are lost here in America, but I believe we shall be found.' Art and confession lead to prophetic wisdom, a pure confession of truth, and the ultimate aim becomes to produce the bookless book that would see and say everything anew.

V

Wolfe was not the only writer of the Thirties with ambitions to transcend the book:

This then? This is not a book. This is libel, slander, defamation of character. This is not a book, in the ordinary sense of the word. No, this is a prolonged insult, a gob of spit in the face of Art, a kick in the pants to God, Man, Destiny, Time, Love, Beauty ... what you will. I am going to sing for you, a little off key perhaps, but I will sing. I will sing while you croak, I will dance over your dirty corpse. ...

So began *Tropic of Cancer* (Paris, 1934; New York, 1961), the first of the 'Tropics' sequence of Henry Miller, a writer who in many ways aimed to reverse or affront all the tendencies and values of the decade. In a time when the expatriates came home, he wrote in expatriate Paris, and his books were printed there, not to be published in the U.S.A. until the 1960s, excluded not because of their avant-garde content but because of their sexual explicitness, violent eroticism, apparent perversity. Miller's refusal to write a 'book' was a deliberate assault on all established concepts of art, and above all to the notion of literary responsibility and social allegiance. Miller is a crucial reminder that the novel of radical extremity took other than directly social form in the Thirties; he is rightly seen now as a fore-runner of post-war experimentalism and post-modernism. The Thirties notes are present: a strong naturalist content, especially in the evocation of his immigrant childhood and life as an urban rogue in Brooklyn; a large transcendental intention, very American, though based on a grand dissent and on Taoism, surrealism, and European anarchist as well as American philosophies; the need for the book that does more than a book can, confessing, prophesying, transforming and touching life's 'reality' directly. However conventional politics, progressive and optimistic views of history, and celebration of America were not for Miller; the burdens American writers were taking up Miller hoped to leave behind when, in 1930, penniless, he moved not to atelier but to *clochard* Paris and made his own distinctive contribution to the new surrealist arts of outrage and atrocity.

Miller's novels were to be Thirties anti-novels – even though, as Leslie Fiedler once said, they are genuine Depression novels too, written out of a sense of economic chaos, historical lesion, and political pain. But at the same time they react against all the conventional and responsible attitudes and judgements – liberal humanism and bourgeois guilt, political rationalism or utopian expectation. It is easy to glimpse in Miller's writing the proletarian novelist he might have been but refuses to be. He was born in Brownsville, Brooklyn, New York, son of a tailor of German immigrant stock, and spoke German himself until he went to school; he grew up the street-wise city boy in the ghetto, in a world of deprivation and excitement, grossness and possibility, where violence and sensitivity, sexual adventure and romantic literariness, were always in equivocal combat. Miller had radical inclinations, admired Jack London and Emma Goldman, and was attracted to theosophy and anarchism. He took up, much as Steinbeck had, the endless round of menial odd jobs and rapid hirings and firings that now seemed required for any literary career; he was variously a clerk, an employee in his father's tailoring shop, a ranch hand in California, a garbage collector, bellhop, statistician, editor, and through a trick personnel manager of the messenger service at Western Union, where he himself now wildly hired and fired, in fury against 'the whole system of American labor, which is rotten at both ends'. He hated the place he was born in, and everything his parents endorsed or approved; an assiduous reader, he found that books inflamed him to further revolt. He turned to manual labour and vagabondage, resolving to reject books and make a living with his hands, but felt ceaselessly suspect, betrayed by his language and his ideas. 'I had no principles, no loyalty, no code whatsoever. . . . I usually repaid kindness with insult and injury. I was insolent, arrogant, intolerant, violently prejudiced, relentlessly obstinate,' he explained later in *The Time of the Assassins* (1956), a study of his literary hero Rimbaud which is even more a study of his second such hero, the author himself.

This history was to come into his second 'Tropic' book, *Black Spring* (Paris, 1936; New York, 1963) and yet more into the third, *Tropic of Capricorn* (Paris, 1939; New York, 1962), and then again into his later series *The Rosy Crucifixion* (made up of *Sexus*, 1945; *Plexus*, 1949; and *Nexus*, 1960), written when some partial reconciliation with his homeland had occurred, and his desire to outrage had somewhat softened. But Miller's initial tale was one of dissent, severance, and withdrawal from a home he disliked, a New York he detested, an America with whose culture and citizens he felt nothing in common. In 1924, abandoning his job with Western Union to become at last a writer, Miller felt confirmed in his view of himself as the one true artist, the dispossessed genius cast aside by all – the gangster genius of the dissenting, romantic-anarchic tradition he would always celebrate, of those who 'lived like scarecrows, amid the abundant riches of our culture'. The artist had to be the eye outside, the outsider and undersider, and his task was self-ejection: 'All my life I have felt a great kinship with the madman and the criminal...,' he observed in his 'Brooklyn Bridge' essay in *The Cosmological Eye* (1945). 'To me the city is crime personified. I feel at home.' If social indignation was strong, the stance excluded a direct political solution, and it led to no humanistic message: 'Today I am proud to say I am *inhuman*,' he would write in *Tropic of Cancer*, 'that I belong not to men and governments, that I have nothing to do with creeds and principles.' Nor was he a writer of American celebration; he saw America as the 'air-conditioned nightmare', a 'huge cesspool', the heartland of modern sterility, and himself as the writer totally deracinated – as he put it in *The Cosmological Eye*, he was not an American but a 'cosmological' writer. This all logically led to expatriation, and expatriation led to *Tropic of Cancer*, his first, most affronting, and still surely best book.

Tropic of Cancer is the story, more fictionalized than it looks, of Miller's poverty-stricken life as an amoral genius in Paris, satisfying above all because it is not America: 'America three thousand miles away,' he cries, 'I never want to see it again.' Paris, though, while itself eaten away with cancer and excremental flow, permits the new art which is not art, and 'One can live in Paris – I discovered that! – on just grief and anguish.' Behind the book are many Thirties ideas: of modern historical debasement and sterility, the waste land and the dead city confirmed by economic apocalypse; of the reality of the obscene; of the need for a subjective anarchistic surrealism that works towards self-liberation, in terms of a new psycho-history that is built on Groddeck and Rank, and encapsulated in the image of the double womb – the womb one regresses into, avoiding rebirth; the world as womb, permitting a rebirth of consciousness. This surrealistic sexual historiography has much of the occult in it. The sense of universal corruption is necessary for the enterprise: culture, especially American, has broken down, the ecstatic man has disappeared, 'The world is pooped out. . . .' This apocalyptic world, 'a world used up and polished like a leper's skull', calls for an obscene resurrection, a mystery recreated around the complex psychic mystery of the vaginal hole: 'If anyone knew what it meant to read the riddle of that thing which today is called a "crack" or a "hole", if anyone had the least feeling of mystery about the phenomena which are labelled "obscene", this world would crack asunder. . . . If there is only a gaping wound left then it must gush forth though it produce nothing but toads and bats and homunculi.' In fact what gushes out is not only a confessional cry hunting its way towards prophecy, but a wild vision, like a surrealist painting, in which the flow from the womb and the flow from the city alike pour out images of sex and death, sterility and birth, excrement and flowers.

Paris was more for Miller than a setting for poverty-stricken expatriation, an alternative city for his rebellion; it provided an unexpected rootedness, 'a soil so saturated with the past that however far back the human mind roams one can never detach it from its human background,' to contrast with the American void. It also gave him much from its dominant experimental movement, surrealism. In *Tropic of Capricorn*, Miller, trapped in the *fourmillante cité* of dead souls, New York, recognizes himself as 'perhaps the unique Dadaist in America, and I didn't know it.' His enterprise, like the surrealist one, went beyond literature into post-literature, beyond art into outrage, beyond reason into the flooded unconscious, beyond form into an apocalyptic randomness, a second-order chaos that was to echo the chaos of the existing and open to the chaos of the new, transformed world. His prose becomes passionate, visionary, often incoherent, always comic, drawing on bawdy and invective both for outrage and authenticity. Miller's books are sometimes read as frank sexual realism; in fact they are books of the grotesque, and the writing seeks often to follow the chaotic flow of consciousness ('chaos is the score upon which reality is written'), which is made occult by the violations the 'I's of his books can score against the cancered environment. A central iconography is of sex, death, excrement, resurrection, with sex portrayed as a destructive act, a violation of this particular regressive female womb, in the interest of the visionary recovery of the male self. The condition of rebirth – or of rebirths, for Miller is reborn rather more frequently than the surrounding environment might suggest is possible – is precisely the persisting sterility and corruption.

Tropic of Cancer ends, like most of Miller's books, with a visionary recovery, raising the possibility of a return to America. *Black Spring*, a set of apocalyptic scenes reaching back into his American past, attempts more elaborate prose experiments. *Tropic of Capricorn* then reaches further into the American past, starting from the existential premise that 'Once you have given up the ghost, everything follows with dead certainty, even in the midst of chaos.' The book begins in a mixture of cunning acquiescence in and rage with the American system ('. . . in the bottom of my heart there was murder: I wanted to see America destroyed, razed from top to bottom . . .') and is dominated by the sexual imagery of 'The Ovarian Trolley' – the diseased ovaries of Hymie's wife, the vaginal wound that spawns the paradoxes of 'The Land of Fuck', the land of life and of death, of the womb as corruption and resurrection. Beginning in social rage, Miller gradually learns to look on everything that is happening around him as if he were a spectator from another planet, picking up a cabbage leaf from the gutter to hold it in his hand and see it as its own universe, finding the city insane and himself a great witnessing eye above the world, a man shedding his skin in a succession of layers. The structure of the telling is loose, disorderly, associative; the aim is clear – the creation of a new life, where 'Equilibrium is no longer the goal – the scales must be destroyed.' Capricorn, 'renaissance in death', can now balance Cancer, 'the extreme point of realization along the wrong path'. And life becomes a hairline walk between the two.

The energy and obscene vitality of Miller's early novels are sustained through their power of apocalyptic fantasy; in them the underdog becomes exploiter-redeemer because he has nothing to lose and everything to gain. With the war, Miller returned to the States, assaulting it in *The Air-Conditioned Nightmare*, a record of his travels round the continent, but finally settling, in 1944, at Big Sur in California. There he wrote extensively and, as his earlier books were no longer banned in the States, or were republished there, he became a guru of the new radicalism, the Beat Generation, the voice of American romantic anarchism. *The Rosy Crucifixion*, re-covering the early ground from a more speculative point of view, is largely a text of visionary celebrations. Miller came to be seen as the type of post-Marcusean man, detached from the conservatism of the maternal womb, free to enjoy bodily and spiritual consciousness; as such, his work deeply influenced many writers of the late Fifties and Sixties, re-opening the path of visionary surrealism. This was one Miller, but another is the subject of George Orwell's early essay on him, 'Inside the Whale' (1940), which saw him as the new quietist, the writer in a dead and corrupted world, enduring and recording the world process without political solutions, a 'completely negative, unconstructive, amoral writer', a 'Whitman among the corpses'. Both views of Miller are enlightening. He was a potential optimist, his mysticism and metaphysics finally pointing the way back to American transcendentalism. But in his notable early work the tension between nihilism and self-discovering vitalism is the key, and it is there that he creates both a remarkable obscene comedy of despair and a striking surrealist form.

Miller was not the only American writer of the Thirties to look at European surrealism for a way to write the times. So did Djuna Barnes, another expatriate, in *Nightwood* (1935), a complex, dense fantasy-novel of psycho-pathological disturbance and tragic horror. And, even more importantly, so did Nathanael West, whose apparently eccentric work proves now to belong firmly in the tradition of American comic grotesquerie, and who shared with Miller a vision of a world of total inhumanity hovering between dream and nightmare, and ever on the edge of apocalypse. Born Nathan Weinstein, the son of Jewish immigrants, in New York in 1903, he went to Brown University, acquired a talent for dandified imposture, and took the name West on moving to Paris in the late Twenties. His was a brief expatriation, but it confirmed his avant-garde disposition and his interest in surrealism – though a part of his talent undoubtedly owes much to his friendship with the American humorist S. J. Perelman. In Paris West worked on *The Dream Life of Balso Snell*, a parodic text published there in 1931. It is a surreal comedy about an American poet innocent who wanders into the womb-world of the Trojan horse through the posterior opening, and finds it 'inhabited solely by writers in search of an audience'. This opens the (rear) door to pastiche and parody of many literary styles, a generalized mockery of art that dislodges past forms and even recent modernism, including the work of Joyce. It is a creative writer's notebook, a striking act of apprenticeship. West was always to be an idiosyncratic writer, with some obvious limitations: his desire to mock, undercut, make art into a kind of comic strip with puppet-like agents, often looks like bad writing, and at times, as in parts of *Balso Snell*, it is. Yet exactly those qualities, which displace prior artistic conventions and ideas of art's humanism, were to prove his real resource, as his work developed through three more novels – *Miss Lonelyhearts* (1933), *A Cool Million* (1934), and *The Day of the Locust* (1939) – before it was cut off by his sudden death in a car accident in 1940.

It is with *Miss Lonelyhearts* that West achieves a coherent vision, a lasting tone, founded on a perception of the pain and anguish underlying the myths of American society. *Miss Lonelyhearts* is a black farce about a newspaperman who actually tries to respond to the sufferings displayed in the letters he receives from readers of his agony column. But grotesquerie is not just a condition displayed by the sufferers; it is also a dominant fictional device. West dissolves any direct concept of character, turning all his agents, including 'Miss Lonelyhearts', into rhetorical figures or objects, comic automata whom we see through the jerks of their flesh, the independent, broken life of their bodies, which come to seem masterpieces of bad design. Yet this too becomes a basis for pain and pathos, for the human figure itself becomes inadequate for the suffering it is invited to bear. Meaningful being is divided off from the absurd actions of the body and the impulses of the will; hence his characters live in a state of semi-crazed illusion, a collective dream of desire which readily tips into violence. Of all this Miss Lonelyhearts, the sensitive man, is the focus, becoming a maddened and inadequate Christ unable to offer any true redemption. Against his failed Christ is set the Antichrist, the witty, indifferent, predatory editor Shrike, who mocks the hero into attempting the 'miracle' of bringing love to one of the surrounding victims, the crippled Doyle – an attempt that leads to his useless and absurd death. The book offers a soft centre and a hard face; throughout pathos is both created and taken away, generating a black comic tone that resembles some of Twain's late work, and that some of the black humorists of the Sixties were to echo. West's theme is clearly human yearning, as much in its grotesquerie as its pathos – a natural enough theme, he implied, for a society where dreams of success and desire were prevalent, yet emerged in distorted and freakish forms, above all in the world of Depression and urban deprivation.

The sense of historical pain and political disaster implicit in *Miss*

Lonelyhearts becomes explicit in *A Cool Million*. A satire on the lore of the American dream and the Horatio Alger success myth of rags to riches, its 'hero' is a classic fictional innocent, Lemuel Pitkin, the American good boy who never loiters on his way home from school. Parodically told in a variety of mock styles, the book then reverses the ancient plot, substituting misfortune for fortune. His home foreclosed upon by a wicked squire, who wants to sell it to an interior decorator, Lemuel seeks the good offices of 'Shagpoke' Whipple, former President of the United States and president now of the Rat River National Bank, who explains that, poor, honest, and born on a farm, his applicant cannot but succeed. Lemuel is then quickly robbed, imprisoned, and has his teeth taken out – the first of a series of dismemberments as he tries to pursue his innocent fate in the land of the American dream. He loses an eye, a thumb, his scalp, a leg, and is finally shot at a political rally. 'Through his martyrdom the National Revolutionary Party triumphed,' Whipple announces, 'and by that triumph this country was delivered from sophistication, Marxism and International Capitalism. Through the National Revolution its people were purged of alien diseases and America became again American.' The all-American boy thus wins his final apotheosis. A satire on nativist politics and myths, the book depends on a fictional energy where violence, dismemberment, and distortion are, again, not only the subject but the artistic method: all the harshness and abstraction of satire is drawn upon. West's most political book, *A Cool Million* penetrates the distortions of society, the process by which dream becomes corruption, exploitation, and violation of innocence, myths become misleading legends. The theme leads naturally to West's next novel, about the great American dream-factory, Hollywood.

The Day of the Locust is naturally to be compared with Scott Fitzgerald's *The Last Tycoon*; the two Hollywood novels were written about the same time, and from a similar experience of working as a screenwriter. Fitzgerald's book, however, is primarily about the studio world, West's about the frenzied and bitter dreamers who surround it – the crowds that pour into this city of possibilities, fantasies, myths, and religions, expressed in their most extreme and artificial form. Towards Hollywood come the distorted, strange creatures of a dislocated American life, themselves fantasists, whose overwhelming boredom, as they grow gradually 'tired of sunshine and oranges', moves towards violent frustration, with themselves as well as with the illusory world around them. The book starts amid the fantasy of the studio sets but moves to the equal fantasy of the world outside, the world of cults and sects, sports and sensations, circuses and clowns, life-styles and promises, and the daily diet on the news of 'lynchings, murder, sex crimes, explosions, wrecks, love nests, fires, miracles, revolutions, wars'. Hollywood is a dream in a land of dreamers, who want ever more sensation and are ready for a violence beyond boredom, solitude, repression, and anger. West has something of Sherwood Anderson's interest in his individual grotesques, with their mixture of expression and repression, their 'drained-out feeble bodies and their wild disordered minds'. They are figures both bizarre and lost – like the 'poorly made automaton' Homer Simpson, with his murderous body; the sex symbol Faye Greener, with her sexless sexual invitation, which is not to pleasure but to struggle, 'hard and sharp, closer to murder than to love'; her father Harry, the 'bedraggled Harlequin' trying to find sympathy and meaning through his clowning; the pugnacious dwarf Abe Kusich. But West's theme is the crowd itself, and he does not enter individual consciousness, but shows wild collective sensations, or the nervous psychic springs of action in a world where life is a meaningless performance, the need is for extreme sensation, and the fundamental human lot one broken between desire and infuriated despair.

Notably, West also explores, through a central figure appropriately called Tod Hackett (the allusions to violence and death are explicit), the artist who might represent such a world. Tod is a set-designer and painter whose intention is to paint *The Burning of Los Angeles*, an apocalyptic modern canvas. As he hunts his subject, he witnesses the growth of a rising scream of fury. The notes of apocalypse sound, and though Tod's aim is less to satirize the crowds who wait to be galvanized into existence than to 'paint their fury with respect, appreciating its awful, anarchic power and aware that they had it in them to destroy civilization', he holds apart from the mob. Finally at the picture première, the mob riots and loots; Tod, though hurt and throwing his stone at the crowd, is none the less able to fix at last on the violent detail of his painting, which will be an elaborate and surreal *Guernica*, created with suffering *and* detachment, depicting both the mob seeking to purify the land, and the artist himself, both present and apart. So situation and painting merge as the novel ends, with the book itself secreting an insight into its method.

West finds his equivalent for Tod's style of art in his short-take techniques, drawn from screen writing and the strip cartoon. Like Tod, he stands inside his vision, a victim, while seeing that the important thing *is* the vision, which therefore becomes one not of total satirical detachment but of pathos and sadness. West constructs his own surreal canvas, expressing a dream-like motion filled with extraordinary images – the dead horse in the swimming pool, the cock fight, and so on – as well as a comic formalism. His last and most self-aware book is a tragi-comic, troubled portrait of the artist in an apocalyptic age – a speculative reminder that Thirties fiction was not solely an affair of reportage and protest fiction, but also of a new experimentalism.

6 Liberal and Existential Imaginations: The 1940s and 1950s

Guiltlessness. Our fat Fifties cars, how we loved them, revved them: no thought of pollution. Exhaust smoke, cigarette smoke, factory smoke, all romantic. Romance of consumption at its height. Shopping for baby food in the gaudy trash of the supermarkets. Purchasing power: young, newly powerful, born to consume. To procreate greedily. A smug conviction that the world was doomed. Beyond the sparkling horizon, an absolute enemy. Above us, bombs whose flash would fill the scene like a cup to overflowing.

John Updike, 'When Everyone Was Pregnant', in *Museums and Women* (1973)

He asked himself a question I still would like answered, namely, 'How should a good man live; what ought he to do?'

Saul Bellow, *Dangling Man* (1944)

I

The Japanese attack on Pearl Harbor in 1941 not only precipitated America into its second world war of the century; it also marked another sharp redirection of national development. The nation united against the totalitarian adversary, and with military spending the economy recovered; a decade racked with economic and political problems and doubts about the future of the capitalist system was at an end. From the war, the United States emerged the one outright victor, a superpower which had initiated the nuclear age when it dropped its atomic bombs on Hiroshima and Nagasaki in 1945. Postwar America became a land of unprecedented affluence; within a short time real incomes doubled and the United States became the exemplary consumer economy, generating a remarkable inner cohesion and what looked to many intellectuals an age of new conformity. But the war had also implicated Americans in the mounting disorders of the modern world; she was unable, as she had in 1918, to withdraw to her own continent and mind her own business. In the new global balance of power American influence and engagement spread; America now represented individualist capitalist democracy against a wall of rising collectivism, in a troubled and anxious age when the hot war was almost immediately followed by a cold one. With whatever misgivings, Americans had entered the historical mainstream, and an earlier state of innocence had clearly ended. That sense of engagement with a bloodied modern history, perplexing, terrifying, and apocalyptic, was to become part of the new spirit that emerged, over the years of war and uneasy peace, in American fiction.

A sense of historical fracture was in any case apparent throughout the fiction of the west. In Europe, a number of the major modernists had died around the war's beginning – Yeats in 1939, Virginia Woolf and James Joyce in 1941 – and a whole phase in the modern arts seemed over. German and Italian fiction had virtually to reconstitute itself after the collapse of the social order; French fiction developed the new existential novel of Sartre and Camus; British fiction was responding to its new welfare state and post-imperial world with a new spirit of realism. In American writing, similarly, a transition was apparent, signalled by the deaths of a number of the major experimental figures – Fitzgerald and West within a few days of each other, in Hollywood in 1940, Sherwood Anderson in 1941, Gertrude Stein in 1946, in a newly liberated Paris, still asking on her deathbed 'What is the question?' Other notable figures from the Twenties and Thirties continued to write; the fact that Hemingway, Faulkner, and Steinbeck all became Nobel Prize laureates in the late 1950s and early 1960s showed the growing international power and prestige of American fiction. Their modernism became better understood, but all three showed signs of being beyond their best work, and could hardly represent the spirit of the post-war generation. The problem of succession came into doubt, and there were those who suspected that the affluent, conformist new America would discourage serious development of the novel. In *After the Lost Generation* (1951) John Aldridge argued that American writing was now too bereft of moral or mythological community to generate serious art; Malcolm Cowley's *The Literary Situation* (1954) claimed that the co-option of American intellectuals by the new academicism and corporatism would produce an age not of the creative arts but of criticism and scholarship. As late as 1959, when a new generation had clearly emerged, Irving Howe was still arguing, in 'Mass Society and Post-Modern Fiction', that it was virtually impossible to relate individual and community adequately in the new America, 'a relatively comfortable, half welfare and half garrison society in which the population grows passive, indifferent and atomized'.

This sense of change was already apparent in the novels of the 1940s, which show a marked ideological uncertainty and a consciousness that the old boundaries had been broken by America's entry into war. So, in a novel that sharply caught the new mood, *Dangling Man* (1944), Saul Bellow presented a hero who, finding himself bereft of all political and social certainties as he awaits military induction, reacts by turning inward in an attempt at existential self-recovery; he fails, and looks to the army with relief, crying 'Long live regimentation!' The price of regimentation was the theme of Norman Mailer's war novel, *The Naked and The Dead* (1948), and the ideological emptiness it produced in post-war America the theme of his *Barbary Shore* (1951), in which the central character is lost in 'the air of our time, authority and nihilism stalking one another in the orgiastic hollow of this century'. Many notable war novels, often from new writers, came out of the experience of young Americans within the military machine, and on the European and Pacific battle-fields: John Hersey's *A Bell for Adano* (1944), Gore Vidal's *Williwaw* (1946), John Horne Burns's *The Gallery* (1947), Irwin Shaw's *The Young Lions* (1948), James Gould Cozzens's *Guard of Honor* (1948), John Hawkes's *The Cannibal* (1949), Herman Wouk's *The Caine Mutiny* (1951), James Jones's *From Here to Eternity* (1951). As after World War I, the war became, for these and later writers, a fundamental turning point. But, as Malcolm Cowley noted, World War I seemed to generate a fiction of great technical experiment, whereas, with exceptions like John Hawkes, this first stage of war fiction emerged in the form of conventional naturalism – though it would produce more complex successors later.

Yet that naturalism was now largely bereft of ideological consciousness, depicting, instead, a world in tragic disarray or what J. D. Salinger would call 'squalor', so vast as to be beyond explanation. Books like *The Naked and the Dead* were less about war than the coming of a world where liberal optimism or direct political action appeared powerless before a new massing of forces, military, industrial, technological, political, which limited the action of the self. A similar dark naturalism also appeared in novels of the neon city of violence, disorder, and psychic extremity, like Willard Motley's *Knock on Any Door* (1947), Nelson Algren's *The Man With the Golden Arm* (1949), Chandler Brossard's *Who Walk in Darkness* (1952). In some ways works of high realism, these books are also an exploration of urban landscapes of horror and nightmare, of a society vast, overpowering, historically lost. In them rising post-war affluence turns towards horror, the central figures into social victims or else conscious violators of social values. Critics began to notice in the new fiction a retreat from the self, and a massing of society as an adversary force, which gave this desperate realism a different flavour from that of Thirties naturalism. It bore some relation to another striking tendency of the Forties — the emergence of a group of new writers, many from the South, a number of them women, with a strong disposition towards Gothic and grotesquerie, and a concern with the problem of intractable human evil. Books like Carson McCullers's *The Heart Is a Lonely Hunter* (1940) and *The Member of the Wedding* (1946), Eudora Welty's *A Curtain of Green* (1941), *The Robber Bridegroom* (1942), and *Delta Wedding* (1946), Truman Capote's *Other Voices, Other Rooms* (1948), and *The Tree of Night* (1949), and Flannery O'Connor's *Wise Blood* (1952) and *A Good Man Is Hard to Find* (1955) mingled a high formal sophistication with a dark vision of decadence and evil, producing a fiction of Gothic finesse. Sharing naturalism's bleak report on social and psychic conditions, this fiction reacted against it in its exact formal concern, its move away from the urban setting and the masculine matrix, above all in its refusal to give a sociological account of human experience and evil. Set often in small Southern communities, the central characters frequently children, the damaged or disabled, these books created a world in which experience is both socially and emotionally twisted, so that the fantastic and the true mysteriously interweave, and (as in *The Heart Is a Lonely Hunter*) broken communication and failed love are prevailing conditions. Evil and loneliness can lead to a pure existential exposure, or perhaps in the direction of a religious awareness in which knowledge of evil is a step towards truth. The emotion of horror and metaphysical disorientation links these writers with a fiction of extreme new grotesquerie developing in the work of John Hawkes, Paul Bowles, James Purdy, and others; but beyond chaos is often the redemption of ritual and form, generating a stylistic precision shared with writers like John Cheever, J. D. Salinger, or John Updike.

Thus along with the weakening of ideological commitment came a qualification of naturalism, a growing preoccupation with form and with moral and metaphysical complexity. There was much talk of a 'new liberalism', post-ideological and deeply conscious, in the world of holocaust and possible atomic annihilation, of the power of human evil, of man's exposure in a dark world. And, in *The Liberal Imagination* (1950), Lionel Trilling saw the means for expressing this new sense of complexity as, exactly, the novel – the form that penetrated beyond ideology to the deeper impulses that generated it, perceived the complexity of reality and the mixed nature of good and evil. His own novel, *The Middle of the Journey* (1947), had already explored the theme by returning (as many writers now did) to the ideological world of the Thirties, setting in exemplary conflict the radical Nancy Croom – with her 'passion of the mind and will so pure that, as it swept through her, she could not believe that any-thing that opposed it required consideration' – and Maxim Gifford, the Party renegade who converts to Catholicism and hopes to find there a vision not of universal innocence but universal guilt. Between these two ideologues and totalists is the hero John Laskell, who discards both options in favour of a liberal pluralism which accepts the shapelessness of experience, the complex contingency of life, the endless interweaving of good and evil – who in effect stands for the curious openness that is the gift of fiction itself. In related vein, Mary McCarthy, in novels like *The Oasis* (1947) and *The Groves of Academe* (1952), cast her cold ironic eye on naïve utopianism and liberalism. Though not complex formalists, these writers repre-sented a new spirit in fiction, seeking to make the novel more than a politics, rather a way into a history no longer open to innocent ideological interpretation. One possible result was a modern absurd-ism, a writing left pained and almost silent in front of an onerous and dark history, dividing self from society; another was a writing of new realism, looking for a more complex reconciliation of the two.

A new generation of writers was powerfully emerging, and behind them was a double heritage. There was the heritage of realism and naturalism, concerned with changing history, social experience, the developing machine of society and the city, the pressure on the self, there was also the heritage of modernism – not just the optimistic modernism of a Dos Passos or a later Faulkner, but of those bleaker European figures, like Dostoevsky, Mann, Joyce, and Kafka, who had made modernism a response to nihilism and historical disorder.

Not surprisingly, some of the best new writers were those who had reason to think of themselves as survivors and victims of war and holocaust, and those whose entire intellectual heritage had been transformed by the events of 1941–5. Jewish intellectuals had often followed the radical path into and out of communism, had been pre-occupied by European intellectual life and its modernist arts. It was they who could speak most validly for the six million victims of the old world order, see the dangers of totalitarianism in politics and art, and speak most firmly for a new humanism. By the Fifties, a signifi-cant new group of Jewish-American novelists had appeared. Their work drew on the Yiddish tradition (brought to the States particu-larly by Isaac Bashevis Singer) and on Russian and European modernism – especially that part of it concerned with the disman-tling of the self by an intolerable modern history. In Saul Bellow, Norman Mailer, Bernard Malamud, and Philip Roth, one can see the transformation of the older tradition of Jewish-American writing. Now the theme was less the immigrant victim struggling for place and recognition in the New World; rather it was that of the Jew as modern victim forced by history into existential self-definition, a definition that was not solely religious, political, or ethnic. As Leslie Fiedler said, in this fiction the Jew now became the type of modern man, 'the metropolitan at home, though expert in the indignities, rather than the amenities, of urban life'. Many of the titles – *The Victim, Goodbye Columbus, A New Life* – allude to the old myths, either of ultimate promise or of fear of victimization, but the books became complex explorations of man's place as beneficiary or exile in the contemporary world, and were largely conducted as meta-physical enquiries, speculations on the predicament of disoriented modern man in a world of urban anonymity, behavioural indiffer-ence, and the totalitarian massing of social force. Humanism was the aim, but it was hard to forge in the face of disjunctive modern experience; the desire was to link the history of single individuals with the larger processes of society, but those individuals were also seen as alienated, victimized, dislocated, materially satisfied but spiritually damaged, conformist yet anomic, rational but anarchic. The mood of these books went beyond the rural innocence and epicality of earlier American writing, drawing on the dark modernity of post-industrial society in an attempt to face Bellow's question: How should a good man live, what ought he to do?

There were similar developments in Black fiction; following on from Richard Wright, the Black too became an image of the existential and displaced hero, the dark other in American culture. Ralph Ellison's *Invisible Man* (1952), owing clear debts to Dostoevsky's *Notes from Underground*, evoked the namelessness and exposure felt by the modern Black, but not only the Black ('Who knows but that, on the lower frequencies, I speak for you?'). Ellison's outstanding novel mixed naturalism, expressionism, and surrealism; while a novel of liberal sympathies, it is also a novel about the disappearance of self and the collapse of moral perspective, and it ends in an apocalyptic riot that both expresses and seeks to purge American disorder, as if in response to the narrator's comment that 'the mind that has conceived a plan for living must never lose sight of the chaos against which the pattern was conceived'. The book explores moral problems, yet, says the unnamed narrator, 'When one is invisible, he finds such problems as good and evil, honesty and dishonesty, of such shifting shapes that he confuses one with the other, depending upon who happens to be looking through him at the time.' Ellison's obvious successor was James Baldwin, writing a new Black novel of violence, suffering, and despair. *Go Tell·It on the Mountain* (1953) portrayed the attempts of a suffering Black family to find hope through religion, and *Giovanni's Room* (1956) is a sensitive exploration of a homosexual relationship between a Black and a white in Paris; by *In Another Country* (1962), however, Baldwin's intensified political indignation had made his fiction into an indictment of the racial gangrene at the centre of all things.

In most of these works, angry or despairing, a humanistic desire is present. As with the Jewish writers, the books are dominated by a sense of the absurd situation of the self, the individual's need to withdraw from a history which silences him or makes him invisible and is beyond his capacity to control or master. Yet this absurdist theme is persistently tempered, in liberal fashion, by a desire for civility, a desire to re-attach the individual virtuously to society, and so give him a value beyond that of mere determinism or victimization. In the new fiction there was a new tension between the claims of alienation and accommodation, between the discrete, separated individual and the system, the absurd, victimized, or comic self and a disordered history. The result was a fiction deeply conscious of alienation and anomie, often voiced in the despairing intonations of modernism, yet also turned towards society and moving back towards realism. Its heroes were often 'philosophical' heroes, seeking to make sense of lives made absurd by society and history; yet that society and history needed to be registered in all their new and commanding detail. Earlier naturalism had been largely raw, accumulative, denotative, driven by a deterministic picture of man; earlier modernism had often shown man as a discrete consciousness and had sought form and insight outside history. Now the elements seemed to merge, in a complex equation of uneasy absurdist existentialism and revived self-doubting liberalism. The result was frequently an oblique realism – an image of tragi-comic disorder and displacement that still insistently alluded to a real external world.

A new generation of distinct temper was therefore emerging in American fiction, of such power as to give American post-war fiction a remarkable international reputation. The writing of this generation caught the flavour of a new America that was influencing the world: urban, affluent, conformist, disoriented, well-equipped, very modern. Indeed the modernity of the new affluent mass society helped generate the sense of novelty within the writing – a writing now multi-ethnic, often Europeanized, distanced from the familiar, often agrarian, images of past American fiction. Despite the doubts that affected the critics, who suspected that the great American tradition was dying, a period ensued in which the novel seemed a central form for expressing the directions and struggles of new American culture. The new generation was markedly different from that of Hemingway, Faulkner, and Fitzgerald. There was, after all, a wide variety of new voices: the Jewish-American writers like Bellow, Malamud, Roth, Edward Lewis Wallant, and Chaim Potok, writing of the trivialization of evil in a world of rising affluence; the Southern writers like McCullers, Welty, O'Connor, and Capote, with their new formal grotesque; the Black writers like Wright, Ellison, and Baldwin, portraying the Black less as social victim than as a figure of modern invisibility; the writers who had come from the tradition of European experiment to write of modern exiles and emigrations, like Singer and the Russian Vladimir Nabokov; the authors of modern religious displacement and urban unease like Salinger, Cheever, and Updike; and finally, as the new liberal compound began to dissolve, writers who broached a more extreme social dissent, like Jack Kerouac and William Burroughs. For the tense 'liberal' compromise of the fiction of the Forties and the Fifties was not to last; it did, however, produce a period of remarkable American fiction of world-wide appeal and influence.

II

The new Jewish-American fiction had its most favourable antecedent in the work of Isaac Bashevis Singer. Born in Poland, he emigrated to the United States in 1935, and continued to write in Yiddish. Slow to be translated, his books, like the novels *The Family Moskat* (in English, 1950) and *The Magician of Lublin* (1960), and the tales of *Gimpel the Fool* (1957) and many other volumes, crossed the ancient world of peasant and ghetto Poland and its supernatural past with life in modern America, in bizarre, ironic ways; they undoubtedly helped link younger Jewish-American writers with the European stock of Jewish literature. The story 'Gimpel the Fool' was translated by the most substantial and enduring of the Jewish-American writers to emerge in the Forties and Fifties, Saul Bellow. Bellow, born in 1915 in Canada of immigrant Jewish parents, and growing up, with strong political interests, in the Chicago of the 1920s and 1930s, published his first short story in *Partisan Review* in 1941. He soon began to display, in the novels that followed, a sceptical view both of realism and modernism that would prove characteristic of a number of his contemporaries. His work displays a deep Jewish humanism, a concern to affirm man, to explore moral and metaphysical questions, to confront displacement and alienation, yet to move towards transcendental answers. The European intellectual heritage haunts nearly all his characters, who are the heirs of modern romanticism, always concerned to defend their inner claim, the vital speaking out of self, against a world where man seems no longer to have a place, and where beyond the ego there is the failing city, the accumulating, oppressing mass of things, the forces of modern diminution. World and consciousness divide, yet Bellow's heroes – often but not always Jewish, usually male and intellectual or semi-intellectual – are driven by mental desire towards an ambiguous relationship with others, with society itself, with nature and the universe ('the universe itself being put into us, it calls out for scope,' cries Henderson), with man's biological tenure on the earth. Historical and social existence contends with mythical and metaphysical existence, the end being the reconciliation evident in Bellow's own fictional codes, which usually take the form of a complex contractual renewal between self and world.

So, in *Dangling Man*, Bellow's first novel – a war novel, though set not on the battlefields but in a denatured Chicago – Joseph, the central character, is waiting to be drafted. A marginal man, a Communist sympathizer in the pre-war years, his aim is to know himself, 'to know what we are and what we are for, to know our purpose, to seek grace'. The quest goes inward, from social life into his own private room, where the 'perspectives end in the walls'. Politics, human relations, and the city all having denied him an assured self, he discovers his existential dilemma, his existence without essence in a hostile world. Yet, he notes, it *is* a historical world, and 'we have history to answer to'; it is also a moral world, and we must ask what a good man should do. The book shows the inheritance of Dreiserian naturalism (a debt Bellow confessed) in its sense of the mechanistic yet forceful modern city, but also that of the diary literature and the soul-searching literature of anxious modernism, the works of Dostoevsky, Kafka, above all of Sartre and Camus, whose *La Nausée* and *L'Etranger* had recently been published and had had strong impact in the United States. Yet finally it is a specific quarrel with Thirties ideology and with modernist alienation that the book conducts. Joseph, suspended between the need for social assertion and an empty inner freedom, finds his answer in neither; he therefore turns to an enforced confession of engagement in the war itself, cancelling his freedom by entering the army. The ambiguous ending can be read as a stoical movement towards engagement with community, or as a dangerous compromise between a broken liberalism and modern force – a dilemma Norman Mailer also explores, in his war novel *The Naked and the Dead*. What distinguishes Bellow's novel is the vein of Jewish metaphysical rhetoric, much concerned with what Joseph calls *le genre humain*, and the rituals of improving suffering. It is this rhetoric that qualifies the existentialist anxiety and points the way towards Joseph's limited, compulsory acceptance of the inadequate world, making the novel more than a fable of bleak self-nullification.

Bellow's next novel, *The Victim* (1947), is set in what would be his other main urban location – a naturalistic, oppressive New York filled with mechanical, impersonal jostle. Its hero, Asa Leventhal, lives irritably in a petty bourgeois world of offices, street crowds; a world anonymous, structured, inexplicable, managed, as he sees it, by mysterious black lists and arbitrary decisions. In Bellow's city, a dense agglomeration of misery and competition, survival is a

Darwinian fight, but the aim of survival is essentially moral, and the urban landscape a landscape of the spirit which must be realized as reality and made a condition of growth and self-renewal. The novel establishes a thread of remote connection and moral responsibility linking Leventhal, the Jew, uncertain of his place in the order of things, and Allbee, the Gentile, who rises from the crowd to blame Leventhal for the loss of his. Leventhal's first instinct is to shift the blame elsewhere; but, gradually and uncertainly, he comes to recognize a wider responsibility, the need to attach a value to man, even though he still does not know his own place in the world or the role of the individual in it. The lesson is learned in part through a dense central chapter in which a group of Jewish characters attempt to take man's measure, asking what is not more than human, or less than it, but human exactly. The question was Bellow's own, and he proceeded to advance it by writing, during the Fifties, a new kind of novel. Breaking with his tight, Europeanized, soul-searching, *Angst*-ridden form, he moved towards an exuberant comedy – a mode that would reach from the comedy of suffering to the ideal of aspiration towards human grandeur, and sustain an appeal to the transcendental and eternal as a fundamental element of style and form. His next books, *The Adventures of Augie March* (1953), *Seize the Day* (1956), and *Henderson the Rain King* (1959), so mark a new stage in his writing; the first and last, especially, are rhetorically rich picaresque fictions in which confident comic heroes encounter nature, the universe, and the gods of being and meet them with a full flood of discourse.

The Adventures of Augie March starts amid the Farrell-like naturalism of Depression Chicago, 'just plain brutal and not mitigated'; but Augie March is a self-creator who believes a man's character is his fate, and he sets out to be a Columbus of the near at hand, a Huck Finn lighting out beyond containing conditions towards a mythic sense, an awareness of the 'axial lines' that guide us, a sharp sense of history (he comes to know Trotsky), a recognition of 'nature': 'It takes some of us a long time to find out what the price is of our being in nature, and what the facts are about your tenure,' Augie notes. 'How long it takes depends on how swiftly the social sugars dissolve.' Augie does find limits on his life – man is both good and evil, history dark, nobody is special, mass and accumulation crowd round us, deadening the self – but he is Bellow's first hero to be larger rather than smaller than the world he lives in, and he is displayed to us with enormous comic force. The picaresque method means, however, that the book is somewhat loosely structured; Bellow moves towards a greater formal tightness in his next two Fifties novels. *Seize the Day* is in fact a novella, very tightly told, the story of one day in the life of Tommy Wilhelm, failed actor, poor husband, a *schlemiel* who meets in Dr Tamkin, the marvellous confidence man of the book, someone who promises to set his life in order – as, in the end, he obliquely does, by losing Tommy's money but revealing to him his common membership in mortal humanity. And *Henderson the Rain King*, Bellow's most ambitious novel of the Fifties, returns to comic picaresque but supports it with a complex mythical structure by setting most of its story in an imaginary Africa. It is to this dry, prehistoric land, and to two exemplary tribes, that Eugene Henderson, Bellow's first non-Jewish hero, an extravagant WASP millionaire with a careless and undistributed energy but a desire for service, goes when he realizes that he is unfit to live among men. In Africa he returns to the primal bases of life and feeling, in nature, culture, and the animal kingdom, measuring his massive strength against the creature world and discovering, again, the limits of its social use. Henderson – with his 'grun-tu-molani', his will to live, his belief that truth comes in blows, his desire to ask T. S. Eliot's nightingale, which tells us that humankind 'cannot stand very much reality', just how much *un*reality it can stand – journeys into the complex places of consciousness; he ends up appropriately enough in Newfoundland, still in flight, still the abundant comedian of his own self-assertion, but the closest thing to a successful man Bellow depicts.

The turn into the Sixties brought another change in Bellow's work. The liberal moral novel was under growing pressure from a rising sense of historical absurdity; a number of his own contemporaries, like Philip Roth and Norman Mailer, changed sharply in form, or fell into silence, as did J. D. Salinger. Bellow noted in an essay that the modern novelist now appeared to feel defeated by a vast public life which dwarfed him as an individual, encouraging him and his characters to become giants in loathing or fantasy; the humanism of the novel was, he complained, being dislodged. Picaresque self-assertion now seemed less possible; in *Herzog* (1964), which still seems Bellow's best novel, Moses Herzog is a 'suffering joker' caught in a 'shameless and impotent privacy', a state of comic but desperate madness. He is a distressed Jewish scholar and intellectual with a complex family and marital history, moving through New York and his home town Chicago, and quarrelling, in letters addressed to the great dead ('He wrote to Spinoza, *Thoughts not causally connected were said by you to cause pain. I find that is indeed the case* . . .') and the not so great living, with their pessimistic answers to the problems of the world, their abstract historicism, their darkening humanism. Herzog's attempt is to resist the apocalyptic thoughts of late romanticism, to throw off the 'reality-instructors' who would explain to us the need to claim the inalienable modern therapeutic right to alienation, conspicuous suffering, psychic extravagance. Yet Herzog is a man of great inward pain; desiring, in Bellovian fashion, to be 'a marvelous Herzog', or prince, he is fatally attracted to the city of destruction. In this learned and self-demanding book, Bellow sets himself no less a task than that of defining a modern selfhood that does not yield to fashionable romanticism, the 'five-cent syntheses' offered by a troubled age. Herzog suffers in history, modern boredom, pluralism, and despair, all moving in formless motion through his own mind; this is a book set primarily *within* consciousness, and there is a parallel formlessness or oblique design in the novel's structure – until, finally, both Herzog and the book transfigure the plurality of words and explanations into significant silence. Bellow ends the book on a new affirmative transcendental-ism, a balanced contentment to rest in human occupancy and to know the oneness in things; Herzog ends it in silence, his letters, for the moment, lapsed, his mind at peace.

Bellow followed this fine book with *Mr Sammler's Planet* (1970), which proved to be his bleakest, most ironic novel. Sammler is an ancient one-eyed survivor from modern European culture with its progressive Wellsian hopes, and from their bleak product and anti-thesis, the German concentration camps, in which Sammler has been left for dead. But now, curiously surviving, detached, almost beyond his human life-span, he has become resident in a New York City of the age of post-humanism, irrationalism, florid romanticism, 'hyper-civilized Byzantine luxury'. *Sammler* is an apocalyptic novel, about New York as an over-populated, sexually barren or debased waste land breeding revolt, violence, and evil, and about conscious-ness mysteriously transforming as it adapts to the world of moonshot, the opening out of American life towards inter-planetary space, so that 'finalities are demanded, summaries'. Weighed down by the burden of modern mass history and by psychic excess,

Sammler attempts to reconstitute the stony planet on which he still lives. The book's dark detachment from the radical-romantic apocalypticism of ego-ridden America in the late Sixties takes it nearer than any of Bellow's earlier novels to social and historical disillusion. But his comic euphoria persists, and so does his sense of transcendentalist affirmation; the book ends by reaffirming, though now in more mystical terms, the power of the human contract, the need, by living a worthy life under the aspect of death, to forge a connection with the universe.

In Bellow's next book, *Humboldt's Gift* (1975), the sense of extreme historical disorder remains, but the pessimism softens; the novel has the tone of an enquiry into what forms of art are appropriate to a world of cultural exhaustion, where mass is greater than self, *it* than *we*. It is another book about a survivor, Charlie Citrine, recalling a non-surviving modernist antecedent, his old friend and mentor the intellectually assimilative, anguished poet Von Humboldt Fleischer, who has set Charlie on the path to literary success but has himself died in a flophouse. Now rich, Charlie wanders through his home city of Chicago in the Seventies, where monetary and emotional capital are all in disorder, material mass outruns sense, art is implicated with crime and violence, the mafiosi have wives taking Ph.D.s, and the policemen are versed in modern psychiatry. In the face of this massing of force, a new gnosticism and mysticism haunts the book, but the lesson Charlie draws from Humboldt's legacy is one of comic survival. In 1976, Bellow was awarded the Nobel Prize for Literature, reinforcing the sense of many that he was the leading American writer of his generation, recognizing, too, the power of his defensive humanism. Bellow's one novel since the Prize, *The Dean's December* (1982), is a strong, sombre book set in Chicago and in Bucharest, a revived meditation on his essential themes. It confirms the later Bellow as the novelist of a world which has lost cultural bearings, moved into an age of boredom and terror, violence and indifference, private wealth and public squalor. Chicago is a city of 'wounds, lesions, cancers, destructive fury, death' and Bucharest a world of cruel political manipulations, a politics of pain. Both societies deny the dignity of death, and death, increasingly for Bellow the meaning of life, the point from which we judge our tenure, becomes the object of thought. Albert Corde, Bellow's late hero, the man of feeling, attempts humanistically to reconcile not just two political orders but two ways of knowing: his own, the journalist's, and that of his Rumanian-born wife Minna, the astrophysicist, the world of terra firma, the world of space. The ending, as Corde, back in America, ascends towards space in the elevator of the Mount Palomar observatory, is a resonant symbol, but one more oblique than many earlier Bellow endings, riddled with the ambiguities of the unreconciled. The tone is muted and far less comic than in Bellow's earlier books; if not his most perfect novel, this is his most serious and concerned.

Bellow's career displays the powerful struggles of the humanistic fiction's strained development in post-war America; and we can see parallel developments in other Jewish-American novelists. Their achievement has gone in many directions: from the anguished yet comic stories of the late poet Delmore Schwartz (*The World Is a Wedding*, 1948), Bellow's model for Von Humboldt Fleischer, to the dark tales of Edgar Lewis Wallant (*The Pawnbroker*, 1960), to the comedy of Stanley Elkin (*A Bad Man*, 1967), close to black humour. The novelist who most interestingly compares and contrasts with Bellow is Bernard Malamud, writing far more explicitly about ghetto life, Jewish mores, traditional themes of suffering and ethnic identity, drawing more directly on the mythic and magical elements of the European Yiddish tradition. These moral and fantastic qualities are interwoven with a vein of naturalism in a fiction whose theme is life as an imprisonment which must be transcended. Suffering and ill luck bring Jew and Gentile together, though the Jew offers his traditional expertise in the area. This fate is comic; Malamud's heroes are sad-funny hunters looking for a new life beyond the imprisonments of conventional existence. The ironic relation between the real and the prospective self is mirrored in Malamud's speculative view of the relation between life and art; he sees art as a mysterious formal transcendence none the less produced from dross and misconduct. In his best work a form of symbolic realism, in which mythic processes and structures work behind an apparently solid surface, arises from a dense prose and a persistent comic awareness – often seen at best in his excellent short stories, like those in *The Magic Barrel* (1958).

Malamud's first novel, *The Natural* (1952), apparently his least Jewish book, is a mythic reworking of the Grail legend in a baseball context. Around the popular sport to which so many American dreams attach, it mockingly evokes the great quests of American fiction, from Ahab's to Huck Finn's, while pursuing Malamud's essential, and Jewish, themes: the rediscovery and ironic renewal of life in a seemingly dead world, the passage through suffering, the conflict between 'the life we learn with and the life we live after that'. His fine second novel, *The Assistant* (1957), shifts to a more naturalistic mode and Jewish setting, exploring the economic and moral pains and imprisonments of a poor Jewish grocer, Morris Bober, trying to make a decent life in a small store in the New York ghetto, slaving away always to make a loss. Into his world of absurd decency comes Frank Alpine, a small-time Italian hoodlum who first holds up the store but then returns in guilt to work for Bober, while still finding the grocer's passivity and capacity for suffering ridiculous: 'the one that has got the biggest pain in the gut and can hold onto it longest without running to the toilet is the best Jew,' he says. But, like *The Victim*, the novel pursues moral re-connection: Frank, the comic rogue, comes, through wrong-doing, lust, confession, self-loathing, and finally absurd sacrifice, himself to Jewishness, ending by falling into Bober's grave, accepting circumcision, taking on his role. *A New Life* (1961), set in a college on the West coast of American pastoral, now suburbanized, deals with the same theme of victimization producing absurd redemption. S. Levin, formerly a drunkard, comes there hoping to leave necessity and find freedom, only to end up with a new life tattered and unpromising, as he goes off with a less than glamorous heroine who promises only care and dull domesticity, but offering a small promise all the same.

A clearer call to moral and political revolt comes in *The Fixer* (1966), Malamud's most directly political novel, about the Russian pogroms of the Tsarist period before the First World War, when so many Jews fled to America. The story of the Jewish handyman Jakov Bok, who sets off from the *shtetl* seeking a new life in the city of St. Petersburg, only to be falsely accused of the ritual murder of a Christian child, it explores the origins of that dark sense of suffering underlying his comic themes. Bok, imprisoned, refuses the surrender of freedom to fate, and acquires not now a deeper heroism but a politicized, revolutionary Jewishness, made ambiguous by its involvement with the Bolshevik revolution on which the book ends. But the theme stands somewhat obliquely to Malamud's work, as was apparent when he published *Pictures of Fidelman* (1969), a group of linked stories written over a long period. The central character is a modern artistic farceur wandering the golden land of art, Italy, and finding sordidness, forgery, and deceit; out of these comes art. The absurd map of relationships interlinking life, love, and art is also the subject of *The Tenants* (1971), the book that reflects, as *Sammler* had done for Bellow, the late Sixties stresses, by contrasting two writers. The appropriately named Jewish writer Harry Lesser is attempting to make up for past failures by creating masterpieces, and the Black revolutionary Willie Spearmint sees art as action and writes as an act of violence. Gradually Willie, the figure of violence and sexuality, withdraws into aesthetic creation; Lesser, meanwhile, is increasingly caught up in the tempting sexuality and violence of Willie's Black world. This fable of two models of art Malamud had himself tried ends in energetic hatred, the destruction of manuscripts, and the collapse of the book's own text, a parable of the modern crisis of form. With *Dubin's Lives* (1979), Malamud attempts his reconciliation. A very domestic book, about an elderly biographer in a marriage 'more happy than many but not as happy as some', a rabbinical, obsessed man of sorrow, understanding, and pity, it is a quietly serious and ambitious work. Dubin records the lives of others because he cannot live one of his own, until he falls in love with a commonplace young girl, recovers sensuality, and finds that art is indeed achieved at the expense of lives, one's own or those of others. Long, slow, worked out in intense human detail, the book is a summing up of Malamud's themes, rendering that awareness of life as both imprisonment and redemption which has always been his strongest concern.

Where Malamud's fiction points to a possible strange recovery of the Jewish moral and artistic heritage, the novels of the somewhat younger Philip Roth are about its dissolution; indeed a good deal of Roth's work is an explicit comment on his own heritage from other writers, and his difficult relation to it. Born in 1933, Roth established himself with a novella, *Goodbye Columbus*, and several related stories in 1959; the novella is a sharp satirical portrait of affluent suburban Jewry in the 'swamp of prosperity'. The hero momentarily mistakes this for the recovered American dream, but, if *The Assistant* suggests that the Jew might gain from avoiding American materialism, *Goodbye Columbus* suggests he can lose in the new affluence; and all Roth's early work – including his long, Jamesian moral novel *Letting Go* (1962), set in student Chicago, and *When She Was Good* (1967) – displays a new America where the Jew, severed from faith and moral direction, struggles in a new secular world with a new sexuality, and humanism runs aground between rigorous traditional ethics and new narcissistic desires for personal freedom. During the 1960s, Roth's attempt to write a fiction of ethical control and exact literary management was conspicuously transformed under new pressures. In a 1961 essay he remarked on the unreality and absurdity of the contemporary American history about which novelists are expected to write ('. . . the American writer in the middle of the twentieth century has his hands full in trying to understand, describe and then make *credible* much of the American reality'), and noted that the historical descent into unreality made realism less and less possible. His work now began to express this growing sense of historical unreality, and a growing doubt about the claims of 'ethical Jewhood'; it moved towards the confessional and the fantastic, to the problems of art and the disturbing power of the European modernist inheritance, especially that from Kafka. *Portnoy's Complaint* (1968) pursued the theme of the collapse from the ethical into a new narcissism; *Goodbye Columbus* Freudianized, the novel is written from the standpoint of a character, the endlessly masturbating Portnoy, adrift in his own experience, who cannot consciously control and direct his story, but only confess it to a professional, the analyst Dr Spielvogel. The Jewish son who fulfils the parental social expectations but cannot realize himself sexually, and so presents himself only in the modes of disorder, guilt, and self-exposure, Portnoy has a life with no development, only extended symptoms. About male emasculation, the power of the Jewish mother, and the function of guilt in the Jewish household, the book is a notable instance of contingent, free-form art – right to the last page, where the language ceases in a scream, and the analyst comes in to start over from the beginning and offer a new order, the therapeutic one, to the material.

Roth's change of form, an exemplary development of the Sixties, led him towards a new kind of creative accomplishment, based on open rather than tightly managed formal methods. *The Breast* (1972) took the theme and mode towards modernist Kafkaesque allegory in its tale of another emasculated Jewish professor who turns, in his confused sexuality, into a gigantic female breast. Roth's novels were becoming metaphysical comedies of desire, of failed sexual fulfilments in the world both of new permissive sexuality and new feminism, in which Jew and *shiksa* make love and seek new secular reconciliations – only to find the haunting Jewish note of guilt and pain, now driven down to the level of deep psychic and historical disturbance. This called forth new and more fantastic fictional methods, often grounded in confessional techniques transliterating into fantasy. *The Great American Novel* (1973) was Roth's attempt at a self-conscious, reflexive fiction, borrowing from and parodying Malamud's *The Natural* to sum up the stuff of American fiction. He was, however, far more successful with *My Life as a Man* (1974), in which, in the persona of Peter Tarnopol, Roth reflects on his own past moral seriousness and on the way 'useful fictions' both plot and disguise the needs and issues of an author's personal life. Even the confessional mask of Tarnopol *is* a mask, though he drives as close to factuality as he can in the book's last story; so art and moral seriousness are revealed as disguise, 'literature' a danger, and median reality an illusion lying between formal self-concealment and pure confession. The confessional-fantastic mode develops in *The Professor of Desire* (1977), which complicatedly reintroduces the 'hero' of *The Breast* at a more realistic level, as he struggles between erotic narcissism and his sense of obligation to the Jewish 'survivors'. Appropriately the story moves to Prague, and to Kafka's grave – indeed to the extraordinary figure of 'Kafka's whore', who concentrates the tense problem of the modern muse and the sexual prompt of modern art. *The Ghostwriter* (1980) extends the complex confessional parable; in the house of an older Jewish writer much resembling in reputation Isaac Bashevis Singer, the hero imagines himself making love to Anne Frank, while his father accuses him of betraying his heritage. Roth's theme is the Jewish writer in crisis, needing to probe the political, literary, sexual, and psychic content of his materials; he has become, of all the recent Jewish novelists, the voice of maximum unease, a witness to the pressure on the writer in a narcissistic modern America.

III

But the sense of moral, ethical, and formal stress, so evident in these Jewish-American writers, and at its most intense in Roth, was not confined to Jewish writers. Though part Jewish, J. D. Salinger is hardly to be put in a Jewish tradition. His *The Catcher in the Rye* (1951), which became a student classic, is also about the strenuous attempt to trace responsibility, to transcend separation and difference, in a world of falsehood, hypocrisy, and stress. Its success turned on its bringing alive as a moral universe the linguistic as well as social milieu of a middle-class adolescent schoolboy in New York caught at the point of pre-social and pre-sexual innocence. Holden Caulfield is adult and sophisticated enough to know the world, with its adult 'phoneys', its pick-ups, bars, hotels, and show business; and when he is expelled from his prep school he makes his way in picaresque fashion through that world, telling his own story. But, caught on the cliff over which one falls into adulthood, his preference is for innocence: for his younger sister Phoebe, for the ducks on the lake in Central Park, for the Museum of Natural History, for the things that look too 'damn nice' to damage, and to which he grants a semi-religious sanction. Holden's ethic turns on semi-articulate emotions, deep instinctive responses, a validated sensitivity. Though read as a novel of protest, *The Catcher in the Rye* is in fact an attempt to discover a lyrical religion of innocence that can be set over society, yet can only point the way towards collapse; Holden ends under medical treatment, refusing to grow up. The stress of the age seems so great that Salinger, both here and in many of *Nine Stories* (1953), can only see the child's world as real and the adult world as intrinsically damaging, a place where love is perpetually sacrificed to squalor.

In his later work – the group of long, linked stories collected as *Franny and Zooey* (1961) and *Raise High the Roofbeam, Carpenters and Seymour: An Introduction* (1963) – the religious dimension of Salinger's work becomes more central and not a little cloying, though the complexity and formality of his art also increases in proportion. The stories, about the Glass family – the wise children, fragile young intellectuals, of two vaudeville entertainers who have won public acclaim on a radio quiz show – turn on a sequence of semi-Buddhist revelations deriving largely from Seymour Glass, the oldest and wisest of the whizz kids, whom Salinger had earlier depicted as a suicide in 'A Perfect Day for Bananafish' (1948). The stories aspire towards a philosophy of total inclusion, of the stuff and persons of the universe: Zooey Glass's revelation to his hysterical sister Franny is that the world is the ugly Fat Lady out there, and that that cancered Fat Lady is 'Christ Himself, buddy'. But this, part of the store of wisdom of the Glasses, gained at the expense of neurosis throughout the family and the death of Seymour, is oddly reductive, since the Glasses are a withdrawn Elect, living outside the world with a philosophy of almost total exclusion of others. Moreover the building up of Seymour as saint and guru involves a process of artistic inflation so considerable that Salinger seems to have difficulty in controlling it. He does so through a highly specu-lative style, alternating moments of exacting description with patterns of multiple narration, moving the witness around the family, and granting the principal narrator, Buddy Glass, an intense writerly anxiety which seeks to break through the dishonesty of fiction to absolute truth. The deceits necessary to sustain the work as fiction struggle with the manner and bring it to crisis. Aspiring to transcendent silence, Buddy apparently falls silent, as Salinger has too, as though the stress of exactness and honesty, and the conse-quent psychic tension, were too great to sustain.

A similar sense of difficulty shows in the work of a far more prolific writer, John Updike, who also mixed a very precise formal-ism with a rising note of historical concern. Updike studied at the Ruskin School of Art in Oxford, and the revelation of form, the moment of aesthetic revelation in the contingencies of life, was to become a concern throughout his writing. Closely associated, like Salinger, with the *New Yorker* magazine, he came to notice in 1959 with a novel, *The Poorhouse Fair*, and a collection of short stories, *The Same Door*. During the early Sixties he published a group of stories with a strong autobiographical constituent, set around Olinger in the rural Pennsylvania landscape of his own boyhood, and then gradually moving towards the recording of young domestic life in New York. *Rabbit, Run* (1960) is the story of an ordinary *homme moyen sensuel*, Harold 'Rabbit' Angstrom, an ex-basketball player caught in domesticity, a man of spontaneous actions trying to live with some kind of instantaneousness in a reduced world. *The Centaur* (1963) is a conscious attempt to reactivate Greek myth in the modern world, a legend about a father–son relationship based clearly on Updike's own upbringing. Throughout these early works runs the theme of a lost sacramentalism, a fall into a shabby secular world which the individual and the artist might have the power to redeem through moments of action, love, or intense formal awareness. The theme focused particularly on young marriage, and Updike increasingly became the novelist of modern bourgeois matrimony. With some forays outside, like the excellent *Bech: A Book* (1970), stories about a Jewish-American writer travelling in Eastern Europe which allow Updike to reflect on the nature of the Jewish-American fictional mode, he built up a clearly delimited world, of modern couples, solemn, sexy, and delicate, just marrying, living in

New York attics and lofts, bringing home bottles of wine after work. Often artists or writers, they share with their creator a taste for epiphany, finding in marital and sexual turmoil, and in the detailed happenings and contingencies of daily domestic life the need for a revelation, an unexpected reward, so defying the emptying of life in the age of religious loss through the use of small domestic forms and rituals.

Updike's formal preoccupations have always been played against a detailed sense of historical change (as was apparent in his developing series about 'Rabbit' Angstrom: *Rabbit, Run* was followed by *Rabbit Redux*, 1972, and *Rabbit Is Rich*, 1982). The stuff of particular decades and historical moments has always been important to him, and his fiction during the Sixties began, like that of other writers, to change very noticeably. Apocalyptic feelings intensify, the domesticity begins to strain and shatter; his short stories shift in setting to the well-heeled Connecticut and Massachusetts shoreline commuterland, where the houses are Old Colonial and babysitters no problem, and while the husbands work in the city the wives sit on the beach, watching the sky shade, until the planes and cars come in and the couples become couples again. In the novel *Couples* (1968), set in the Kennedy era, Updike erotically depicts a troubled world where, against a backcloth of historical disturbance, adultery becomes, in a complex blasphemy, the revelation and sacrament as religion wanes and collapses. So, too, does marriage itself; in *Marry Me* (1976), the new ritual of the age, in 'the twilight of the old morality', is divorce, as the now middle-aged couples attempt to recover, through sex as sacrament, through 'Bodily Ascension', the old mystery – a theme that passes also into his stories of the Seventies (*Too Far To Go: The Maples Stories,* 1979). Updike's domestic world is always a register of political and historical change; some of his books look to that political world directly, as in *The Coup* (1979), set in the dry African republic of Kush, about an anti-American dictator reflecting on American follies, but in most history meets round the marriage bed. Updike's work can appear realistic and local, but its resonances are greater; his essential concern is with transcendental form and the pressure against it of a compelling but disquieting history; his novels of domesticity are really novels of social anxiety and secular unease.

If much of the spirit of the Fifties was expressed in an attempt to recover liberal realism, to seek formal elegance and compactness, to make literature into a serious moral and formal enterprise, an enhancement of and a shaping of life, the best writers displayed that attempted realism as a mode under strain, shaken and disturbed by the extremity of contemporary history: 'It is as though these novelists, and the characters they create, have been shaken loose by the amount and the violence of the history America had passed through (America, it must be remembered, has until late been unaccustomed to history),' observed one critic, R. W. B. Lewis. The sense of discontinuity between individual and society, between formal control and social tremors, is manifest in many of these writers, and it heightens in the Sixties – in Bellow's comedy of disordered consciousness in *Herzog*, in Roth's confessions, Salinger's silence, Updike's divorces. It is apparent in other writers too: in the work of John Cheever, who, in *The Wapshot Chronicle* (1957), *The Wapshot Scandal* (1964), and most notably in *Falconer* (1977), explores the shattering encounter between the apparently stable world of middle-class domestic America and a new era of psychic extremity and historical nightmare; or in the comic existentialism of the early John Barth, who presented in *The Floating Opera* (1956) and *The End of the Road* (1958) a universe of weatherless contingency in which identity is absent, prescriptive grammar impossible, and there is no reason for living but equally none for committing suicide. It is also apparent in the grotesque images underlying the formal elegance of the Southern writers, and in the work of novelists like James Purdy (*Malcolm*, 1959; *Cabot Wright Begins*, 1964) or Terry Southern (*Flash and Filigree*, 1958), written in the spirit the Sixties would call 'black humour', a humour derived from historical and existential despair. It is equally evident in the rising anger of James Baldwin as his work moved from the formal exactness of *Giovanni's Room* to the fury of *In Another Country*, where apocalyptic images abound, and force can no longer be gainsaid or wrongs resolved. The attempt to contain contemporary experience within a formal and moral frame may have been one essential direction of the Fifties, but the pressure to break that form and express a modern extremity was another.

IV

The writer who most obviously displayed this struggle between the claims of form and the urgencies of historical immersion is Norman Mailer, whose endeavour has been increasingly to incorporate and express the disturbed psycho-political history of the post-war age.

Mailer has always offered himself as a writer searching for a new order of consciousness, in face of a history that seems destructive of feeling, sexuality, and realized being; and in *Advertisements for Myself* (1959) and other books of essays he has put on public record his struggle to be a writer of historical investment rather than purified art. *The Naked and the Dead*, his first book, was formally naturalistic, a work of reportage about war's violence, nature's intractable indifference, the victimizations of the military machine, intersected with experimental passages of the 'Time Machine', a device intended to connect army life with the jungle world of American society. Mailer conventionally takes naturalist types – the petty racketeer, the Southern cracker, the Brooklyn Jew, the Montana wanderer – and puts them on to a Pacific battlefront where 'the individual personality is just a hindrance'; but he stressed that the book was 'a parable about the movement of men through history', and that larger history and the nature of the modern encounter with it is the main theme. Mailer's concern, here and thereafter, is the massing of power, and its psychic consequences; his General Cummings explains that the war is not fought for ideals but is a 'power concentration', and 'You can consider the army as a preview of the future.' The insufficiency of the liberal mind in the face of this 'power morality' is manifested in the collapse of Lieutenant Hearn, which suggests that in Mailer's coming world liberalism will be weak and powerless. Instead it is through immersion in power and totalitarian energy that existing power concentrations can be resisted, and Mailer's work from this point onward moves quickly away from reformatory liberalism into a neo-sexual anarchism.

His next book, *Barbary Shore*, explored the political wasteland of post-war America; with *The Deer Park* (1955), at one point intended as part of an eight-part sequence of box-in-box novels, he began to seek a connection of new circuits, through a path of existential self-discovery primarily won through sexuality and apocalyptic violence. Set in the Hollywood of the McCarthyite anti-Communist purges, this novel identifies the politics of the movies with the chaos of national politics, and the Californian desert spaces around Desert D'Or with contemporary American history. As Mailer explained, his aim in both books was to build a contemporary psychology of politics, a union of Marx and Freud; the writer's task was, he said, to unite the subjective with the historical, the sexual body with the social body. At the centre of the project was the image of the romantic-revolutionary savage who is at once sexually harmonious and historically evolutionary; the figure is, inescapably, Mailer himself. *Advertisements for Myself* shows him squaring up to Hemingway's existentialism and commitment to style through action, and to Faulkner's technical complexity, and trying to merge the two in order to take on responsibility for the evolving style and consciousness of his own generation. Form or craft as such is no longer the essential issue; 'Craft is very little finally,' he said, for consciousness and performance were the great necessities, and writing was a merging of self-awareness and a report on the psychic and social workings of a cancerous history. Mailer's attempt to become the writer as immersed historical performer reached its strongest expression in his essay 'The White Negro' (1957, reprinted in *Advertisements for Myself*), where he explained that the age called for a new hero, the white Negro or the 'hipster', to react against the totalitarian order: 'One is Hip or one is Square (the alternative which each new generation is beginning to feel), one is a rebel or one conforms, one is a frontiersman in the Wild West of American night life, or else a Square cell, trapped in the totalitarian tissues of American society, doomed willy nilly to conform if one is to succeed.'

The essay dramatizes the Manichean struggle into which Mailer felt the writer must throw himself in American culture. One fictional outcome was *An American Dream* (1965), an unselfconsciously obscene, semi-autobiographical novel told in the first person by Stephen Rojack, 'a personality built on an abyss', a man both of wild inner desires and large political ambitions. The book becomes a sex-and-power fantasy, seeking to draw into Rojack's responding consciousness both those political and psychic forces that order and shape American society, and the extra-territorial and supernatural powers of salvation and damnation at work in the world. Mailer's concern is again with the fantastic interweaving of the psychic, sexual, and political worlds, the pubic and the public; *An American Dream* is a dark nightmare that turns towards an apocalyptic redemption. Another possible mode was fictionalized journalism; Mailer developed it most fully in *The Armies of the Night* (1968). Subtitled 'History as a Novel, The Novel as History', the book, about an actual protest march on the Pentagon over the Vietnam war, seeks to merge reportage and the novelistic dramatization of the active consciousness of one participant, Mailer himself, which alone can give perspective on what is recorded by the media as 'historical fact'. Mailer's work since has gone closer to journalism than fiction, though *Why Are We in Vietnam?* (1967) is a Reichian fantasy relating an Alaskan bear hunt to the violence of the Vietnam war; but it has always sought to portray that alliance of consciousness with the anarchy and disorder of the social psyche which expresses itself as history, so moving away from a controlling form, a concern with the individual life, or a humanist view towards the exploration of that dream world of sex and violence Mailer now saw as the age's true politics.

Mailer's suggestion, in 'The White Negro', that the new experiments in the form of the novel were arising from behavioural experiment, from romantic disaffiliation, the hip life-style, youthful protest, the underground culture of drugs and homosexuality, seemed confirmed as the Fifties developed. In 1952 Paul Bowles, an expatriate in Tangier, brought out his novel *Let It Come Down*, about degenerate exhaustion and exposure, drugs and sexuality; in 1953 William S. Burroughs, also in Tangier, brought out under the pen name William Lee his novel of homosexuality and addiction, *Junkie*; in 1955, J. P. Donleavy published in Paris his erotic novel of expatriate disaffection, *The Ginger Man*. A culture of alienation and deviation was meanwhile finding a voice at home in the 'Beat' movement. The term was reputedly coined as early as 1952 by Jack Kerouac, drawing on associations with the spontaneous beat of jazz and the beatific joys of oriental mysticism – two streams vital to the 'Beat' writing that now emerged in quantity, to voice the spirit of a new young generation in revolt against the conformity and respectability of Lonely Crowd America. This mood found its poetic expression in Allen Ginsberg's frenzied free-line long poem 'Howl' (1955), and Kerouac's parallel fictional text, *On the Road* (1957). Written in a 'spontaneous bop prose', celebratory and defiant, *On the Road* moved beyond Salinger's fragile mysticism to a drop-out philosophy, celebrating the freeing journey west, out of the technological city, and the inner journey towards a new emotional and physical freedom achieved through movement, jazz, and drugs. In *The Subterraneans* and *The Dharma Bums* (both 1958), Kerouac moved further both into oriental mysticism and the culture of drugs and disorientation. By the early Sixties, this romantic anarchism, emphasizing instinct, provisionality, and mysticism, spontaneous and loose in form, came to seem the new aesthetic. As much behavioural as formal, often rejecting the security and fixity of print for the instantaneousness and immediacy of performance, Beat writing was of a piece with improvised poetry, the happening, the spontaneous event, the multi-media performance, the new global village sensibility. Kerouac's methods, appropriately loose, influenced a number of writers in the Sixties, like Hubert Selby and John Rechy, who went further with his sense of hallucinatory naturalism, but without his spontaneous poetic energy.

Of more importance as an experimenter was William S. Burroughs, whose sequence *The Naked Lunch* (1959), *The Soft Machine* (1961), *The Ticket That Exploded* (1962), and *Nova Express* (1964), came to represent Beat fiction on its avant-garde and surrealist edge. Burroughs adopted for these books a new mode of presentation, advertised as the 'cut-up', 'fold-in' method 'of Brion Gysin'. It was in fact a mode clearly derived from the French surrealist movements of the 1920s and 1930s, allying collage presentation with hallucinatory and fantastic systems, and drawing on 'junk' in two senses, of drugs and cultural rubbish. Burroughs's work assimilates the floating detritus and the loose images of contemporary life; it also reflects the hallucinatory sense of exposure, the disaffiliated withdrawal from objects that follows drug dependence. The *dreck* of the daily word, the commanding power of media systems, the fantasies of popular science fiction, merge through the cut-up method with the homoerotic fantasies of the author to create a transformed and modern fantasy, concerned with the endless warring powers of the Nova universe. Burroughs has called his books 'satires', but this suggests a control which their form denies. They see and challenge a world of oppressive, authoritarian systems run by policing forces which attempt to defeat and contain the free play of consciousness, and in this sense satirize a distorted, plot-ridden, and science-managed age; but at the same time Burroughs has described himself as a 'cosmonaut of inner space' and his fictional world of violent plots and disfiguring obscenities coincides with his own inner fantasies. The result is a satirical grotesquerie in which there can be no stable object of indignation, only a condition of outrage, accusing the world while indulging the homoerotic and sadistic fantasies of the self. Burroughs's methods are in fact parodic, and his books are post-humanist, unstable and volatile texts attempting to penetrate at various points a world far gone in obscenity, barbarity, technological systematization and violence in which the human subject is dissolved, by an imagination in much the same condition. In this respect they break the difficult frontiers of fantasy, opening out the world of the subject on to the loveless system; as such they represent a crucial transfiguring of the tradition of the surreal, the fantastic, the paranoid, and the obscene into the post-humanist novel of the American 1960s and 1970s.

While Burroughs was beginning, during the 1950s, to sketch a new transgressive apocalyptic experimentalism which sought to dislodge dominant systems of language, and to use the materials of science fiction and junk as the basis for a new prose, another significant experimentalist was challenging the realistic and referential base of the novel from a very different standpoint and tradition. This was Vladimir Nabokov, whose work comes out of the Russian tradition of comic grotesquerie (Gogol is an important source for his writing); it was developed late in the Symbolist period of pre-Revolutionary Russian fiction, with its preoccupation with the elusive relation of word to world, and also reflects the linguistic disquiets and modernist disorders of European fiction between the wars. Nabokov's earlier novels were written in Russian and German in the various European cities to which the Russian Revolution of 1917 exiled him. In 1940 he moved to the United States, having already begun in Paris his first English-language novel, *The Real Life of Sebastian Knight* (1941), an effort at writing a 'true' biography which disintegrates amid literary paradoxes and problems of identity. So began the 'love affair with the English language' which resulted in a sequence of novels, including *Bend Sinister* (1947) – written, Nabokov explains, by 'an anthropomorphic deity impersonated by me', *Lolita* (1955), *Pnin* (1957), *Pale Fire* (1962), *Ada, or Ardor: A Family Chronicle* (1969), *Transparent Things* (1972), and *Look at the Harlequins* (1974). These, with Nabokov's earlier books, since translated into English, amount to a major enquiry into the nature of fiction and fictionality in which the word does not attach referentially to the thing, in which types and structures of fiction are subjected to endless mockery, narrators may be madmen, liars, or practised deceivers, the names of characters puns, anagrams, or emblems, and fictional development through acrostics or word golf. Appropriately the artist becomes an exile amid language and cultural forms and structures, and his central characters – the Humbert Humberts, the Pnins, the Charles Kinbotes and Van Veens – are cast in a world of contingent disorder intensified by the fact that increasingly that

world is the United States, a world Nabokov shows a fascinated difficulty in constituting.

Nabokov was to become an essential influence on the American
novel of the Sixties because of his nominalism, his assumption that
the world is named into existence. Art becomes both a cosmic and a
comic game of knowledge, a fictive acrostic with transcendental
properties which can do no more than create the illusion of reality
and the sense of an escaping transcendence. His work has patently
decadent origins, being a narcissistic engagement with the
ephemeral, the doubled, the mirrored, the enclosed. His heroes are
obsessive game-players, chasing transcendent butterflies with
linguistic nets, seeking in some fleeting imprint of reality to hold on
to a lasting image from which they are none the less perpetually to be
exiled. Like Burroughs, Nabokov finds in the novel a parodic proliferation of forms; unlike him, he depends on subtle dispersions of
the fictional impression, and so brings into the foreground the
essentially rewritten and parodic nature of all text. Yet an essential
faith in the novel form remains, because that form displays the way
we constitute a sense of 'reality' – a word, Nabokov stresses, that
means nothing except in quotes. The need to invent and to live in
the pleasure of the mind is thus crucial. In *Lolita*, his best-known
novel, the ageing émigré Humbert Humbert, chasing his American
nymphet, the child-woman caught on the elusive turn between innocence and experience, is chasing that which cannot be had but which
must be desired. He is also chasing or is chased by his own double,
Quilty, whom he murders in order to sustain his own guilt ('Guilty
of killing Quilty'). The book itself is a literary gallery; the America
he crosses from motel to motel is a world of punning clues construct-
ing both a plot and a 'reality'. Humbert becomes a figure of the
decadent artist in pursuit of his symbol, fleeting and erotic, and the
appropriately named nymphet, Dolores Haze, a sophisticated metaphorical substitute for the ambiguous and elusive myth of America
itself. An equally complex allusive system underpins *Ada*, with its
similar structure of doubles and mirrors (Ivan Veen incestuously
loves his 'cousin' Ada Veen), its setting at Ardis Hall (which appears
'on the gentle eminence of old novels') on the planet Anti-Terra,
which is close to the landscape of both Russian and American
fiction, parodically superimposed one on the other. Parody indeed is
the dominant mode, but out of it comes the serious need of the artist
to subvert reality and defeat time. The essence of Nabokov's art is to

display both the means and the epistemological necessity for regarding fiction as a constituted world contending with the systems by which we assert the solidity of reality, but also to display the pleasures of the imagination engaged in the pursuit.

Nabokov's work can be related to the grotesque black humour that was now emerging as an essential strain in the new American fiction, but even more to the scepticism about fiction's claim to record or assert the real which was to become dominant in the 1960s. Indeed Burroughs and Nabokov both point to the way in which the naturalist mode in American writing was beginning to come under doubt – on the one hand from the sense that not just the human subject but the word systems that gave that subject a sense of order and significance were disintegrating in the face of violent and murderous forces, and on the other from a nominalist anxiety about the nature of fiction itself and its capacity to name life and the world into existence. The pressing sense of disorder in post-war American fiction seemed, by the end of the 1950s, to be generating a fluidity in if not a dissolution of forms and genres – displacing habitual conventions of realistic reportage, breaking the humanist discourse of moral control, and exposing a world in which language was no longer capable of naming or fixing the enormities of contemporary experience nor the imaginative mind able to suborn history and society directly into fiction. Yet despite the rise of fantasy, disordered perception, and parodic structures, based in Nabokov on literary allusion, in Burroughs on 'junk', the sense of the immensity of historical processes, of the dominance of plot and system and the force of language programmed from outside, makes this experimentalism more than pure play; it becomes a cultural event, a stylistic resolution responding to displacement. Thus the novel found itself responding obliquely, both in political awareness and in formal and textual anxiety, to the world of late twentieth-century post-technological life. The striking thing was that these developments were not simply a naturalistic literary protest but a radical-aesthetic revolt as well; in the 1960s a spirit of fantastic and historically pained experimentalism was to create a quite new stylistic phase in the novel.

7 Postmoderns and Others: The 1960s and 1970s

Ghosts, monsters, criminals, deviates represent melodrama and weakness. The only horror about them is the dreamer's own horror of isolation. But the desert, or a row of false shop fronts; a slag pile, a forge where the fires are banked, these and the street and the dreamer, only an inconsequential shadow himself in the landscape, partaking of the soullessness of these other masses and shadows; this is the 20th Century nightmare.

Thomas Pynchon, V. (1963)

'I began to write fiction on the assumption that the true enemies of the novel were plot, character, setting and theme, and having once abandoned these familiar ways of thinking about fiction, totality of vision or structure were really all that remained.'

John Hawkes, in an interview (1965)

I

Nothing marked the turn from the 'tranquillized' Fifties more clearly than the election, in 1960, of John F. Kennedy to the Presidency of the United States. Kennedy's promise of a 'New Frontier' in American life, his appeal to youth, his sense of historical purpose and his cultural sympathies drew intellectuals towards him, and even into the 'Camelot' court of his brief Presidency. In *The Presidential Papers* (1963), Norman Mailer plotted the links between the President and his own anarchistic radicalism; and Rojack, in his *An American Dream* (1965) is a Kennedy acquaintance, conducting a seemingly parallel battle against cancerous growth and false powers. Other novelists displayed similar fantasies of the intellectual as historical performer and government adviser – Gore Vidal in his knowing, élitist Washington novels (*Washington, D.C.*, 1967; *Burr*, 1974; and *1876*, 1976), Roth in *Portnoy's Complaint* (1969), Bellow in *Humboldt's Gift* (1975), Jerzy Kosinski in *Being There* (1971),

Joseph Heller in *Good as Gold* (1979). But the complex, strained relation between public and personal life was also being explored in other ways; it was during the Kennedy Presidency that Roth noted the stupefying unreality of contemporary American history, and Bellow a massing of public life so great that 'private life cannot maintain a pretence of its importance' – with complex consequences for the novel. It was not far from this thought to the suspicion that history itself was an absurd fiction, a massive plot commanding the individual yet dissolving all stable reality. American fiction at the beginning of the Sixties was enlarging its themes and looking historically outward; it was also reappraising the forces loose in the world, and the question of the individual's power to face them. The history novelists now explored was somehow beyond individual existence and the measure of reason; it was a history of distorting power plays, large conspiratorial structures, huge technological systems, apocalyptic threats to survival.

These themes became pressing in older writers and new ones. Burroughs's *Naked Lunch* (1959) and its sequels saw a contest between inner space and overwhelming political systems; John Barth's *The Sotweed Factor* (1960) took the historical novel and turned it into matter for pastiche. In 1961 came Joseph Heller's anti-war novel, *Catch-22*, about a World War II no longer depicted naturalistically, but as a grotesque and absurd fantasy that applied to contemporary America. Kurt Vonnegut's *Mother Night* (1961) was another of the many books that returned to the absurdities of wartime Europe, seen through the eyes of a writer whose science-fiction methods were to generate numerous images of human insignificance. Ken Kesey's *One Flew Over the Cuckoo's Nest* (1962) saw American power as authority ruling and containing a madhouse; the most remarkable new writer of the time, Thomas Pynchon, produced in *V.* (1963) an endeavour to reconstitute world history while insisting on the disintegrative, entropic processes functioning through it. Fiction might indeed be drawn from the domestic back into the historical world, but its images were disquieting – images of pattern, power, process, and system, of the struggle of animate against inanimate, of diminished self against increased force. Novelists might then celebrate an unpatterned, resistant awareness to history, system, and code; they might, though, point to something yet bleaker, the entry of system into the very heart of the self, rendering humanism impossible and life absurd. These themes run through early Sixties writing; but when, in 1963, Kennedy was assassinated, and then the war in Vietnam escalated, the sense of horror increased, and the tension between massive public history and the dwarfed artistic imagination pushed writers into examining the potential of the form they possessed. It was the writers of the historical grotesque who now seemed most relevant, like John Hawkes, who – ever since *The Cannibal* (1949) – had been using the landscape of historical violence for a fiction of inner psychic exploration, or Vonnegut – who made his relation between science fiction and the agonies of modern history explicit in *Slaughterhouse-Five* (1969), which moves between the wartime fire-bombing of Dresden and the imaginary planet Tralfamadore, in a spirit of what he identified as 'gallows humour', a tragi-comic response to the defeat of the subject by the social and historical world.

In many of these books, history is seen not as a haunting progress, but as a landscape of lunacy and pain; the doubting of a rational and intelligent history leads to a mocking of the world's substance, a sense of inner psychic disorder, a cartooning of character, a fantasizing of so-called 'facts' or actualities, and a comic de-nominalization. History is itself shown as fictional, not in order to dismiss it but to subvert it; new imaginative structures were generated which both encountered and questioned the world's ugly presentness. American fiction in the Sixties found itself deserting the humanistic and realistic centre of much previous novel-writing. One direction in which it moved was towards a fantastic factuality, attempting to penetrate the fictionality of the real. A 'non-fiction novel', Truman Capote called his *In Cold Blood* (1966), a novel-like reportage about the murder of an innocent middle-American Kansas farm family by two wandering psychopaths, one America encountering a dark other one. Though this genre was hardly original to the Sixties, it expressed its stylistic anxieties – as did Norman Mailer in *The Armies of the Night* (1968), where the relationship between historical actuality and fiction is exactly considered, the way we 'construct' a reality examined. Anxiety about reportorial subjectivity also became explicit within journalism itself. A 'new journalism' emerged, and its leading exponent, Tom Wolfe, claimed that it had taken over from the 'boring' novel, using its methods – scene-by-scene construction; full recording of dialogue; interiorization of third-person viewpoint; detailed explication of social mores and the hungers expressed in style and status – to record what Wolfe called the 'crazed obscene uproarious Mammon-faced drug-soaked mau mau lust-oozing Sixties' (fictional discretion was not something he took over). Though Wolfe and other 'new journalists' – Hunter S. Thompson, Seymour Krim, Jimmy Breslin, and Joan Didion, herself a good novelist – were inclined to emphasize the stylistic innovation of their methods, their main contribution was to a journalism now ready to confess to authorial subjectivity. But formal mergers were very much in order, and the factualized novel continued its elaboration, in such works as William Styron's *The Confessions of Nat Turner* (1967), based on an actual slave rebellion, E. L. Doctorow's *Ragtime* (1975), and Robert Coover's *The Public Burning* (1977).

One motif of the Sixties was therefore a new, self-examining hyper-realism which drew the novelist towards reportage, and reportage towards fictionality, so challenging 'innocent' realism. But a significant other step away from realism was in an opposite direction – towards what one critic, Robert Scholes, called 'fabulation', and others perceived as a new 'fictionality' in fiction. The period saw a notable revival of surrealism and fantasy, often insisting, à la Nabokov, on the utter fictionality of *all* attempts at naming, structuring, and ordering experience, and on exploring the novel's own inward mechanisms; the result was an era of 'self-reflexiveness' in the novel. It went along with a new fascination with the springs of creativity and narrative, and the tactics of fantasy and grotesquerie, all evidently shaped by the need to react artistically against the horror and grossness of the historical world. As modern critics have argued, fantasy is not an outright escape from reality, rather a mode for interrogating the real, dispersing and displacing its forms, creating its expectations only to displace them. Much Sixties fiction becomes fantastic through its assault on the historical and the real; it arises, that is, from defined historical landscapes and processes. The strain of black humour which dominated the early part of the decade explored the manifest absurdity of contemporary society and of any rational response to it: this is the spirit of the fiction of Heller and Vonnegut, Bruce Jay Friedman, Thomas Berger, Terry Southern, Alfred Grossman, Stanley Elkin. But as the decade went on, the sense of experiment intensified, and the direct historical reference often weakened; fiction, unable to form coherent meaning, celebrated its own loss of signification, rejected pre-formed views of reality, and sought to create its own provisional, liberated worlds of creative consciousness.

These developments were partly the reflection of an international move towards experimentalism in the novel, manifest in the impact on American writers of the French *nouveau roman*, of Nabokov, Borges, and Beckett, and of Latin American magical realism. But there were also close affiliations with the counter-culture that, stimulated by rising protests about civil rights, free speech, and the Vietnam war, dominated the later part of the decade. The counter-culture was not solely political; it saw itself as a new avant-garde, a new surrealist consciousness, expressing an age in which outward violence could be countered by an inward spirit. Post-humanistic, messianic, mystic, shamanistic, provisional, it was rooted in youth, drawing on psychic and psychedelic experiment, expressing the post-culture of the new global village, in which a glut of new styles appeared to be available simultaneously, and without rational design or order. This new psycho-political awareness deeply affected Sixties fiction. Its directly political aspect was evident in a greatly radicalized Black fiction: the work of Black writers like John Oliver Killens (*And Then We Heard the Thunder*, 1963), John A. Williams (*The Man Who Cried I Am*, 1967), and William Melvin Kelley (*Dem*, 1969) is a revolt against white consciousness. But it also stimulated a new Black surrealism, a vein of apocalyptic fantasy – evident in the work of Ishmael Reed, author of the free-form text *The Free-Lance Pallbearers* (1967) and the mock western *Yellow Back Radio Broke-Down* (1969), and the more poetic and coherent experiments of Clarence Major (*All-Night Visitors*, 1969). Other writers celebrated the hippie youth spirit, as did Kerouac and, later, Richard Brautigan; the drug and psychedelic culture, as did Burroughs and Kesey; or the new shamanism, as did Thomas Berger and William Eastlake. But the new spirit was more than a new subject, a new indignation, or a new set of cultural values; it pointed towards a new sense of form, or indeed to a pervasive new merging of forms.

A sense of ungovernable stylistic glut, formal multiplicity and interfusion, artistic synaesthesia, dominated the Sixties arts. Signs seemed to outrun signification; styles, in the imaginary museum of multiple forms, fascinated but became styleless, offering themselves as parody. There was much talk of a new tendency, postmodernism, which was the sum of the styles: the term suggested a return to the experimental and avant-garde spirit of modernism, but also a revolt against modernism's high seriousness and hope for formal coherence and transcendence. In an essay of 1967 John Barth saw among the time's most self-aware writers a new 'literature of exhaustion', following on from Borges and Nabokov; it was a writing that betrayed 'the used-upness of certain forms or exhaustion of older possibilities', and suggested the end of the era of the referential text. And with the appearance of such books as John Hawkes's *Second Skin* (1964), Thomas Berger's parodic western *Little Big Man* (1964), Jerzy Kosinski's *The Painted Bird* (1965), Robert Coover's *The Origin of the Brunists* (1965), Thomas Pynchon's *The Crying of Lot 49* (1966), William H. Gass's *Omensetter's Luck* (1966), and Barth's own *Giles Goat-Boy* (1966), a new experimental tendency or revised stylistic equation did seem to be emerging. The year 1967 saw publication of Richard Brautigan's *Trout Fishing in America*, and Donald Barthelme's anti-novel *Snow White*; the key radical year of 1968 saw Barth's intermedia exercise *Lost In the Funhouse: Fiction for Print, Tape, Live Voice*, Gass's *In the Heart of the Heart of the Country*, Kosinski's *Steps*, Ronald Sukenick's *Up*, and Steve Katz's *The Exaggerations of Peter Prince*. A body of fiction had appeared marked by scepticism about generic types, disposition to parody, ironic inversion, 'meta-fictional' insistence on its own chosen modes of signification, and on the capacity to challenge the stability of what is signified.

The nature of this new mood could be read variously. In some writers the move was towards anti-realism and nominalism – the belief, that is, that we call the world into existence by naming it. Hence text could manifest only the creative invention and artifice of its own existence, speculate about the performance of the fictional act, function as a game or exercise in provisional assertion. Narratives of every kind, whether by journalists, historians, sociologists, or other presumed constructors of 'truth', offered no truths logically prior to those of a novel; all partook of universal fictionality, and since both past fictions and other forms of prose structure paralleled new ones, a crisis of intertextuality, a problem in the making of modern style, arose; the novelist lived in a world of unattached signifiers, suggesting both a historical crisis and a new creative opportunity. History now reached into the heart of text. Much of this experimental Sixties fiction is concerned with the enormous powers at work in the modern world, the impact of war and the coming of an era of 'nothingness', the presence of imposed plots and patterns conditioning and containing all discourse, making man as language user a programmed instrument of the system. For, where

earlier writers might respond to the powers of the world with a victimized naturalism, these writers tended to find the victimization
present in the very explanatory structure they used, language itself.
In some sense this disabled the form and structure of novels; at the
same time it could generate new imaginative fusions, as the novel
sought not just to re-invent itself but to display the nature of its
inventive process, offering itself as a form of re-naming, a form of de-
creation leading to re-creation. If it displayed the defeat of text by the
weight of the past and the domination of fixed systems, it might also
produce a new reality – 'open-ended, provisional, characterized by
suspended judgments, by disbelief in hierarchies, by mistrust of
solutions, dénouements and completions, by self-consciousness issu-
ing in tremendous earnestness but also in far-reaching mockery...,'
said one critic.

The prevailing paradox was summed up by Ronald Sukenick in
the title of his *The Death of the Novel and Other Stories* (1969), where
he noted that, in 'the world of post-realism', all absolutes have
become problematic, literature does not exist, and 'The contemporary writer – the writer who is acutely in touch with the life of which
he is a part – is forced to start from scratch: Reality doesn't exist.
God was the omniscient author, but he died: now no one knows the
plot. ...' The conviction of living in an age of epistemological re-
definition was shared with, and undoubtedly fed by, the development in France of the *nouveau roman*, and the related intellectual
movements of structuralism and, later, deconstruction; but the
tendency also had a distinctly American face that was most evident
in its comic and parodic texture, its 'cheerful nihilism'. Writers like
Donald Barthelme indicated that they found the 'deadly earnest'
note of French fiction inimical; some stressed the optimism of the
new American modes. Not surprisingly, the question of whether
these developments really marked a large new direction in the
twentieth-century novel, of comparable significance to modernism,
concerned the critics. It was also a question as to whether the various
experimental gestures had much in common, since they displayed
widely different preoccupations and could be defined in many ways
– as a literature of silence or a literature of noise and redundancy, as
a minimalist process or one of free and open creative invention, as an
art of deconstruction but also an aleatory art, as an art of philosophical absurdism but also as an art of hopeful provisionality. The term
'postmodernism' still remains vague, but what it describes and

attempts to define has been a fundamental challenge to the past realism and naturalism in American fiction, and to previous experimentalism; and it has opened up the novel as experimental ground in a time when many old images of America went into dissolution.

If the term is vague, that is partly because of the many new American writers of interest and weight whose widely varying work it has sought to define and associate. Besides Nabokov, Hawkes, Pynchon, Vonnegut, Brautigan, Barth, Gass, Barthelme, Kosinski, and Coover, these include significant successors like Sukenick, Clarence Major, Walter Abish, Raymond Federman, and Steve Katz. Some are self-conscious fictionalists, others playful or serious users of fantasy and grotesquerie; some are writers of intense historical preoccupations, others primarily concerned with the formation of text. Some, like Pynchon, write a fiction of glut, excess, and encyclopedic mass; others, like Barthelme, express a reductive economy, writing a literature of lessness and the left out. Critics trained in structuralist and deconstructionist methods saw these writers as exemplary instances of their view that the new writing displayed the language crisis of the times, and read in the collapse of the traditional alliance of reader and exterior subject, or of an assimilable text written for an easily comprehending implied reader, the late-twentieth-century historical condition. Whether or not postmodernism is the dominant or 'appropriate' style of the age may be questionable; what is certain is that formal and epistemological questions crucial to fiction's nature are being articulated in writers who have extended certain fundamental preoccupations of modernism – notably with fiction as play, game, parody, forgery, and fantasy – and added new challenges to the notion that art is referential and formally coherent. In their works the stable text disappears; the fiction becomes meta-fictional; the reader is invited into novels in novel ways. Raymond Federman has seen the emergence of a new 'surfiction' wherein 'all distinctions between the real and the imaginary, between the conscious and the subconscious, between the past and the present, between truth and untruth, will be abolished'; other critics have offered less aesthetic, more historical explanations, seeing the new novel as a reaction against what Tony Tanner calls 'all kinds of conspiracies against spontaneity of consciousness'.

The phenomenon of postmodernism has been for some predominantly a style or a mannerism, but for others a total, enfolding historical manifestation, the apocalyptic product of a time when the sign has floated free of the signified, authoritative utterance becomes impossible, and only re-naming, re-writing, re-creating can be attempted. For some a latter-day epistemological impasse, it has been for others a great and open freeing of creation. If postmodernism's nature has been disputed or variously explained, so has its degree of dominance in late-twentieth-century American fiction. For the late Sixties it appeared, in its synthesizing drive and parodic abundance, a crucial break with previous realism and naturalism and with previous generic and regional tendencies, so that older categories and groupings – 'Southern fiction', 'Jewish-American fiction', 'Black fiction' – appeared increasingly senseless; any style was open to intersection, reformulation, and parody. By the Seventies the creative abundance had hardened towards mannerism and there was already talk of post-postmodernism. The tendency began to merge with the latter-day confessional of male liberationists like Philip Roth and John Irving (*The World According to Garp*, 1978) or female liberationists like Erica Jong (*Fear of Flying*, 1973) and Lisa Alther (*Kinflicks*, 1976), and with the 'culture of narcissism' which the therapeutic Seventies evolved in reaction against the politically and historically anxious Sixties. Writers like John Gardner (*Grendel*, 1971) began to espouse the cause of 'moral fiction', and more recent novels by major practitioners – like John Barth's *Letters* (1979) and John Hawkes's *The Passion Artist* (1979) – have shown signs of a push back towards a self-consciously qualified realism. The surrounding aesthetic debate has somewhat tired, and the harsher economics of the Eighties has produced a mood encouraging to more conservative forms. Yet, in part because the works of postmodernism have been popular as well as avant-garde, and belong as much to the new media as the new bohemia, the transformation from older realism into new systems of creative notation has been of the largest importance, and has had the deepest implications for the novel internationally, because it has questioned the act of imaginative writing at its heart.

II

Though sometimes seen as a movement towards non-referentiality, the experimental drive of the Sixties and Seventies was indeed much concerned with responding to modern history. It has been haunted everywhere by the image of a disabling war, and the note of absurdism and black humour has been crucial throughout. Thus a founding text for the Sixties was Joseph Heller's *Catch-22*, about a group of flyers in a corrupt and benighted Italy carrying out an unremitting series of wartime missions to no apparent intent. Heller's nihilist-absurdist mode was hardly new to American fiction; related images of grotesque absurdity go back to Melville (especially his *The Confidence Man*), Mark Twain, Nathanael West. But the absurdism of *Catch-22* comes from a modern senselessness and is a direct reaction to contemporary history and institutions; the 'catch-22' of the title derives from the U.S. Air Force's view that, to get out of combat duty, you must be certified insane, but, since anyone who wants to avoid combat duty must be sane, it is impossible to get out of combat duty. It is an image of the way man is bound to the system as machine; similar absurd formulae provide the book's structure and become its prime source of black humour. If such bondage is absurd, the only response can be wry anarchy, a perception that there are no just causes, only our corrupt technological system operating unideologically against an enemy system. Enemies are death-bringing forces which are either evaded or not; death is pervasive and purpose absent; the army is staffed by freaks programmed to perform senseless acts; technology, system, and death, rather than culture, morals, values, or significant politics, surround men in this world; 'There are now fifty or sixty countries fighting in this war. Surely so many countries can't *all* be worth dying for,' the book observes. The alternative to the system becomes personal survival, since 'The spirit gone, man is garbage', and all intelligence goes into the skills of evasion – a principle exemplified by the book's hero, Captain Yossarian.

Catch-22 is, like many of the new American novels, a book of systematic denaturing, by society, capitalism, the war organization, disfiguration, de-identification, dehumanization, and death, as well as by the text itself. Comedy creates both the denaturing – the system of paper laws which insists that record is prior to fact, unreality precedes reality, the human being is a function of his role and may suffer every possible humiliation and manipulation – and its alternative, the sense of the absurd which constitutes revolt. Heller's book turns on a comic proliferation of absurd characters: Milo Minderbender, the classic entrepreneur and confidence man; Major Major, who runs his office by only seeing people in it when he is out, and who earns promotion to Major Major Major; Lieutenant

Scheisskopf, whose aim is to produce the perfect military parade, and who does it through attaching technological devices to the men; ex-Pfc Wintergreen, the mail clerk, who is actually running the war. In this world of dehumanization and death, insanity is contagious, and madness both a system and a means of recuperation. There is a pervasive sense of pain and tragedy: Yossarian, inspecting his experiences in the dark ruined city of Rome, finds the Eternal City eternal only in its continuous and chaotic suffering; here too the rule of catch-22 prevails, for God has created a lousy world filled with unnecessary suffering. So survival requires an equal power of absurdity, a manipulation of language. Yossarian decides to live forever or die in the attempt; people are, he believes, trying to murder him, which he can prove because 'strangers he didn't know shot at him with cannons every time he flew into the air to drop bombs on them'. A paranoid with reasons, he finally pursues the possibilities of survival through desertion; but to the end escape remains an elusive and absurd possibility.

In Heller's next two books, *Something Happened* (1974) and *Good as Gold*, the post-war America prefigured in *Catch-22* is made the reality. *Something Happened*, the bleaker of the two, has as its central character and anti-hero Bob Slocum, who works in a corporation office where everyone is afraid of someone else, in order to maintain a suburban middle-class family in which everyone – apart from a brain-damaged son – is afraid of someone else. Though Slocum reflects, 'When I grow up, I want to be a little boy,' he lacks, even more than Yossarian, any real recourse to innocence; in a world of 'logical universal schizoid formation', he shares the universal corruption and lives in a state of guilty complicity. So does Bruce Gold, the half-malign and half-sympathetic anti-hero of *Good as Gold*. The novel is likewise half-way between a homage to and a parody of the Jewish-American novel Heller had been criticized for not having written. Gold is a second-generation Jewish academic who has lost touch with his own ethnic past, and lives without roots in a Seventies world of YMCA joggers and fashionable swinging adulteries. The Jewish theme is important: the old anti-Semitism in this world has ceased, but no one has much time for Jews; liberals have anxious conservative thoughts and Gold himself is abrim with 'fiery caution and crusading inertia'. Nor are his attempts to recover his Jewish past aided by membership in one of the most anguishing and appalling families in all Jewish-American literature. The ironies of 'complete freedom' are brought home when Gold is called in as a specialist in public relations by the President of the United States, and offered the chance to do 'anything you want, as long as it's everything we tell you to do in support of our policies, whether you agree with them or not. You'll have complete freedom.' Both novels portray a social and historical decline leading to entrapped complicity, and Gold's glimpses of ethnic self-recovery seem to offer no more than a standpoint for irony and self-doubt.

Heller's vision of innocence lost, of modern man denatured by system and falling into ironic resignation, brings his work close to that of another novelist of historical pain, resigned passivity, and comic anarchy, Kurt Vonnegut. What lies behind Vonnegut's world is a lost middle-American innocence, fractured by waste, decay, technology. Vonnegut creates that world by drawing heavily on the popular form of science fiction, which not only allowed him to explore scientific systems and processes, apocalyptic situations, and space–time variation and relativity, but also the tones of sentimental folksiness. His novels mix the spirit of pulp fiction with experimental methods and anxious historical preoccupations. His first book, *Player Piano* (1952), is a dystopian novel about the technological future, set in the company town of Ilium, New York, and built on the irony that, when men revolt against the technological plenty and human uselessness of the computerized, machine-run future world they live in, they at once start to re-create the same sort of system. In *The Sirens of Titan* (1959), a more elaborate science fiction, Vonnegut invents his imaginary planet Tralfamadore, and see the earth's achievements – Stonehenge, the Great Wall of China – as signals designed to guide flying saucers through the galaxy. The senselessness and pathos of human history are more directly treated in *Mother Night*, set in Europe under Fascism, and about the double agent Howard Campbell, who commits 'the crime of his times' by serving evil too openly, good too secretly. With *Cat's Cradle* (1963), Vonnegut turns to the nuclear apocalypse, and creates the religion of Bokononism, founded on 'harmless untruths' – just like a novel. *God Bless You, Mr Rosewater* (1965) comes back to the more familiar historical world to examine how philanthropy might amend the world of corporatism and technology. Vonnegut's books by now were successful and influential, largely because of their tone, hard to characterize yet always easy to catch. Both naïve and sophisticated, resigned and bitter-sweet, that tone is passive before the powers of history, system, and fate, a world that functions as a vile joke; it also expresses an awareness of the consolation of human fantasies, and seeks to celebrate philanthropy, kindness, goodness. Absurdist because it suggests that the only possible response to the world is an agonized laughter, it leads the characters towards conspiracy with the horrors in which they live, yet also towards a life of harmless innocence.

That resigned anxious voice was the author's own, as he made clear in his most powerful book, *Slaughterhouse-Five: Or, The Children's Crusade*, written, he says folksily on the title-page, by 'a fourth-generation German-American now living in easy circumstances on Cape Cod (and smoking too much), who, as an American infantry scout *hors de combat*, as a prisoner of war, witnessed the fire-bombing of Dresden, Germany, "the Florence of the Elbe", a long time ago, and survived to tell the tale. . .' Vonnegut proposes in the book that all his previous science fictions have been displacements from a central event in his life too terrible to record; he also insists on the imaginative value of that displacement, on fantasy's importance in trying to make sense of the senseless. Again, fictions become responses to history and horror; 'real' horror forms one essential component of the book, the process of fantastic displacement the other. Vonnegut converts himself into Billy Pilgrim, a childlike, gentle-natured but emotionally damaged optometrist from Ilium, New York, who is none the less concerned, like his narrator, with the making of 'corrective lenses'. In the 'real' world, Billy suffers the author's experience of capture in war, imprisonment in the Dresden slaughterhouse, and chance survival from the fireball which destroys the city. In the world of fantasy, Billy is displaced further, being kidnapped and taken to Tralfamadore – partly a pathological location, partly a place that opens the door of alternative knowledge, for here time has been desynchronized, historical cause and effect interrupted. Billy adjusts to the Tralfamadorian view of things – men are machines, life is experienced in instants, affection wastes, fatalism ('So it goes') is the only response, and even novels are written in another manner, where there is 'no beginning, no middle, no end, no suspense, no moral, no causes, no effects', where messages are multiple and synchronic but, 'seen all at once, they produce an image of life that is beautiful and surprising and deep'. The method proposed is that of the book itself, which both expresses and reacts against the world of the actual and the coherent and generates 'harmless' fictions which both defamiliarize and reconstruct.

Speculating about the tactics of historical displacement, the means of composition, the rights of fiction to transform 'known facts', the nature of the imagination, *Slaughterhouse-Five* thus becomes Vonnegut's most 'postmodern' novel. One of the imaginative fictions of history which recur centrally in the postmodern experiment, it also recognizes the problems of fiction's potential for humanism. 'Harmless fictions' might free us from a bleak world, but they can also generate enslavements of their own; as Billy is a prisoner in Tralfamadore as well as Dresden, so characters are victims of their author's imagination, 'listless playthings'. In *Breakfast of Champions* (1973), Vonnegut's vision of a polluted, junked, raped contemporary America, he poses the problem of whether his characters are the victims of such a society, or of his own vision. He resurrects his author surrogate, Kilgore Trout, who has appeared in earlier novels, and makes him responsible for the madness of one of his characters, Dwayne Hoover, driven insane by Trout's imaginative vision. Behind Trout, Vonnegut himself explains the problem: 'It's a big temptation for me, when I create a character for a novel, to say that he is what he is because of faulty wiring, or because of microscopic amounts of chemicals which he ate or failed to eat on a particular day'; and at the end of the book, much like Jefferson freeing his slaves, Vonnegut 'frees' his characters – only to compound the fictional paradox further, since there is nowhere for them to exist except in his own imagination. And indeed in later books Vonnegut has called them back again, in novels like *Slapstick* (1976) and *Jailbird* (1979) where, after the experimental venture of his middle work, the folksy and more popular Vonnegut has returned, his more complex experiments apparently forsaken.

The effort to use experimental fictional forms to reach towards and recover a spirit of American innocence can also be seen in the work of Richard Brautigan, another author very insistent on intruding his own presence and tone into his storytelling. A younger writer whose roots lie in the California hippie scene and in Sixties radicalism, Brautigan has been too readily cast as a writer of naïve fictions, and as a celebrator of that California beach and hippie life-style that followed on from the worlds of Henry Miller and Jack Kerouac. Brautigan certainly exploits that connection; his first novel, *A Confederate General from Big Sur* (1964), plays solid images from the American past, above all those arising from the Civil War, against the latter-day skirmishings of his contemporary 'confederate general', Lee Mellon, as he battles with hippie irony against ideology and system. But Brautigan's effort is also to create a modern text, dissolving old national narrative. He writes about the ironizing of the world, the waning of pastoral myths of innocence and of escape from social constriction into nature; he shows the power of old images and then of the endeavours of the imagination to dissolve them, both through the struggles of his fictional outsiders, and of the poetic imagination itself. If the world wanes, the writer's exuberant comic imagination thrives; form in its collapse promises recovery, the fixities of time, space, and ideology dissolve, and *A Confederate General* ends both in a characteristic sadness and in hyperactivity of the creative imagination, as it generates 'more endings, faster and faster until this book is having 186,000 endings per second'.

The same notion of dissolving the solidity of the world through the freedoms of imagination dominates Brautigan's next book, or 'writing', *Trout Fishing in America* (1967), 47 brief chapter-essays cast in the mode of the angler's notebook, an old pastoralizing form that permits Brautigan to celebrate his West Coast world. But on that world a mechanical age has imposed itself, generating mechanical images; from their juxtaposition come strange mergings and contrasts, a new discourse. Old linguistic sets generate new fantasy and invention: thus the title phrase itself, 'Trout Fishing in America', keeps transforming, becoming place, person ('Trout Fishing in America Shorty'), and an essential principle of imaginative independence. Mind and metaphor can recover the animate from the inanimate – as when, in a marvellous passage, the narrator visits the Cleveland Wrecking Yard and there buys a used trout stream. Signs thus detach from their systems, grow indeterminate, generate invention; phrase becomes *dreck*, redundancy, and reforms as a new basis for textual creation.

Brautigan's effort to recover an animate from the inanimated world is yet more evident in his next book *In Watermelon Sugar* (1968), a surreal fantasy set in a peaceable community called iDEATH, where, amid the remnants of a technological America, the inhabitants make a gentle world of watermelon sugar, much like a fiction itself. With its apparent restitution of an innocent pastoral world, the book is open to sentimental reading; but it is also about the decentreing of the subject, the death of the self (iDEATH), about consciousness fading and changing, objects displacing into pure phenomenal existence, then being recovered as random ikons. As in other post-modern texts, words lose their fixity and attachment to things, becoming fluid, just like watermelon sugar. Brautigan is parodying fixed writing and solid forms, and his next books mock the generic fixities of fiction itself. *The Abortion* (1971), sub-titled 'An Historical Romance', attempts to collapse the library of literature itself, which now includes Brautigan's own past books; *The Hawkline Monster* (1974), sub-titled 'A Gothic Western', merges two seemingly incompatible forms, the classic adventure Western and the Gothic novel of horrors, displacements, and estrangements; *Willard and His Bowling Trophies* (1974), sub-titled 'A Perverse Mystery', dissolves all the suspense and expectation of mystery writing to create a text for fictional play. These books are attempts at the dissolution of forms, the breaking of serial orders, the collapse of nominative pro-cesses and identities, the substitution of free invention for static mimesis. More recently, *The Tokyo-Montana Express* (1980) has emphasized the poetic and conceptual underpinnings of his work – its emphasis on the instant, the sense of severance from the past, the awareness of the dissolution of classic identity, the claims of the fluid moment. It illuminates the serious postmodern 'game' of his work, a work that proposes the wasting of old forms and orders, the exhaus-tion of writing, but the powers of recovery the image offers to the imagination, as intertextuality generates new forms, parts without wholes that invite radical re-connection. Brautigan has proved vastly more than an innocently hippie writer, rather an author of gnomic knowledge and imaginative discovery whose spirit of saddened yet finally optimistic imaginative hope would pass on to a number of literary successors in the Seventies.

III

But if one way to respond to the aggressive historical landscape of the Sixties was to move through experimental fantasy to a recovered imaginative innocence, there were other writers for whom the imagination was far more compromised, more grotesquely com-pounded into the disturbed psychic world of the times. Among the most powerfully compelling of these authors has been John Hawkes – a somewhat older writer whose first book, *The Cannibal*, appeared as early as 1949, but who found a natural place in the experimental company of the Sixties and Seventies. A writer of the imaginative grotesque, for whom ideas of imaginative innocence were illusory, Hawkes himself traces his debts firmly to American Gothic (the work of Faulkner, Djuna Barnes, Flannery O'Connor) and European surrealism (especially Lautréamont and Céline); but his work is also deeply shaped by a sense of contemporary historical disturbance, and by complex use of modern images and the devices of indeterminate textual presentation. His writing draws to the full on the dislocative methods of fantasy, dissolving the ego into a landscape that is surreal, grotesque, and metaphorical, and into social structures where laws of authority and victimization are universal. Hawkes's experiment does not work towards recovering the innocent imagination, nor does it produce carefully controlled fictional constructs which insist on their own arts of invention. His books are, rather, the troubled action of the gothic and grotesque imagination, presented as a fundamental state of being and as an ultimate source of the act of writing; Hawkes has spoken of experimental fiction as 'an exclamation of psychic materials which come to the writer all ready distorted, prefigured in that inner schism between the rational and the absurd'. He described his fiction as 'committed to nightmare, violence, meaningful distortion, to the whole panorama of dislocation and desolation in human relationships'; yet at the same time his novels possess a high formal self-consciousness, for their aim is to create not a psychological realism but a structured process of imaginative discovery. Hence their developing systems of psychic images develop according to laws of verbal as much as of psychological coherence.

Yet his world is, he insists, a historical one, and his economy of the grotesque begins in the 'spiritless, degraded landscape of the modern world'. *The Cannibal*, set in Germany over a complicated time-scheme from 1914 to 1945, covers the psychotic rise of Nazi totalitarianism and its post-war impact on the wandering escapees from the Asylum who pass through the barren wastes of a derelict, defeated Germany. *The Beetle Leg* (1951) finds similar images of violence and sterility in the landscape of the American Western desert, but *The Goose on the Grave* (1954), two novellas set in Italy, returns to war-torn Europe and the Fascist imprint that clearly haunts this writer. In *The Lime Twig* (1961) Hawkes turns to the setting of a bleak post-war Britain he had never visited; the landscape thus becomes parodic, a Graham Greene-land of race gangs and violence that serves as an imaginary world appropriate to Hawkes's themes of force and victimization, authority and submission, where maimed minds function in a maimed landscape which is more like a state of consciousness than an outward 'reality'. Hawkes's fiction of the Fifties patently derives from an inner landscape of violence and desire that found expression in fragmentary settings appropriate to it: his novels build up a world of detritus and death, frames and limits, asylums and prisons, islands and desert where inner terror and outward circumstance coalesce. The result is a conscious anti-realism, a dematerialization both of the naturalistically seen universe and of habitual narratives, in order to re-create these anew according to laws of imaginative and psychic intensity. That intensity seems conditioned by the as yet unnamed desires of the writer as much as of the characters he invents, and is fulfilled by the author's own psychic release and then by the commanding processes of the released images themselves. The imaginary world so created acquires intense power as an image, expressing what Hawkes would call in a later book 'clarity but not morality'. The author's own implication in the process is quite clear, in the disposition of the structures of mastery and submission, in the strange identifications made with violent characters – like the Nazi Zizendorf in *The Cannibal,* whose totalitarian view of the word is contrasted with the 'unintelligible military scrawls' of the Americans trying to bring order back to cannibal post-war Germany. For the writer, too, works between the totalitarian word and the incomplete scrawl – the elements he shapes and conditions and those he expresses without controlling.

By the Sixties, Hawkes's methods were intensifying and becoming more complex. Where *The Lime Twig,* because it is told in the third person through multiple narration, still largely exteriorizes its landscape, *Second Skin* is Skipper's first person narration; the method exposes his textual and psychic unreliability, makes the landscape more abstract, and permits a web of complex allusions to Greek myth. This change greatly sharpened Hawkes's work, clarifying its technique and increasing its complexity. His characters now knew that they lived, and lived in, the fantasies of others, in dissolving paradoxes of self, as they kept crossing the duplicitous line of the containing skin. Instead of the decadent displacements of the earlier books, there was something more like a psychoanalytic text, still unreliable and indeterminate, but opening, through the narrators, on to a world of complex psycho-sexual activity, the deeper recesses of fantasy, the places of non-signification of both self and the written word. This increasing self-consciousness and complexity of form developed in Hawkes's next books – *The Blood Oranges* (1971), *Death, Sleep and the Traveller* (1974) (a title taken with appropriate abstraction from a sculpture), and *Travesties* (1976). It sharpened more in *The Passion Artist* (1980), a large imaginative enterprise set in an invented Eastern European city of prisons and iron, exploring the unshuttering of an iron-bound male self through the extreme violence of women, which releases Conrad Vorst, the central character, into flesh. Hawkes is most compelling when, as here, he creates a world of psychic magnitude reaching into incoherence as well as coherence, into significance without direct signification. The novelist as interior discoverer, committed alike to nightmare and formal exploration, he has himself emphasized that he starts with the materials of psychic derangement, but in order to arrive at aesthetic bliss. His novels evolve through psychic melodrama, but also through the growth of complex and ambiguous images and sign systems that, falling under artistic control, acquire the coherence of an artistic object.

Perhaps the most remarkable writer to explore the limits of modern fantasy has been Thomas Pynchon, whose economy of the grotesque also starts in the historical world, and in the cultural and psychic disorders of Nazi and wartime Europe and America. Pynchon has played form against history in ways as complex as his view of history itself. The theme was laid down early, in the short story called 'Entropy' (1960), which takes up Henry Adams's reflections on the dislocation of mind in the modern multiverse, his conviction that energy is running loose towards entropy, moving from differentiation towards sameness, and so into the heat death of culture. Pynchon has been personally very elusive, but it is known that he studied engineering at Cornell, and worked for a time for the Boeing Corporation; his books are all marked with a high degree of technical knowledge. The character Callisto, in 'Entropy', shares this knowledge and reflects, in his protected and hermetically sealed room, on such matters, while a vastly more physical party is being held downstairs by Meatball Mulligan, one of the directionless, frenetic, body-centred men who become alternative central figures in Pynchon's frequently binary structure. Typically, neither commands the story; Pynchon does not create figures who can contain the sum of the inchoate yet encyclopedically explicable world through which they move or, in Callisto's case, stand motionless. For the dominant presence in Pynchon's writing was always to be the text itself, functioning by an elaborate and often expository discursiveness working on the interface between two levels of experience, two systems – a closed one, Callisto's, and an open one, Mulligan's; a language of control and a language of disorder. Beyond both characters is an apocalyptic and a technological world, generating non-human systems that require a response from consciousness. The text mediates between the world of hyperactivity and excess and the world of hermetic containment – the essential postmodernist mannerism that would guide Pynchon's subsequent work.

Two such characters, Benny Profane and Hubert Stencil, and their apparently discrete stories provide the system of double motion out of which Pynchon's first novel, *V.* (1963), is constructed. Profane is identified as the *schlemiel*, the suffering absurd comedian of Jewish fiction, the sailor and street man who 'yoyos' in physical oscillation and frequent violence through the urban, mechanical, and underground world of this populous book. Often in the company of the 'Whole Sick Crew', he is a tourist through the streets and sewers of the present, experiencing its lovelessness and its drift towards inanimation; his only function to want. Stencil appears to be on a significant quest: described as 'a century's child', born in 1901, and therefore a citizen of Henry Adams's multiverse (like Adams, he refers to himself in the ironic, detaching third person), he is seeking the remnants of the Virgin in the Dynamo world. His father, a former British spy, has left behind him gnomic clues pointing to a great conspiracy behind modern history, and whereas Profane lives in a world of signlessness, Stencil enters one of assertive signs and apparent patterns, pointing to the hidden importance of the lady V., who has somehow been involved in a variety of twentieth-century historical events, from the Fashoda crisis to the siege of Malta in World War II, and who may possibly be Stencil's own mother. His quest is both for a fulcrum identity and the pattern or meaning of modern history; it proves centreless, for V.'s identities are plural and the problem is not only who she is, but what. Using the oblique approach of 'attack and avoid', Stencil seeks to be the meaning-giver of the book, and his attempt at the recovery of a master historical plot leads him into or through many central modern events, in which the letter V. significantly functions, its meaning spreading from the spread thighs of sexuality to the capital of Malta, Valletta. Its historical logic seems to be the emptying of a significant human history and its sacrifice to mass and mechanism, a transfer apparently finally turning on the Second World War.

The paradox of *V.* is that its enormous historical and social bulk is so constituted that it may be disordered, dismantled, and doubted. We can see this deconstruction occurring with V. herself, 'a remarkably scattered concept', a human figure moving through many identities and stages of decadent narcissism and sexual perversion down to Stencil's final dream of her as a plasticated technological object, a shifting letter also attached to a historical process of progressive de-animation. Stencil comes personless back from the past, Profane moves through an aimless present, the empty street of the modernworld where identity and ego are voided, 'tourism' prevails, the inanimate becomes the face of animate. The paradox goes further: Stencil and Profane are effectively the two compositional principles of the book, the pattern-maker and the man of contingency, the constructive and the deconstructive. They hunt the lettered sign and seek in some fashion to construct or elude the world, but their quest is less a discovery of meaning than a loss of meanings, or rather a disorderly and chaotic excess of them, for the book proceeds by proliferating data in excess of possible system. Pynchon both creates and de-creates his own characters (as he does with the elusive non-character V. herself), giving them personality and personlessness, names and namelessness (for the names are parodies), figuration and disfiguration. Yet what is reduced is compensated for by excess: the historical matter of the book is extraordinarily dense and powerfully created, and the novel indeed functions at a high level of referentiality, massing itself round the 'facts' of history and geography, granting weight to the 'objective' voice of the author. *V.* may be a text about indeterminacy, even an indeterminate text. But it is not a totally lexical book, a pure word-play, a novel without a subject.

In his next book, *The Crying of Lot 49*, Pynchon moved to a tighter, funnier mode of tragic farce. Set in the hyper-technological, hyper-therapeutic society on the lapping edge of the non-human or inanimate Pacific, it is the story of a suburban California housewife, Oedipa Maas, who leaves the world of Tupperware parties to decipher and execute the cryptic will of her dead ex-lover Pierce Inverarity, a tycoon in San Narciso. Active in various technological enterprises, Inverarity has been mysteriously implicated in the affairs of a complex underground conspiracy and postal system, variously known as WASTE and the Tristero, the meaning of which may be America itself. *Lot 49* can be seen in the line of earlier surreal-absurdist California fiction, such as Nathanael West's or Terry Southern's, a Space Age sun belt tale of hyper-technology and psycho-analytic narcissism, Oedipa herself being in analysis. But the book is itself a decadent-enigmatic object; just as Oedipa is caught, through Pynchon's image of the Mexican tower, in the narcissistic possibility that we construct from our subjective imprisonment the tapestry of the world, so Pynchon himself creates images of self, story, and history that are stripped towards their enigmatic but possibly empty centre. Oedipa's paranoia arises from her entry into a world where the laws of the fantastic dominate but will not necessarily yield significance, as Pynchon creates but does not resolve the possibility of arriving at sign or meaning through penetrating the web of musical codes, historical system and counter-system, plays and signals. Oedipa moves through randomness without reaching revelation, wondering whether 'the gemlike "clues" were only some kind of compensation. To make up for her having lost the direct, epileptic Word, the cry that might abolish the night.' But Pynchon ends the book at an auction before the crying of the possibly revelatory lot 49, and it remains in its ambiguity, 'another mode of meaning behind the obvious, or none'. Language, sign, and cipher work in the book, as in cybernetic America itself, towards mystery which is redundancy, towards sophisticated forms containing insignificance. Yet Pynchon also raises the possibility of 'underground' recovery from the empty, personless space, through alternative frequencies, such as, perhaps, the oblique codes of his own book.

These codes reappear in Pynchon's 460-page summative novel *Gravity's Rainbow* (1973), a work of such density and complexity that it has been seen as the late-twentieth-century *Ulysses*, the exemplary post-modernist text. Certainly the book, with its elaborate plot and its plotlessness, its massive accumulation of data and 'characters' (over 400 of them), disables any brief summary. Again it is a novel of data in excess of system; again the book disestablishes the codes we are initially tempted to read into it, particularly those associated with the conventional humanism and historicity of fiction. Again, though, history as referential subject is overwhelmingly present; the book is set, like many contemporary American novels, in what one critic calls 'the crucial, explosive, fecund nightmare of all our psychoses and all our plots', the Second World War, seen as a total modern system. The metaphor for this is the trajectory of the supersonic rocket, the German V2, with its gravity-shaped curve of aspiration and destruction, with its complex physics and meta-physics, its human scientific input and its technological indifference, its power of noiseless, signal-less, and apparently random annihilation. Like all randomness in Pynchon, this raises the paradox of the plotted and the plotless, and a key story in the book is that of Lieutenant Tyrone Slothrop, of American Puritan descent (like the author himself), who has been given behaviourist conditioning at Harvard by a German scientist, and is now attached to the British forces. The rockets fall on London on sites coinciding exactly with the sites of Slothrop's sexual conquests, suggesting not only the analogy between phallus and rocket but also the absurdist possibility that Slothrop is programmed into a massive scientific, military, and economic conspiracy – that, indeed, there is a vast contemporary construct into which everyone is incorporated, adapted to or turned into rocketry, that sex and death lie together, that energy is annihilating system. Against the London episodes are set those in the post-war Zone in Germany, after the collapse of the Third Reich, a place of defeat and disorder (not unlike that of Hawkes's *The Cannibal*), systemlessness and broken patterns. The rocketry evokes paranoia, the seamless chaos anti-paranoia; through these forms of perception many of the characters engage in a clue-hungry search for a 'Real Text' that never emerges – again, a textless text like the book itself.

The inner problems of the book are again those of the novelist attempting to constitute the modern novel. Again the book has a massive excess or overassertion of reference, historical data, scientific exposition, yet it dissipates its own referentiality by constant displacements towards the fantastic, to illusion, dream, theatre, by an ever-widening proliferation of generic types. 'Secular history', it says, 'is a diversionary tactic,' and the narrative method expands from encyclopedic science and reportorial realism through comic-strip devices and music-hall songs to abstracted metaphysical speculation. Its discourse is now phenomenological, now nominalist, now psychological-fantastic, and now semiotic. Again there is character-disintegration as human figures become random and story sequence fails ('There ought to be a punchline, but there isn't,' we are told as Slothrop falls into fictional disintegration. 'The plans went wrong. He is being broken down instead, and scattered'). Bafflement about life on these interfaces engages those within the book; it is shared with the reader, enfolded in a wealth of matter without structural finites and hence left in a condition of indeterminacy, resulting from the parodic clustering of forms and the linguistic systems of multi-registration. Pynchon may seem to programme the book with his own defeat, producing what one critic has called 'a work of low message value at the zero degree of interpretation', but there is also evidently a gnostic aim, a thrust towards a new metaphysical creativity, its anxious historical pressures transferred to the reader to display the paradox of literary transaction. Pynchon's novels are central to modern American writing. Historically alert and histori-cally conditioned, they are cybernetic novels generating, like the world itself, information in excess of mastery and systems in excess of relationship, displaying what has been called a 'paranoid' style to deal with the entropic world of random and dehumanizing energy, yet creating textual energy and generic and linguistic proliferation on a huge scale in an attempt to redeem the word. At the beginning of the century, at the start of Adams's modern multiverse, Dreiser was able to conceive of a world in which inhuman energy was greater than human, in which person becomes object, object person; Pynchon takes that enquiry far beyond any naturalism, into an enquiry into the text itself, into the problem of communication it poses, the structurelessness it creates, and the post-humanist space that language must enter to find the way to a significant sign.

IV

Pynchon's massive enterprise has its parallels in other American novels – most notably in the work of William Gaddis, whose *The Recognitions* (1955) was a remarkable exploration of fiction and forgery, and whose second novel *JR* (1976) is an encyclopedic novel about modern money, with a cybernetic theme. But other potent versions of the postmodernist impulse existed, especially in the novel of self-conscious fictionality, the novel that exposed the novelist as artificer and sought to explicate the form's inherent *as if*. Of the writers who have exemplified this nominalist tendency and chosen to introduce the reader into the workshop of composition, John Barth, a novelist who has long insisted on his dissent from mimetic realism ('What the hell, reality is a nice place to visit but you wouldn't want to live there, and literature never did, very long,' he once said), is central. His earlier novels, *The Floating Opera* (1956) and *The End of the Road* (1958), are comedies of existential absurdity. The first treats a suicidal hero from the point when he decides, the world being meaningless, to commit suicide, to that at which he decides, the world being meaningless, to stay alive ('There is, then, no "reason" for living (or suicide)'); the second introduces a first-person but personless hero ('In a sense, I am Jacob Horner,' he begins), a weatherless man without feeling or sense of purpose, who, after being given 'mythotherapy', goes to teach grammar in a college, and finds his problems summed up in the contrast between 'descriptive' and 'prescriptive' grammar. Drawn into adultery with a colleague's wife, which ends in a bungled abortion and her death, he reverts to weatherlessness, and the black comedy ends as he is directed to the railroad terminal, an apt place for an ending to occur. These books express the feeling that there is no significant text in the world, and they thus lead the way to Barth's fiction of the Sixties, which went on joyously to celebrate textuality and intertextuality. *The Sotweed Factor* is a marvellous exercise in pastiche, a pseudo-history of Barth's local domain of Maryland, where most of his fiction is set, telling the mock-story of its founding poet Ebenezer Cooke through the romping mannerisms of the novelists of the eighteenth century. *Giles Goat-Boy* comes closer to Pynchon's themes; it is a parody myth for modern times, set on the campus of the modern cosmos, a global semi-allegory about competing computers with alternative political programmes, and about life's other generic divisions: mind and body, human and animal, male and female. Appropriately divided into 'reels' and 'tapes', it takes cybernetic form, calling up structures of traditional myth to introduce the fractures and inter-textual allusions that the ethically weakened modern writer, conscious of writing his writing, feels compelled to introduce into his story.

Barth's 'literature of exhaustion' was evolving; his fictions showed signs of spiralling round themselves, turning into rewritings of prior rewritings, generating intertextual allusions not just to the works of other authors but to the author's own. Story arrests, tales within tales, techniques for asserting and withdrawing stylistic authenticity, enquiries into the history of narrative, form the method, with at the centre a bewildered author. *Lost in the Funhouse* is founded on the Möbius strip, and is a mixed group of items for print, tape, and live voice, open to multiple re-fashioning. The book attempts a radical redisposition of the materials of authorship; of the author himself, presented as lost in the funhouse of his own creations, fragmenting, subdividing, losing order and seriality, moving through various textual and verbal systems to find himself as a speaker. The three novellas of *Chimera* (1972) then return to narrative's origins, in that founding story of stories, *The 1001* (or *Arabian*) *Nights*, and the Greek myths of Perseus and Bellerophon. The opening tale, the 'Dunyazadiad', updates the story of the most successful of all story-tellers, Scheherazade, who, by endlessly generating plots, counter-plots, and narrative suspense, saved her own life. Barth himself appears in the story as a genie, only to confess his own lostness: 'I've quit reading and writing; I've lost track of who I am; my name's just a bundle of letters; so's the whole body of literature: strings of letters and empty spaces, like a code I've lost the key to.' The chimera of *Chimera* is the elusive reality at the heart of fiction – that which justifies its bewildering array of devices, multiplication of narrators, tales-within-tales, its ciphers, hieroglyphs, letters and alphabets, mazes and labyrinths, writings and rewritings, its approaches, suspenses, deferrals, and consummations. Indeed Barth uses the analogy between foreplay, deferral, and consummation in sexuality and in fiction to spiral towards the narrative heart, to discover that 'the key to the treasure is the treasure', the being of the story the meaning of the story; fictional being is being, discourse about realities a reality.

Chimera postulates many more stories than it tells, including a failed or blocked book called *Numbers* and another called *Letters*. In 1979 appeared a novel called *Letters*, written by but also to an author, John Barth. Functioning according to a complex alphabetical code, it sought over 772 pages to put together, through epistolary means, the central characters of all Barth's previous books and stories. Breaking down the discreteness of the fictions Barth had already written, it took the form of a self-disfiguring monument, while revealing that there was a monument there to disfigure, the existence of his own writings. But it also reached back through the stock of the Anglo-American tradition of the novel as such, introducing a new muse, Germaine Pitt, Lady Amherst, a visitor from the literary circles of Britain. The path is towards realism, though Lady Amherst disappoints by declaring: 'I am *not* the Great Tradition! I am *not* the ageing Muse of the Realistic Novel!'; as might many a contemporary British writer. Since then, Barth has offered us *Sabbatical* (1982), another work of exposed piping and service-ducts, a narrative Beaubourg, equipped with footnotes and *two* assumed authors, one male and one female. A story of sea-voyaging and sea-mysteries, again set off Maryland, it goes back to the sea-story origins of narrative – origins that have been particularly important for the development of American fiction. *Sabbatical* is Barth's attempt at a modern version of the American romance novel, drawing on its twin traditions of terror and sentimentality. Twins are everywhere, even down to the twin authors, representing in their marriage the generative source of creativity.

Barth's sense of the erosion of story and then of its potential for replenishment has led him toward a writing of encyclopedic scale; for other writers the exhaustion of story has appeared more complete, pointing the way to fictional minimalism. The most notable instance is Donald Barthelme, author of two anti-novels, *Snow White* (1967) and *The Dead Father* (1975), and several extraordinary collections of short fictions, including *Come Back, Dr Caligari* (1964), *Unspeakable Practices, Unnatural Acts* (1968), *City Life* (1970), *Sadness* (1972), *Guilty Pleasures* (1974), consisting largely of parody articles, *Amateurs* (1976), and *Great Days* (1979). Barthelme proposes a more inexorable lapse of realism from the days of our dead fathers. 'At the Tolstoy Museum we sat and wept. Paper streamers came out of our eyes,' begins the story 'At the Tolstoy Museum' in *City Life*, and we may take Tolstoy to be the great realist whom we replace by the paper streamers of the present. As another of his volume titles suggests, Barthelme is haunted by sadness about the displacement of reality in a world of inauthentic experiences, *dreck*, and junk language; but it is precisely the tactics of displacement that make up the procedure and technique of his works. A phrase in *Snow White*, 'fragments are the only forms I trust,' is often quoted as central to his methods; certainly his stories and novels depend on a progressive decentring of the apparent topic – Robert Kennedy, for example, in the story 'Robert Kennedy Saved from Drowning' in *Unspeakable Practices, Unnatural Acts* – in order obliquely to compose its existence. What is composed is also conspicuously de-composed, in a dissolution of the subject, a cool parodying of the verbal tropes that might have been thought to produce meaning or emotion. If character is introduced, it is questioned and often finally made absent ('Yet it is possible that it is not my father who sits there in the center of the bed weeping. It may be someone else, the mailman, the man who delivers the groceries...,' runs 'View of My Father Weeping', in *City Life*); absurdist instances and images develop; stories are shown proliferating through chance images or ideas which may lead to an ending or none at all ('etc.', is how the above-quoted story ends). Where Barth's work is self-reflexive because it hungers for something to narrate, Barthelme often proceeds by negating any subject, so that all possible content is manifested as disorder, and object-references and statements exist without being rationally juxtaposed to each other, generating new combinatory systems while confusing the levels of story. Barthelme is sometimes taken as the source of a modern meaningless text, but he is better read as a writer conscious of the absences he creates, indeed a writer of sadness, pointing to the spaces of a self-negating world, while using and pointing up the materials it offers. His structures and phrases are taken from the public action of language, and he has described his method as collage: 'The point of collage is that unlike things are stuck together to make, in the best case, a new reality. The new reality, in the best case, may be or imply a comment on the other reality from which it came and may also be much else. It's an *itself*, if it's successful.'

Barthelme's notion of the fictional imagination constituting a new reality, using novel methods of deletion, distortion, and re-combination in order to do so, would seem no novelty in a discussion of poetry; it is because of fiction's inheritance of asserted empirical reality that it seems novel. But such notions have become part of the thinking of many of the more serious American novelists of the last two decades, and imparted a growing sense of euphoric yet self-sceptical invention. 'Reality is not a matter of fact, it is an achievement,' remarks one of these novelists, William H. Gass, in his critical book *Fiction and the Figures of Life* (1970), also remarking that the good novelist must keep us 'kindly imprisoned in his language, there is literally nothing beyond.' Gass's fiction – the novel *Omensetter's Luck*, the novella *Willie Master's Lonesome Wife* (1968), the short-story collection *In the Heart of the Heart of the Country* – displays its creator's nominalist philosophical background, his consciousness of the discrepancy between language and reality, and also his aim of using the slow, complex workings of fiction to find a possible embrace between the text and the world. *Willie Master's Lonesome Wife*, like much of Barth's work, draws explicitly on the erotic analogy between the sexual act and the

relation between writer and reader, and through complex typo-
graphy and the shape and form of the book-object itself it seeks to
fashion words into transfigurative images and metaphors, through
deconstruction to reconstruction.

'The novelist uses familiar mythic or historical forms to combat
the content of those forms and to conduct the reader . . . to the real,
away from mystification to clarification, away from magic to
maturity,' writes another of the younger experimentalists, Robert
Coover, addressing Cervantes, in one of the 'Seven Exemplary
Fictions' of his story collection *Pricksongs and Descants* (1969),
adding: 'And it is above all to the need for new modes of
perceptionand fictional forms able to encompass them that I,
barber's basin on my head, address these stories.' The reconstitution
of forms for reality's sake is the principle behind Coover's novels,
*The Origin of the Brunists, The Universal Baseball Association, Inc.,
J. Henry Waugh, Prop.* (1968), and, above all, *The Public Burning* –
which deals with a crucial moment of recent American history, the
execution for spying of the Rosenbergs, but transfers that actual
event to the figurative realm by making their executions a public
burning in Times Square. Times Square is not only a public meeting
place but a source of 'history', for here the recording pages of *The
New York Times* are created; and Coover goes on to analyse the
fictions of fact by looking back through the newspaper's files and
then displaying the alternative record of the imagination. He relates
abstracted figures like Uncle Sam to actual ones like Vice-President
Richard Nixon, who soliloquizes his own life story, in an extraordinary imaginative gesture, in the novel, to show that fiction does
not simply assist history; it can draw it into the subjective, reality-
searching standpoint of fiction, which then produces ever compli-
cating principles of fantasy, elaborate transformations of text, new
combinations of genres and artistic materials. Like Barth, Coover,
while responding to the urgencies of history, sees that the quest also
goes into the origins of story, which are both timeless and international. And that internationality, too, has been a crucial note in
modern American fiction – in the experiments of the French-
American Raymond Federman (*Take It Or Leave It*, 'an exaggerated
second hand tale to be read aloud either standing or sitting', 1976),
the Polish-American Jerzy Kosinski (from *The Painted Bird*
onwards), or the Austrian-Jewish-American experimentalist Walter
Abish (*Alphabetical Africa*, 1974). Abish's novel *How German Is It*

(1980) is another formally very exacting return to the subject of Germany, in its flat modern materialism a world of signs without meanings under which dark meanings hide, where crisis relations between history and form persist, where the writer's task is to unlock the hidden code and penetrate the chaos inside. His work, bleak, detached, and bearing strong stylistic resemblances to that of Italo Calvino or Peter Handke, reminds us that 'postmodernism' is a more than American phenomenon, a ranging quest of the troubled contemporary imagination to find a style that faces our kind of world.

V

Now, in the Eighties, it is possible to dispute the degree to which the experimental American writing of the last two decades is a fiction of creative novelty, presenting us with the potential for a new concept of fictional style. The search, in writers like Barth and Coover, for the old origins of narrative and the novel, and their alert recognition that the novel as a modern form emerged in the seventeenth and eighteenth centuries from processes of generic and narrative re-combination resembling their own, is equally a confession that many contemporary writers have been searching for the meaning of fiction at its roots, and that such an enterprise is not entirely novel and contemporary. Many of the laws of invention in the new writing are lasting laws of fantasy – though they here function in a changed world of secularity, barrenness, high scepticism, and de-serialization of the imagination. We call these writers 'postmodern' to emphasize their contemporaneity, and because they break with modernism in their pursuit of far looser, vastly more random and more combinative structures; perhaps they are more appropriately to be called 'post-realist', since their persistent challenge is to the structures of plausibility, the modes of inner coherence, and the confident referentiality of realistic fictions, their assertion that they record a pre-textual reality. What has been remarkable about the achievement of these new writers is that their response to the contemporary historical situation has driven them into essential questions about the nature of story and modern stylistic citizenship. To some extent the phase shows signs of being over; John Barth has written of a new 'literature of replenishment', rather than of exhaustion, and John Gardner, himself a notable fantasist, author of *Grendel*, has argued in his book *On Moral Fiction* (1978) that the 'theory of fiction as mere language' evades the question of literature's moral power and influence. As innovation has tended to become simple convention and mannerism, such disquiets have increased, and may well produce a reaction in the fiction of the Eighties.

American fiction of the post-war period has produced two striking versions of the modern novel which have had an importance vastly more than American. In that period, the novel has grown much more international; its major performers are now emerging world-wide. In that enlargement of fiction, we have seen, coming from many directions and fictional traditions, numerous versions of the style of the late modern, the articulate form appropriate to the second half of the twentieth century. It has been a period of creative instability leading to creative renewal, a period of outstanding new talents and extraordinary new versions of the novel. For, at its best, the novel is not simply an infinitely repeatable type, a body of habitual and therefore apparently innocent styles and modes of expression, a set of fixed sub-genres open to local modernization by fresh authors; it is an ever-changing act of apprehension, belonging in the world of our changing thought, our changing history, our changing ways of naming experience, and it cannot stand still. It is not surprising that contemporary fiction has been preoccupied with our presence in history, with the rising of systems, the dehumanizing of experience, the death of the subject; nor is it surprising that it has looked enquiringly at its own history as a form, challenged past modes of imaginative expression, and sought to call on new acts of the creative imagination. In that enterprise, the American novel has been of ever-increasing centrality and importance, a key point of responsiveness to, and assimilation of, more widespread fictional change. This book has been a study of some of the main forms of expression that have developed since 1890 within the modern American novel, and of a period when American fiction has moved from marginality to centrality. For, though always tempted to assert its Americanness, and then to assert that Americanness as a distinctive and different form of mythography, the novel in America has grown steadily more international, not just in its readership but in its aesthetic nature. If the novel is, at best, a deep apprehension of what it means, in a changing world, to utter ourselves, structure our experience, name our world into being, then over the course of the century the best American fiction has become a literature of primary enquiries into the means of doing exactly that.

The American Novel Since 1890
A List of Major Works

The following list is necessarily selective, but it extends beyond the authors covered in the text. Not all works by authors mentioned are included; dates are of American publication.

MARK TWAIN (1835–1910)
The Adventures of Huckleberry Finn (1884); *A Connecticut Yankee at King Arthur's Court* (1889); *Pudd'nhead Wilson* (1894)

HENRY JAMES (1843–1916)
The Portrait of a Lady (1881); *What Maisie Knew* (1897); *The Wings of the Dove* (1902); *The Ambassadors* (1903); *The Golden Bowl* (1904); *The Art of the Novel* (prefaces, ed. R. P. Blackmur) (1934)

WILLIAM DEAN HOWELLS (1843–1916)
The Rise of Silas Lapham (1885); *A Hazard of New Fortunes* (1890); *Criticism and Fiction* (essays) (1892)

SARAH ORNE JEWETT (1849–1909)
The Country of the Pointed Firs (1896)

KATE CHOPIN (1851–1904)
The Awakening (1899)

HAROLD FREDERIC (1856–98)
The Damnation of Theron Ware (1896)

HENRY BLAKE FULLER (1857–1929)
The Cliff-Dwellers (1893)

ABRAHAM CAHAN (1860–1951)
Yekl: A Tale of the New York Ghetto (1896); *The Rise of David Levinsky* (1917)

HAMLIN GARLAND (1860–1940)
Main-Travelled Roads: Six Mississippi Valley Stories (1891); *Crumbling Idols* (essays) (1894)

EDITH WHARTON (1862–1937)
  The House of Mirth (1905); *The Custom of the Country* (1913); *The Age of Innocence* (1920)

STEPHEN CRANE (1870–1900)
  Maggie: A Girl of the Streets (1893); *The Red Badge of Courage* (1895)

FRANK NORRIS (1870–1902)
  McTeague (1899); *The Octopus* (1901); *Responsibilities of the Novelist* (essays) (1903)

THEODORE DREISER (1871–1945)
  Sister Carrie (1900); *Jennie Gerhardt* (1911); *An American Tragedy* (1925)

WILLA CATHER (1873–1947)
  O Pioneers! (1913); *My Antonia* (1918); *The Professor's House* (1925)

ELLEN GLASGOW (1874–1945)
  The Battle-Ground (1902); *Barren Ground* (1925); *Vein of Iron* (1935)

GERTRUDE STEIN (1874–1946)
  Three Lives (1909); *Tender Buttons* (1914); *The Making of Americans* (1925)

SHERWOOD ANDERSON (1876–1941)
  Windy McPherson's Son (1916); *Winesburg, Ohio* (1919); *Dark Laughter* (1925)

JACK LONDON (1876–1916)
  The Call of the Wild (1903); *The Sea-Wolf* (1904); *The Iron Heel* (1907); *Martin Eden* (1909)

UPTON SINCLAIR (1878–1968)
  The Jungle (1906)

CARL VAN VECHTEN (1880–1966)
  Nigger Heaven (1926); *Spider Boy* (1928)

DAMON RUNYON (1884–1946)
  Guys and Dolls (1932)

RING LARDNER (1885–1933)
  The Love Nest (1926)

SINCLAIR LEWIS (1885–1951)
Our Mr Wrenn (1914); *Main Street* (1920); *Babbitt* (1922)

RAYMOND CHANDLER (1888–1959)
Farewell, My Lovely (1940)

CONRAD AIKEN (1889–1973)
Blue Voyage (1927)

KATHERINE ANNE PORTER (1890–1980)
Pale Horse, Pale Rider (1939); *The Leaning Tower* (1944); *Ship of Fools* (1962)

HENRY MILLER (1891–1980)
Tropic of Cancer (1934); *Black Spring* (1936); *Tropic of Capricorn* (1939)

DJUNA BARNES (1892–1982)
Nightwood (1936)

MICHAEL GOLD (1892–1967)
Jews Without Money (1930)

J. P. MARQUAND (1893–1960)
H. M. Pulham, Esq. (1941)

E. E. CUMMINGS (1894–1962)
The Enormous Room (1922)

DASHIELL HAMMETT (1894–1961)
The Maltese Falcon (1930)

JEAN TOOMER (1894–1967)
Cane (1923)

JOHN DOS PASSOS (1896–1970)
One Man's Initiation: 1917 (1920); *Three Soldiers* (1921); *Manhattan Transfer* (1925); *U.S.A.* (1937)

F. SCOTT FITZGERALD (1896–1940)
This Side of Paradise (1920); *The Great Gatsby* (1925); *Tender Is the Night* (1934); *The Last Tycoon* (1941)

WILLIAM FAULKNER (1897–1962)
Soldier's Pay (1926); *Sartoris* (1929); *The Sound and the Fury* (1929); *As I Lay Dying* (1930); *Light in August* (1932); *Absalom, Absalom!* (1938)

ERNEST HEMINGWAY (1898–1961)
   In Our Time (1925); *The Sun Also Rises* (in England: *Fiesta*) (1926); *Men
   Without Women* (1927); *A Farewell to Arms* (1929); *For Whom the Bell Tolls*
   (1940); *The Old Man and the Sea* (1952)

VLADIMIR NABOKOV (1899–1977)
   Bend Sinister (1946); *Lolita* (Paris, 1955; USA,1958); *Pale Fire* (1962); *Ada:
   or Ardor* (1969)

THOMAS WOLFE (1900–38)
   Look Homeward, Angel (1929); *Of Time and the River* (1935); *You Can't Go
   Home Again* (1940)

JOHN STEINBECK (1902–68)
   In Dubious Battle (1936); *Of Mice and Men* (1937); *The Grapes of Wrath*
   (1939); *East of Eden* (1952)

ERSKINE CALDWELL (1903–   )
   Tobacco Road (1932); *God's Little Acre* (1933)

JAMES GOULD COZZENS (1903–78)
   Guard of Honor (1948); *By Love Possessed* (1957)

JAMES T. FARRELL (1904–79)
   Young Lonigan (1932); *The Young Manhood of Studs Lonigan* (1934);
   Selected Essays (1964)

ISAAC BASHEVIS SINGER (1904)
   Gimpel the Fool (stories) (1957); *The Magician of Lublin* (1960)

NATHANAEL WEST (1904–41)
   Miss Lonelyhearts (1933); *A Cool Million* (1934); *The Day of the Locust*
   (1939)

JOHN O'HARA (1905–70)
   Appointment in Samarra (1934); *BUtterfield 8* (1935); *Ourselves to Know*
   (1960)

ROBERT PENN WARREN (1905)
   All the King's Men (1946); *World Enough and Time* (1950)

HENRY ROTH (1907–   )
   Call It Sleep (1934)

RICHARD WRIGHT (1908–60)
  Native Son (1940); *The Outsider* (1953)

EUDORA WELTY (1909–)
  A Curtain of Green (1941); *Delta Wedding* (1946); *Collected Stories* (1980)

JOHN CHEEVER (1912–82)
  The Wapshot Chronicle (1957); *Falconer* (1977); *The Short Stories of John Cheever* (1979)

MARY MCCARTHY (1912–)
  The Groves of Academe (1952); *The Group* (1963)

WILLIAM S. BURROUGHS (1914–)
  The Naked Lunch (1959); *The Ticket That Exploded* (1962); *Nova Express* (1964)

RALPH ELLISON (1914–)
  Invisible Man (1952)

BERNARD MALAMUD (1914–)
  The Natural (1952); *The Assistant* (1957); *The Fixer* (1966); *Dubin's Lives* (1979)

SAUL BELLOW (1915–)
  Dangling Man (1944); *The Victim* (1947); *Henderson the Rain King* (1959); *Herzog* (1964); *Humboldt's Gift* (1975)

JOHN HORNE BURNS (1916–53)
  The Gallery (1947)

JOHN OLIVER KILLENS (1916–)
  And Then We Heard the Thunder (1963)

CARSON MCCULLERS (1917–67)
  The Heart Is a Lonely Hunter (1940); *Member of the Wedding* (1946)

J. F. POWERS (1917–)
  The Presence of Grace (stories) (1956); *Morte d'Urban* (1962)

J. D. SALINGER (1919–)
  The Catcher in the Rye (1951); *Franny and Zooey* (1961); *Raise High the Roofbeam, Carpenters and Seymour* (1963)

JAMES JONES (1921–   )
  From Here to Eternity (1951)

WILLIAM GADDIS (1922–   )
  The Recognitions (1955); *JR* (1976)

JACK KEROUAC (1922–68)
  On the Road (1957); *The Dharma Bums* (1958)

KURT VONNEGUT, JR. (1922–   )
  The Sirens of Titan (1961); *Cat's Cradle* (1961); *Slaughterhouse-Five* (1969);
  Breakfast of Champions (1973); *Jailbird* (1979)

JAMES DICKEY (1923–   )
  Deliverance (1970)

JOSEPH HELLER (1923–   )
  Catch-22 (1961); *Something Happened* (1974); *Good as Gold* (1979)

NORMAN MAILER (1923–   )
  The Naked and the Dead (1948); *The Deer Park* (1955); *An American Dream*
  (1965); *The Armies of the Night* (1968)

JAMES PURDY (1923–   )
  Colour of Darkness (stories) (1957); *Malcolm* (1959); *Cabot Wright Begins*
  (1964)

THOMAS BERGER (1924–   )
  Reinhart in Love (1961); *Little Big Man* (1964); *Vital Parts* (1970)

TRUMAN CAPOTE (1924–   )
  Other Voices, Other Rooms (1948); *Breakfast at Tiffany's* (1958); *In Cold
  Blood* (1966)

WILLIAM H. GASS (1924–   )
  Omensetter's Luck (1966); *In the Heart of the Heart of the Country* (stories)
  (1968); *Willie Master's Lonesome Wife* (1968)

JOHN HAWKES (1925–   )
  The Cannibal (1949); *The Lime Twig* (1960); *Second Skin* (1964); *Death,
  Sleep and the Traveler* (1974); *The Passion Artist* (1980)

FLANNERY O'CONNOR (1925–64)
  Wise Blood (1952); *A Good Man Is Hard to Find* (1955)

WILLIAM STYRON (1925–)
Lie Down in Darkness (1951); *The Confessions of Nat Turner* (1967); *Sophie's Choice* (1979)

GORE VIDAL (1925–)
Julian (1964); *Washington, D.C.* (1967); *Myra Breckinridge* (1968); *Burr* (1974); *Creation* (1981)

JOHN A. WILLIAMS (1925–)
The Man Who Cried I Am (1967)

J. P. DONLEAVY (1926–)
The Ginger Man (Paris, 1955); *A Singular Man* (1963)

HUBERT SELBY (1926–)
Last Exit to Brooklyn (1964); *The Room* (1971)

RAYMOND FEDERMAN (1928–)
Double or Nothing (1972); *Take It or Leave It* (1976)

JAMES BALDWIN (1929–)
Go Tell It on the Mountain (1953); *Another Country* (1961); *Tell Me How Long the Train's Been Gone* (1968)

GILBERT SORRENTINO (1929–)
Imaginative Qualities of Actual Things (1971); *Mulligan Stew* (1979)

JOHN BARTH (1930–)
The Floating Opera (1956); *The Sot-Weed Factor* (1960); *Lost in the Funhouse: Fiction for Print, Tape, Live Voice* (1968); *Chimera* (1972); *Letters* (1979)

STANLEY ELKIN (1930–)
Boswell (1964); *A Bad Man* (1967)

BRUCE JAY FRIEDMAN (1930–)
Stern (1962); *A Mother's Kisses* (1964)

WALTER ABISH (1931–)
Alphabetical Africa (1974)

E. L. DOCTOROW (1931–)
The Book of Daniel (1971); *Ragtime* (1975)

ROBERT COOVER (1932–)
The Origin of the Brunists (1965); *The Universal Baseball Association, J. Henry Waugh Prop.* (1968); *Pricksongs and Descants* (stories) (1969); *The Public Burning* (1977)

SYLVIA PLATH (1932–63)
The Bell-Jar (1966)

RONALD SUKENICK (1932–)
Up (1968); *The Death of the Novel and Other Stories* (stories) (1969); *Out* (1973); *Long Talking Bad Conditions Blues* (1979)

JOHN UPDIKE (1932–)
The Poorhouse Fair (1959); *Rabbit, Run* (1960); *Couples* (1968); *The Coup* (1979)

DONALD BARTHELME (1933–)
Come Back, Dr Caligari (stories) (1964); *Snow White* (1967); *City Life* (stories) (1970); *The Dead Father* (1975)

JOHN GARDNER (1933–82)
Grendel (1971)

JERZY KOSINSKI (1933–)
The Painted Bird (1965); *Steps* (1968); *Being There* (1971); *Blind Date* (1977)

LEONARD MICHAELS (1933–)
Going Places (stories) (1969)

REYNOLDS PRICE (1933–)
A Long and Happy Life (1962)

PHILIP ROTH (1933–)
Goodbye Columbus (stories) (1959); *Letting Go* (1962); *Portnoy's Complaint* (1969); *The Professor of Desire* (1977)

SUSAN SONTAG (1933–)
The Benefactor (1963); *Death-Kit* (1967)

JOHN DIDION (1934–)
Play It As It Lays (1971)

JOHN RECHY (1934–)
The City of Night (1963)

RICHARD BRAUTIGAN (1935–   )
A Confederate General from Big Sur (1964); *Trout Fishing in America* (1967); *In Watermelon Sugar* (1968); *The Hawkline Monster* (1974)

STEVE KATZ (1935–   )
The Exaggerations of Peter Prince (1968); *Moving Parts* (1977)

KEN KESEY (1935–   )
One Flew Over the Cuckoo's Nest (1962); *Sometimes a Great Notion* (1964)

CLARENCE MAJOR (1936–   )
All-Night Visitors (1969); *No* (1973)

WILLIAM MELVIN KELLEY (1937–   )
A Different Drummer (1962); *Dem* (1969)

THOMAS PYNCHON (1937–   )
V. (1963); *The Crying of Lot 49* (1966); *Gravity's Rainbow* (1973)

JOHN KENNEDY TOOLE (1937–69)
A Confederacy of Dunces (1980)

JOYCE CAROL OATES (1938–   )
Them (1969); *Wonderland* (1971); *Marriages and Infidelities* (stories) (1973)

ISHMAEL REED (1938–   )
The Free-Lance Pallbearers (1967); *Yellow Back Radio Broke-Down* (1969); *Mumbo-Jumbo* (1972)

RUDOLPH WURLITZER (1938–   )
Nog (1969)

MICHAEL HERR (1940–   )
Dispatches (1977)

JOHN IRVING (1942–   )
The World According to Garp (1978)

ERICA JONG (1942–   )
Fear of Flying (1973)

Select Bibliography

Modern American fiction has been extensively treated in criticism. The following list includes general studies of the modern American novel, thematic treatments, and studies of particular periods. For work on individual authors, Lewis Leary's *American Literature: A Study and Research Guide* (New York, 1976), provides useful brief information. Fuller bibliographies are in Blake Nevius, *The American Novel: Sinclair Lewis to the Present* (Northbook, Ill., 1970), Donna Gerstenberger and George Hendrick, *The American Novel: A Checklist of Criticism* (2 vols., Chicago, 1961, 1970), and Irving Adelman and Rita Dworkin, *The Contemporary Novel: A Checklist of Critical Literature on the British and American Novel Since 1945* (Metuchen, N.J., 1972).

The main general studies of twentieth-century American fiction largely belong to the 1940s and 1950s, when concern to establish the 'modern tradition' was strong. Key books are Alfred Kazin's early, powerful, but nationalistically oriented *On Native Grounds: A Study of American Prose Literature from 1890 to the Present* (New York, 1942), which can be usefully supplemented by the same author's essays in *Contemporaries: Essays on Modern Life and Literature* (New York, 1962; London, 1963) and *Bright Book of Life: American Novelists and Storytellers from Hemingway to Mailer* (New York, 1973; London, 1974). Similarly nationalist and naturalist in orientation is Maxwell Geismar's coverage in his four volumes: *Rebels and Ancestors: The American Novel 1890–1915* (Boston, 1953), *The Last of the Provincials: The American Novel 1915–1925* (New York, 1947), *Writers in Crisis: The American Novel 1925–1940* (New York, 1942), and *American Moderns: From Rebellion to Conformity* (New York, 1958). A fuller historical study with an excellent modern section is Leslie Fiedler's *Love and Death in the American Novel* (New York, 1960; rev. edn., 1967), supplemented by his *Waiting for the End* (New York, 1964; London, 1965) and *The Return of the Vanishing American* (New York/London, 1968). Other useful general studies are Frederick J. Hoffman's *The Modern Novel in America* (Chicago, 1951) and Joseph Warren Beach's *American Fiction: 1920–1940* (New York, 1960). Though few of these use modern critical methods, they represent founding arguments in the debate. A helpful critical anthology is *Modern American Fiction: Essays in Criticism*, ed. A. Walton Litz (New York, 1963).

Many of the most important studies are thematic, exploring essential themes or tendencies in American fiction. Among the best are Joseph Blotner's *The American Political Novel 1900–1960* (Austin, Tex., 1960); W. M. Frohock's *The Novel of Violence in America* (Dallas, Tex., 1957); Blanche Gelfant's *The American City Novel* (Norman, Okla., 1954); *Psychoanalysis in American Fiction,* ed. Irving Malin (New York, 1965); James M. Mellard's interesting but narrow *The Exploded Form: The Modernist Novel in America* (Urbana, Ill./London, 1980), which concentrates on Faulkner, Heller, and Brautigan; Michael Millgate's *American Social Fiction: James to Cozzens* (Edinburgh and London, 1964); Walter B. Rideout's *The Radical Novel in the United States 1900–1954* (Cambridge, Mass., 1956); and David Galloway's *The Absurd Hero in American Fiction* (Austin, Tex., 1966; rev. edn., 1971). For Southern fiction, see Jay B. Hubbell's *The South in American Literature* (Durham, N.C., 1954) and *Southern Life in Fiction* (Athens, Ga., 1960), John M. Bradbury, *Renaissance in the South: A Critical History of the Literature 1920–1960* (Chapel Hill, N.C., 1963) and Richard Gray, *The Literature of Memory: Modern Writers of the American South* (London/Baltimore, 1977). On Black American fiction, see Robert A. Bone, *The Negro Novel in America* (rev. edn., New Haven/London, 1970), *Modern Black Novelists: A Collection of Critical Essays,* ed. M. G. Cooke (Englewood Cliffs, N.J., 1971), and C. W. E. Bigsby, *The Second Black Renaissance: Essays in Black Literature* (Westport, Conn., 1980). On Jewish-American fiction, see Allen Guttman's *The Jewish Writer in America: Assimilation and the Crisis of Identity* (New York, 1971), Irving Howe's monumental *World of Our Fathers* (New York, 1977), and Abraham Chapman, *Jewish-American Literature* (New York, 1974), as well as the works by Leslie Fiedler mentioned above.

For the 1890s and the rise of naturalism, the best studies are Charles C. Walcutt, *American Literary Naturalism: A Divided Stream* (Minneapolis, Minn., 1956) and Donald Pizer, *Realism and Naturalism in Nineteenth Century American Literature* (Carbondale, Ill., 1966). A brilliant evocation of the decade is found in Larzer Ziff's *The American 1890s: The Life and Times of a Lost Generation* (New York/London, 1967), while Gordon O. Taylor's *The Passages of Thought: Psychological Representation in the American Novel 1870–1900* (New York/London, 1969) is admirable on the treatment of 'consciousness' in the novels of the period. The continuing impact of naturalism on the progressive novel of the 1900s is studied in Robert W. Schneider, *Five Novelists of the Progressive Era* (New York/London, 1965); Jay B. Martin, *Harvests of Change: American Literature 1865–1914* (Englewood Cliffs, N.J., 1967) gives a broad view of the period through to 1914.

For the emergence of modernism on the international scene, including the United States, see *Modernism 1890–1930,* ed. Malcolm Bradbury and James McFarlane (Harmondsworth, 1976), with an extensive bibliography. The topic is explored comparatively, and admirably, in Edmund Wilson, *Axel's*

Castle: A Study in the Imaginative Literature of 1870–1930 (New York, 1931);
an interesting recent study, if rather partial and overnationalistic, is Hugh
Kenner, *A Homemade World: The American Modernist Writers* (New York,
1975). The fundamental changes of style involved have been widely explored
in modern criticism, but especially to be recommended are Wylie Sypher's
Rococo to Cubism in Art and Literature (New York, 1960) and *Loss of the Self
in Modern Art and Literature* (New York, 1962). An important area is
covered in Bernard Duffey, *The Chicago Renaissance in American Letters*
(East Lansing, Mich., 1954), while a good general background to the cultural
changes of the immediately pre-war years is Henry F. May, *The End of
American Innocence: A Study of the First Years of Our Own Time 1912–1917*
(New York, 1959).

The direct impact of war on modern American writers is examined in
Frederick J. Hoffman, *The Mortal No: Death and the Modern Imagination*
(Princeton, N.J., 1964); also see Stanley J. Cooperman, *World War I and the
American Novel* (Baltimore, Ind., 1967). Frederick Hoffman also offers an
excellent introduction to the Twenties in *The Twenties: American Writing in
the Postwar Decade* (New York, 1949) as well as in *Freudianism and the
Literary Mind* (New York, 1977). Malcolm Cowley's *Exile's Return: A
Literary Odyssey of the 1920s* (New York, 1934; rev. edn., 1951) is a key book
of memoirs and analysis; also see the valuable critical essays in his *A Second
Flowering: Works and Days of the Lost Generation* (New York/London,
1973). *The American Novel and the 1920s*, ed. Malcolm Bradbury and David
Palmer (London, 1971), offers essays on the period and the main authors,
with general bibliographies. An admirable historical survey of the period is
William E. Leuchtenburg, *The Perils of Prosperity* (Chicago, 1958).

On the 1930s and the rise of proletarian fiction see Daniel Aaron, *Writers
on the Left* (New York, 1961) and also Leo Gurko, *The Angry Decade* (New
York, 1968). Kazin's *On Native Grounds* and Geismar's *Writers in Crisis*,
cited above, provide valuable material. The reaction of the 1940s is best
found in Chester E. Eisinger, *Fiction of the Forties* (Chicago/London, 1963);
also see John W. Aldridge, *After the Lost Generation: A Critical Study of the
Writers of Two Wars* (New York, 1951), Marcus Klein, *After Alienation:
American Novels in Mid-Century* (Cleveland, Ohio, 1962), and Sidney
Finkelstein, *Existentialism and Alienation in American Literature* (New York,
1965).

The best general survey of the post-war American novel is Tony Tanner,
City of Words: American Fiction 1950–1970 (London, 1971); a broader but
less analytical portrait is to be found in the *Harvard Guide to Contemporary
American Writing*, ed. Daniel Hoffman (Cambridge, Mass./London, 1979).
Three useful collections of essays on the post-war American novel are *Recent
American Fiction: Some Critical Views*, ed. Joseph J. Waldmeir (Boston,
1963), *Contemporary American Novelists*, ed. Harry T. Moore (Carbondale,
Ill./London, 1964), and *The American Novel Since World War II*, ed.

Marcus Klein (New York, 1969). For a more detailed study, see Ihab Hassan's very useful and central *Radical Innocence: Studies in the Contemporary American Novel* (Princeton, N.J., 1961). Howard M. Harper, *Desperate Faith: A Study of Bellow, Salinger, Mailer, Baldwin and Updike* (Chapel Hill, N.C., 1967), Nathan A. Scott, *Three American Moralists: Mailer, Bellow, Trilling* (Notre Dame, Ind., 1973), and *Five Black Writers: Essays on Wright, Ellison, Baldwin, Hughes and LeRoi Jones,* ed. Donald B. Gibson (New York/London, 1970), deal well with major figures.

On the fiction of the 1960s, see Tony Tanner, cited above, and Raymond Olderman, *Beyond the Waste Land: The American Novel in the 1960s* (New Haven, Conn., 1973). Other useful studies as Jonathan Baumbach, *The Landscape of Nightmare: Studies in the Contemporary American Novel* (New York, 1965), Max F. Schultz, *Black Humor Fiction of the Sixties* (Athens, Ohio, 1973), and Richard B. Hauck, *A Cheerful Nihilism: Confidence and 'The Absurd' in American Humorous Fiction* (Bloomington, Ind./London, 1971). On the fictional scene from the writers' point of view, see *The Creative Present: Notes on Contemporary American Fiction,* ed. Nona Balakian and Charles Simmons (New York, 1963), and *The Contemporary Writer,* ed. L. S. Dembo and Cyrena Pondrom (Madison, Wis., 1972). Other useful books are Jerry H. Bryant, *The Open Decision: The Contemporary American Novel and Its Intellectual Background* (New York, 1970), Josephine Hendin, *Vulnerable People: A View of American Fiction Since 1945* (New York, 1978), and John R. May, *Towards a New Earth: Apocalypse in the American Novel* (Notre Dame, Ind., 1972).

On postmodernism, see especially Ihab Hassan, *The Dismemberment of Orpheus: Toward a Postmodern Literature* (New York, 1971), and *Paracriticisms: Seven Speculations of the Times* (Urbana, Ill./London, 1975); *Surfiction: Fiction Now and Tomorrow,* ed. Raymond Federman (Chicago, 1975); Robert Alter, *Partial Magic: The Novel As a Self-Conscious Genre* (Berkeley, Calif., 1975); Robert Scholes, *The Fabulators* (New York, 1967); Mas'ud Zaverzadeh, *The Mythopoeic Reality: The Postwar American Nonfiction Novel* (Urbana, Ill., 1975); David Lodge, *The Modes of Modern Writing: Metaphor, Metonymy, and the Typology of Modern Literature* (London, 1977); Manfred Pütz, *The Story of Identity: American Fiction of the Sixties* (Stuttgart, 1979); and Christopher Butler, *After the Wake: An Essay on the Contemporary Avant Garde* (Oxford, 1980). See also the counter-attack by Gerald Graff, *Literature Against Itself: Literary Ideas in Modern Society* (Chicago/London, 1979). On the 'new journalism', see *The New Journalism,* ed. Tom Wolfe and E. W. Johnson (New York, 1973; London, 1975). More recent developments are discussed in Jerome Klinkowitz, *Literary Disruptions: The Making of a Post-Contemporary American Fiction* (rev. edn., Urbana, Ill., 1980); also see the volumes in the series 'Contemporary Writers', ed. Malcolm Bradbury and Christopher Bigsby (London/New York, 1982–). For a general study of the culture of the Sixties see

Morris Dickstein, *Gates of Eden: American Culture in the Sixties* (New York, 1977); and for the Seventies see Christopher Lasch, *The Culture of Narcissism: American Life in an Age of Diminishing Expectations* (New York, 1978).

Index

Abish, Walter, 163, 184
Abortion: An Historical Romance, The
  (Brautigan), 171
Absalom, Absalom! (Faulkner), 89, 92–3
Across the River and Into the Trees
  (Hemingway), 78
Ada, or Ardor: A Family Chronicle
  (Nabokov), 153–4.
Adams, Henry, 1–4, 20–1, 30, 36, 42,
  57, 67
Adventures of Augie March, The (Bellow),
  136
Adventures of Huckleberry Finn, The
  (Twain), 3
Advertisements for Myself (Mailer), 149,
  150
After the Lost Generation (Aldridge), 127
Age of Innocence, The (Wharton), 36
Air-Conditioned Nightmare, The (Miller),
  120
A la recherche du temps perdu (Proust), 39
Aldridge, John, 127
Alex Maury, Sportsman (Gordon), 107
Algren, Nelson, 129
Allen, Frederick Lewis, 96
All-Night Visitors (Major), 160
Alphabetical Africa (Abish), 184
Alther, Lisa, 164
Amateurs (Barthelme), 182
Ambassadors, The (James), 31–2
An American Dream (Mailer), 150, 156
An American Tragedy (Dreiser), 2,
  25–6, 104
Anderson, Sherwood, 45–52, 56, 72,
  74, 87, 97, 113, 124, 127
And Then We Heard the Thunder
  (Killens), 160
Apollinaire, Guillaume, 40
Appointment in Samarra (O'Hara), 108
Armies of the Night, The (Mailer), 150,
  158

Arrowsmith (Lewis), 56
As I Lay Dying (Faulkner), 89, 92
Assistant, The (Malamud), 141–2
Autobiography of Alice B. Toklas, The
  (Stein), 40
Awakening, The (Chopin), 18

Babbitt, Irving, 44
Babbitt (Lewis), 53–5
Bad Man, A (Elkin), 140
Baldwin, James, 104, 132–3, 148
Barbary Shore (Mailer), 128, 149
Barnes, Djuna, 100, 121, 172
Barth, John, 148, 157, 160–1, 163–4,
  179–85
Barthelme, Donald, 161–3, 182–3
Battle-Ground, The (Glasgow), 29
'Bear, The' (Faulkner) 90–1
Beat Generation, the, 120, 151
Beautiful and the Damned, The
  (Fitzgerald), 64
Bech: A Book (Updike), 146
Becker, G. J., 30
Beckett, Samuel, 160
Beetle Leg, The (Hawkes), 172
Being There (Kosinski), 156
Bell for Adano, A (Hersey), 128
Bellow, Saul, 126, 128, 131, 133–40,
  142, 148, 156–7
Bend Sinister (Nabokov), 153
Berger, Thomas, 159–61
Bergson, Henri, 44
Berlin Alexanderplätz (Döblin), 82
Biely, Andrei, 82–3
Big Money, The (Dos Passos), 83, 86
Black Spring (Miller), 117–20
Blood Oranges (Hawkes), 174
Borges, Jorge Luis, 160–1
Bottom Dogs (Dahlberg), 98, 101
Bourne, Randolph, 45
Bowles, Paul, 129, 151

Boyd, Thomas, 59
Brancusi, Constantin, 42
Brautigan, Richard, 160–1, 163, 169–71
Breakfast of Champions (Vonnegut), 169
Breast, The (Roth), 143–4
Breslin, Jimmy, 159
Brooks, Van Wyck, 45
Brossard, Chandler, 129
Bruccoli, Matthew J., 68
Burke, Kenneth, 107
Burns, John Horne, 128
Burr (Vidal), 156
Burroughs, William, 133, 151–4, 157, 160
BUtterfield 8 (O'Hara), 108

Cabell, James Branch, 64
Cabot Wright Begins (Purdy), 148
Cahan, Abraham, 18, 97, 101–2
Caine Mutiny, The (Wouk), 128
Caldwell, Erskine, 107–8
Call It Sleep (Roth), 102–3
Call of the Wild, The (London), 29
Calvino, Italo, 185
Camus, Albert, 127, 135
Cane (Toomer), 97
Cannery Row (Steinbeck), 110
Cannibal, The (Hawkes), 128, 158, 171–3, 178
Cantos, The (Pound), 85
Capote, Truman, 129, 133, 158
Catcher in the Rye, The (Salinger), 144–5
Catch-22 (Heller), 157, 165–6
Cat's Cradle (Vonnegut), 167
Céline, L.-F., 72
Centaur, The (Updike), 146
Cézanne, Paul, 38, 42
Châtelaine of La Trinité, The (Fuller), 18
Cheever, John, 129, 133, 148
Chevalier of Pensieri Vani, The (Fuller), 18
Chimera (Barth), 181
Chopin, Kate, 18–19
Churchill, Winston S., 18
City Life (Barthelme), 182–3
Civilisation in the United State (Stearns), 61
Cliff Dwellers, The (Fuller), 18

Come Back, Dr Caligari (Barthelme), 182
'Composition As Explanation' (Stein), 38
Composition of 'Tender Is the Night', The (Bruccoli), 68
Confederate General From Big Sur, A (Brautigan), 169–70
Confessions of Nat Turner, The (Styron), 159
Confidence Man, The (Melville), 165
Connecticut Yankee in King Arthur's Court, A (Twain), 4
Conrad, Joseph, 13, 65, 82
Conroy, Jack, 98, 101
Cool Million, A (West), 122–3
Coover, Robert, 159, 161, 163, 184
Country of the Pointed Firs, The (Jewett), 3
Couples (Updike), 147
Coup, The (Updike), 147
Cowley, Malcolm, 42, 63, 68, 97, 127–8
Cozzens, James Gould, 128
'Crack-Up, The' (Fitzgerald), 63, 69, 71
Crane, Hart, 83
Crane, Stephen, 1, 8–13, 19, 30, 46
Crumbling Idols (Garland), 9
Crying of Lot 49, The (Pynchon), 161, 176–7
Cubism, 39, 42
Cummings, E. E., 50, 58–9
Cup of Gold (Steinbeck), 109
Curtain of Green, A (Welty), 129
Custom of the Country, The (Wharton), 35

Dahlberg, Edward, 98, 101
Damnation of Theron Ware, The (Frederic), 18
Dangling Man (Bellow), 126, 128, 134
Dark Laughter (Anderson), 50–1
Darwin, Charles, 2, 28
Daughter of the Snows, A (London), 28
Davis, Richard Harding, 18
Day of the Locust, The (West), 70, 122–3
Dead Father, The (Barthelme), 182
Dean's December, The (Bellow), 139
Death in the Afternoon (Hemingway), 77
Death in the Woods (Anderson), 50

Death of the Novel and Other Stories, The (Sukenick), 162
Death, Sleep and the Traveller (Hawkes), 174
Debs, Eugene V., 43
Deer Park, The (Mailer), 149
Deliverance, The (Glasgow), 29
Delta Wedding (Welty), 129
Dem (Kelley), 160
Democracy (Adams), 3
Dharma Bums, The (Kerouac), 151
Didion, Joan, 159
Disinherited, The (Conroy), 102
Döblin, Alfred, 82
Doctorow, E.L., 159
Documents of Modern Literary Realism (Becker), 30
Dodsworth (Lewis), 56
Donleavy, J. P., 151
Dos Passos, John, 58–9, 62, 81–4, 86, 97–9, 130
Dostoevsky, Fyodor, 130, 132, 135
Dream Life of Balso Snell, The (West), 121–2
Dreiser, Theodore, 22–7, 30, 33, 46, 97, 104, 106, 135, 179
Dubin's Lives (Malamud), 142
Dubliners (Joyce), 47
Duchamp, Marcel, 42–3, 45
Dunbar, Paul Laurence, 18–19

'Early Success' (Fitzgerald), 57, 69
Eastlake, William, 160
East of Eden (Steinbeck), 111
Eggleston, Edward, 3
1876 (Vidal), 156
Eisenstein, Sergei, 83
Eliot, George, 6
Eliot, T. S., 44–5, 59, 137
Elkin, Stanley, 140, 159
Ellison, Ralph, 132–3
Elmer Gantry (Lewis), 56
Emerson, Ralph Waldo, 63
End of the Road, The (Barth), 148, 180
Enormous Room, The (Cummings), 50, 59
Ethan Frome (Wharton), 35
Etranger, L' (Camus), 135
Exaggerations of Peter Prince, The (Katz), 161
Exile's Return (Cowley), 42

Expressionism, 23, 42

Face of Time, The (Farrell), 107
Falconer (Cheever), 148
Family Moskat, The (Singer), 134
Farewell to Arms, A (Hemingway), 59, 76
Farrell, James T., 99, 105–7, 115, 136
Far Side of Paradise, The (Mizener), 68
Father and Son (Farrell), 107
Fathers, The (Tate), 107
Faulkner, William, 51, 58–9, 62, 87–94, 107, 127, 130, 133, 150, 172
Fauvism, 42
Fear of Flying (Jong), 164
Federman, Raymond, 163, 184
Feu, Le (Barbusse), 81
Fiction and the Figures of Life (Gass), 183
Fiedler, Leslie, 117, 131
Fiesta (Hemingway), 74
Financier, The (Dreiser), 25
Fitzgerald, F. Scott, 26, 57–9, 62–9, 71, 87, 95–6, 99, 108, 113, 123, 127, 133
Fitzgerald, Zelda, 64
Fixer, The (Malamud), 141
Flappers and Philosophers (Fitzgerald), 64
Flash and Filigree (Southern), 148
Flaubert, Gustave, 37, 38
Floating Opera, The (Barth), 148, 180
42nd Parallel, The (Dos Passos), 83, 85, 98
For Whom the Bell Tolls (Hemingway), 77
Frank, Waldo, 42, 45, 51, 57, 100
Franny and Zooey (Salinger), 145
Frazer, Sir J. G., 28
Frederic, Harold, 18–19
Free-Lance Pallbearers, The (Reed), 160
Freud, Sigmund, 44, 48, 67, 110, 149
Friedman, Bruce Jay, 159
From Here to Eternity (Jones), 128
Frost, Robert, 45
Fry, Roger, 43
Fuller, Henry Blake, 18
'Future of Fiction, The' (James), 7

Gaddis, William, 179
Gallery, The (Burns), 128
Gardner, John, 164, 185

Garland, Hamlin, 3–4, 13
Gass, William H., 161, 163, 183
Genius, The (Dreiser), 25
'Gentle Lena, The' (Stein), 37
George's Mother (Crane), 10
Ghostwriter, The (Roth), 144
Gilded Age, The (Twain and Warner) 4, 8, 9
Giles Goat-Boy (Barth), 161, 180
Gimpel the Fool (Singer), 134
Ginger Man, The (Donleavy), 151
Ginsberg, Allen, 151
Giovanni's Room (Baldwin), 132, 148
Glasgow, Ellen, 29–30, 34
God Bless You, Mr Rosewater (Vonnegut), 167
'Godliness' (Anderson), 47, 52
Go Down, Moses (Faulkner), 91, 93
God's Little Acre (Caldwell), 107–8
Gogol, Nikolai, 153
Golden Bowl, The (James), 31–3
Goldman, Emma, 43, 81, 117
Gold, Michael, 96–8, 100–1, 105
'Good Anna, The' (Stein), 37
Good As Gold (Heller), 157, 166
Goodbye Columbus (Roth), 131, 142–3
Good Man Is Hard to Find, A (O'Connor), 129
Goose on the Grave, The (Hawkes), 172
Gordon, Caroline, 107
Go Tell It on the Mountain (Baldwin), 132
Grapes of Wrath, The (Steinbeck), 110–11
Gravity's Rainbow (Pynchon), 177
Great American Novel, The (Roth), 144
Great American Novel, The (Williams), 51
Great Days (Barthelme), 182
Great Gatsby, The (Fitzgerald), 26, 59, 62, 65–9
Green Hills of Africa (Hemingway), 77
Grendel (Gardner), 164, 185
Griffith, D. W., 83
Groddeck, Georg, 118
Grossmann, Alfred, 159
Groves of Academe, The (McCarthy), 130
Guard of Honor (Cozzens), 128
Guilty Pleasures (Barthelme), 182

Haeckel, Ernst, 28

Heart is a Lonely Hunter, The (McCullers), 129
Hamlet, The (Faulkner), 93
Handke, Peter, 185
'Hands' (Anderson), 49–50
Harding, President G., 60
Harland, Henry, 18
Harte, Bret, 3
Hawkes, John, 128–9, 156, 158, 161, 163–4, 171–4, 178
Hawkline Monster: A Gothic Western, The (Brautigan), 171
Hawthorne, Nathaniel, 3, 63
Hazard of New Fortunes, A (Howells), 6
'H. D.', 45
Hearn, Lafcadio, 18
Heller, Joseph, 157, 159, 165–7
Hemingway, Ernest, 4, 17, 51, 58–9, 71–80, 94, 99, 113, 127, 133, 150
Henderson the Rain King (Bellow), 136–37
'Henry James' (Stein), 20
Hersey, John, 128
Herzog (Bellow), 137, 148
Heywood, Big Bill, 43
Hicks, Granville, 99
Hillyer, Robert, 81
Hoosier Schoolmaster, A (Eggleston), 3
Horses and Men (Anderson), 50
House of Mirth, The (Wharton), 34
Howe, Irving, 128
Howells, William Dean, 1, 3, 5–7
How German Is It (Abish), 184
'Howl' (Ginsberg), 151
'Hugh Selwyn Mauberley' (Pound), 59
humanism, 2, 78, 131, 134, 139, 142, 157
Humboldt's Gift (Bellow), 139, 156

I'll Take My Stand, 107
Imagisme, 45, 94
Impressionism, 78, 1–13, 19
In Another Country (Baldwin), 132, 148
In Cold Blood (Capote), 158
In Dubious Battle (Steinbeck), 110
In Our Time (Hemingway), 71, 73
Inside the Whale (Orwell), 121
In the Heart of the Heart of the Country (Gass), 161
Invisible Man (Ellison), 132
In Watermelon Sugar (Brautigan), 170

Iron Heel, The (London), 28
Irving, John, 164
Islands in the Stream (Hemingway), 80

Jailbird (Vonnegut), 169
James, Henry, 6, 7, 13, 31–4, 36, 37, 41, 82
James, William, 30–1, 37, 41
Jennie Gerhardt (Dreiser), 25
Jewett, Sarah Orne, 3
Jews Without Money (Gold), 98, 100–2
Jones, James, 128
Jong, Erica, 164
Joyce, James, 39, 47, 51, 61, 82–3, 87, 90, 94, 121, 127, 130
J R (Gaddis), 179
Judgement Day (Farrell), 105
Jungle, The (Sinclair), 27
Junkie (Burroughs), 151
Jurgen (Cabell), 64

Kafka, Franz, 130, 135, 143–4
Katz, Steve, 161, 163
Kazin, Alfred, 7, 22
Kelley, William Melvin, 160
Kerouac, Jack, 133, 151–2, 160, 169
Kesey, Ken, 157, 160
Killens, John Oliver, 160
Kinflicks (Alther), 164
King Coal (Sinclair), 28
Knock on Any Door (Motley), 129
Kosinski, Jerzy, 156, 161, 163, 184
Krim, Seymour, 159

Lady Chatterley's Lover (Lawrence), 59
Last Tycoon, The (Fitzgerald), 70–1
Lautréamont, comte de, 172
Lawd Today (Wright), 103
Lawrence, D.H., 59
Let It Come Down (Bowles), 151
Letters (Barth), 164, 181
Letting Go (Roth), 142
Lewis, R. W. B., 148
Lewis, Sinclair, 45, 53–6, 63
Lewisohn, Ludwig, 100
Liberal Imagination, The (Trilling), 130
Liberator, The, 43
Light in August (Faulkner), 89, 91–3
Lime Twig, The (Hawkes), 172–3
Lindsay, Vachel, 45
Lippmann, Walter, 43, 45

Literary and Philosophical Essays (Sartre), 83
Literary Situation, The (Cowley), 127
Little Big Man (Berger), 161
Little Review, The, 43
Lolita (Nabokov), 153–4
London, Jack, 26–8, 52, 109, 117
Look at the Harlequins (Nabokov), 153
Look Homeward Angel (Wolfe), 113, 114
Lost in the Funhouse: Fiction for Print, Tape, Live Voice (Barth), 161, 180
Lowell, Amy, 45
Lubbock, Percy, 33
Luhan, Mabel Dodge, 44–5
Lynd, Robert and Helen, 53

McCarthy, Mary, 130
McCullers, Carson, 94, 129, 133
McTeague: A Story of San Francisco (Norris), 14–16
Maggie; A Girl of the Streets (Crane), 9–10
Magic Barrel, The (Malamud), 140
Magician of Lublin, The (Singer), 134
Mailer, Norman, 128, 131, 135, 137, 148–50, 156, 158
Main Street (Lewis), 52–4, 63
Main-Travelled Roads (Garland), 13
Major, Clarence, 160, 163
Making of Americans: The Hersland Family, The (Stein), 38–9, 62
'Making of the Making of Americans, The' (Stein), 39, 40
Malamud, Bernard, 131, 133, 140–2
Malcolm (Purdy), 148
Manhattan Transfer (Dos Passos), 62, 82–3
Mann, Thomas, 130
Mansion, The (Faulkner), 93
Man Who Corrupted Hadleyburg, The (Twain), 5
Man Who Cried I Am, The (Williams), 160
Man With the Golden Arm, The (Algren), 129
Many Marriages (Anderson), 50, 51
Marching Men (Anderson), 46
Marry Me (Updike), 147
Martin Eden (London), 28
Marx, Karl, 67, 101, 149
Masses, The, 43

Masters, Edgar Lee, 45, 48
Matisse, Henri, 40, 43, 45
'Melanctha' (Stein), 37
Melville, Herman, 3, 63, 165
Member of the Wedding, The
　(McCullers), 129
Mencken, H. L., 45, 53
Men Without Women (Hemingway), 73
Metropolis, The (Sinclair), 28
Mid Century (Dos Passos), 86
Middle of the Journey, The (Trilling), 130
Middletown (Lynd), 53
Miller, Henry, 116–21, 169
Miss Lonelyhearts (West), 122
Mizener, Arthur, 68
Modernism, 33, 41, 44–5, 48, 61–2,
　82, 86–7, 94, 100, 127, 130–4,
　161–3, 185
Monroe, Harriet, 45
Moore, Marianne, 45
Mosquitoes (Faulkner), 88
Mother Night (Vonnegut), 157, 167
Motley, Willard, 129
Movers and Shakers (Luhan), 44
Mr Sammler's Planet (Bellow), 138, 142
Mrs Peixada (Harland), 18
Museums and Women (Updike), 126
My Days of Anger (Farrell), 107
My Life as a Man (Roth), 144
Mysterious Stranger, The (Twain), 5

Nabokov, Vladimir, 153–5, 159,
　160–1, 163
Naked and the Dead, The (Mailer), 128,
　135, 149
Naked Lunch, The (Burroughs), 152, 157
Nation, The, 44
Native Son (Wright), 103
Natural, The (Malamud), 140, 144
naturalism, 6–17, 19, 23, 25–6,
　29–30, 34, 36, 38, 41–4, 46, 52, 55,
　61, 66, 76, 78, 97, 99, 101, 104,
　108–9, 111–12, 128–30, 32–3, 135,
　140, 162, 164, 179
Nausée La (Camus), 135
New Life, A (Malamud), 131, 141–2
New Masses, The, 98, 102
New Republic, The, 43, 98
New Yorker, 146
Nexus (Miller), 118
Nietzsche, Friedrich, 28, 44

Night Rider (Warren), 107
Nightwood (Barnes), 121
Nine Stories (Salinger), 145
Nineteen Nineteen (Dos Passos), 83, 85
Nixon, Richard M., 184
Norris, Frank, 8–9, 13–19, 23, 47,
　109, 110
No Star Is Lost (Farrell), 107
Notes from Underground (Dostoevsky),
　132
'Notes on the Decline of Naturalism'
　(Rahv), 30
nouveau roman, 160, 162
Nova Express (Burroughs), 152

Oasis, The (McCarthy), 130
O'Connor, Flannery, 94, 129, 133, 172
Of Mice and Men (Steinbeck), 110
Of Time and the River (Wolfe), 113–14
O'Hara, John, 108–9
Oil (Sinclair), 28
Octopus, The (Norris), 16–17, 110
Old Man and The Sea, The
　(Hemingway), 80
Omensetter's Luck (Gass), 161, 183
One Flew Over the Cuckoo's Nest (Kesey),
　157
O'Neill, Eugene, 45
One Man's Initiation (Dos Passos) 59, 81
Only Yesterday (Allen), 96
On Moral Fiction (Gardner), 186
On the Road (Kerouac), 151
'Open Boat, The' (Crane), 9
Origin of the Brunists, The (Coover), 161,
　184
Orwell, George, 121
Other Voices, Other Rooms (Capote), 129
Our America (Frank), 57
Our Mr Wrenn (Lewis), 52
Outsider, The (Wright), 104

Painted Bird, The (Kosinski), 161, 184
Pale Fire (Nabokov), 153
Partisan Review, 98, 134
Passion Artist, The (Hawkes), 164, 174
Pastures of Heaven, The (Steinbeck), 109
Pawnbroker, The (Wallant), 140
People of the Abyss, The (London) 29
Perelman, S. J., 121
'Perfect Day for Bananafish, A'
　(Salinger), 145

Perkins, Maxwell, 113
Petersburg (Biely), 82
Phillips, William, 99
Picasso, Pablo, 39–40, 42
Pictures of Fidelman (Malamud), 141
Pit, The (Norris), 16
Player Piano (Vonnegut), 167
Plexus (Miller), 118
Pnin (Nabokov), 153
Poe, Edgar Allan, 3
'Poetry and Grammar' (Stein), 38
Poetry (Chicago), 43, 45
Poorhouse Fair, The (Updike), 146
Poor White (Anderson), 50
Portnoy's Complaint (Roth), 143, 156
'Portraits and Repetition' (Stein), 38
Postmodernism, 159–64, 168–85
Potok, Chaim, 133
Pound, Ezra, 45, 59, 61, 85
Prairie Folks (Garland), 13
Preface to Politics, A, (Lippmann), 43
Presidential Papers, The (Mailer), 156
Pricksongs and Descants (Coover), 184
Princess Casamassima, The (James), 82
Principles of Psychology (W. James), 30
Professor of Desire, The (Roth), 144
Proust, Marcel, 39, 87, 90
Provincetown Players, 45
Public Burning, The (Coover), 159, 184
Pudd'nhead Wilson (Twain), 5
Purdy, James, 129, 148
Pynchon, Thomas, 156–7, 161, 163, 174–80

Rabbit is Rich (Updike), 147
Rabbit Redux (Updike), 147
Rabbit, Run (Updike), 146–7
Ragtime (Doctorow), 159
Rahv, Philip, 30
Raise High the Roofbeam, Carpenters and Seymour: An Introduction (Salinger), 145
Rank, Otto, 118
realism, 3, 6, 7, 30, 33–4, 43, 99–100, 107–8, 110, 119, 129–30, 132, 134, 148, 163–4, 181
Real Life of Sebastian Knight, The (Nabokov), 153
Rechy, John, 152
Recognitions, The (Gaddis), 179

Red Badge of Courage, The (Crane), 1, 9, 11–12
Red Pony, The (Steinbeck), 110
Reed, Ishmael, 160
Reed, John, 43, 98, 103
Reivers, The (Faulkner), 93
Responsibilities of the Novelist, The (Norris), 9, 13
Ricketts, Edward F., 109
Rimbaud, Arthur, 117
Rise of David Levinsky, The (Cahan), 97, 100
Rise of Silas Lapham, The (Howells), 5
Robber Bridegroom, The (Welty), 129
Roman expérimental, Le (Zola), 7
Roosevelt, Teddy, 36
Rose of Dutcher's Coolly (Garland), 13
Rosy Crucifixion, The (Miller), 118, 120
Roth, Henry, 102–3, 105
Roth, Philip, 131, 133, 137, 142–4, 148, 156–7, 164
Royce, Josiah, 37

Sabbatical (Barth), 182
Sacred Fount, The (James), 33
Sadness (Barthelme), 182
Salinger, J.D., 128–9, 133, 137, 144–8, 151
Same Door, The (Updike), 146
Sanctuary (Faulkner), 92
Sandburg, Carl, 45
Santayana, George, 18, 37
Sartoris (Faulkner), 88–9
Sartre, Jean-Paul, 83, 127, 135
Scholes, Robert, 159
Schwartz, Delmore, 140
Sea Wolf, The (London), 28
Second Skin (Hawkes), 161, 173
Secret Agent, The (Conrad), 82
Seize the Day (Bellow), 136–7
Selby, Hubert, 152
Sense of the Past, The (James), 31
Shaw, George Bernard, 28, 44, 52
Shaw, Irwin, 128
Sheltered Life, The (Glasgow), 30
Sinclair, Upton, 26–8, 52, 97
Singer, Isaac Bashevis, 131, 133–4, 144
Sirens of Titan, The (Vonnegut), 167
Sister Carrie (Dreiser), 22–7, 32
Slapstick (Vonnegut), 169

Slaughterhouse-Five: Or, The Children's Crusade (Vonnegut), 158, 168–9
Snow White (Barthelme) 161, 182
Soft Machine, The (Burroughs), 152
'Soldier's Home, A' (Hemingway), 59
Soldier's Pay (Faulkner), 59, 88
Something Happened (Heller), 166
Sorel, Georges, 44
Sotweed Factor, The (Barth), 157, 180
Sound and the Fury, The (Faulkner) 62, 89, 91
Southern, Terry, 148, 159, 177
Spencer, Herbert, 21
Spengler, Oswald, 67
Spinoza, Baruch, 138
Spoil of Office, A (Garland), 3, 13
Spoils of Poynton, The (James), 7, 31
Spoon River Anthology, The (Masters), 48
Stearns, Harold, 61
Stein, Gertrude, 20–1, 31, 33, 36–41, 44–7, 51, 61–2, 72, 75, 127
Stein, Leo, 37
Steinbeck, John, 17, 99–113, 117, 127
Steps (Kosinski), 161
Stevens, Wallace, 45
Stoic, The (Dreiser), 25
Strike (Vorse), 98
Styron, William, 159
Subterraneans, The (Kerouac), 151
Sukenick, Ronald, 161–3
Sun Also Rises, The (Hemingway), 59, 71, 74–6
surrealism, 100, 121, 132, 159

Tanner, Tony, 163
Take It Or Leave It (Federman), 184
Tales of the Jazz Age (Fitzgerald), 64
Tate, Allen, 107
Tenants, The (Malamud), 142
Tender Buttons (Stein), 40, 67
Tender Is the Night (Fitzgerald), 64, 68–9
Things As They Are (Stein), 37
This Side of Paradise (Fitzgerald), 58–9, 63
Thompson, Hunter S., 159
'Thornton Wilder: Prophet of the Genteel Christ' (Gold), 96
Three Lives (Stein), 37, 47
Three Soldiers (Dos Passos) 59, 82

Three Stories and Ten Poems (Hemingway), 73
Through the Wheat (Boyd), 59
Ticket That Exploded, The (Burroughs), 152
Time of the Assassins, The (Miller), 117
Titan, The (Dreiser), 25
To A God Unknown (Steinbeck), 109
Tobacco Road (Caldwell), 107–8
To Have and Have Not (Hemingway), 77
Tokyo-Montana Express, The (Brautigan), 171
Tolstoy, Leo, 21
Too Far to Go: The Maples Stories (Updike), 147
Toomer, Jean, 97
Torrents of Spring (Hemingway), 51, 74
Tortilla Flat (Steinbeck), 110
Town, The (Faulkner), 93
Transparent Things (Nabokov), 153
Travesties (Hawkes), 174
Tree Of Night, The (Capote), 129
Trilling, Lionel 108, 130
Triumph of the Egg (Anderson), 50
Trois Contes (Flaubert), 37
Tropic of Cancer (Miller), 116, 118, 120
Tropic of Capricorn (Miller), 117, 119–20
Trout Fishing in America (Brautigan), 161, 170
Turgenev, Ivan, 6
Twain, Mark, 3–6, 122, 165

Ulysses (Joyce), 39, 82–3, 177
Uncalled, The (Dunbar), 18
Uncle Tom's Children (Wright), 103
Universal Baseball Association, Inc., J. Henry Waugh, Prop., The (Coover), 184
Unspeakable Practices, Unnatural Acts (Barthelme), 182
'Untold Lie, The' (Anderson), 49
Up (Sukenick), 161
Updike, John, 126, 129, 133, 146–8
U.S.A. (Dos Passos) 60, 62, 83–6, 98–9

V (Pynchon), 156–7, 175–6
Vandover and the Brute (Norris), 14–15
Van Gogh, Vincent, 42
Vein of Iron (Glasgow), 29
Victim, The (Bellow), 131, 135, 141

Vidal, Gore, 128, 156
'Views of my Father Weeping'
  (Barthelme), 182
Virginia (Glasgow), 29
Vonnegut, Kurt, 157–9, 163, 167–8
Vorse, Mary Heaton, 98

Wallant, Edward Lewis, 133, 140
Wapshot Chronicle, The (Cheever), 148
Wapshot Scandal, The (Cheever), 148
Warner, Charles Dudley, 4
Warren, Robert Penn, 94, 107
Washington, D. C. (Vidal), 156
Waste Land, The (Eliot), 59, 87
Web and the Rock, The (Wolfe), 115
Wells, H. G. 13, 44, 52
Welty, Eudora, 94, 129, 133
West, Nathanael, 70, 100, 121–5, 127,
  165, 177
Wharton, Edith, 33–7
What Is Man? (Twain), 5
What Maisie Knew (James), 7, 31
'When Everyone Was Pregnant'
  (Updike), 126
When She Was Good (Roth), 142
White Fang (London), 28
Whitehead, A. N., 39
'White Negro, The' (Mailer), 150–1
Whitman, Walt, 63
Who Walk In Darkness (Brossard), 129
Why Are We In Vietnam (Mailer), 151
Wilder, Thornton, 98
*Willard and his Bowling Trophies: A
  Perverse Mystery* (Brautigan), 171
Williams, John A., 160
Williams, William Carlos, 45

Willie Master's Lonesome Wife (Gass),183
Williwaw (Vidal), 128
Wilson, Edmund, 58, 98
Wilson, Woodrow, 43, 57, 60, 107
Windy McPherson's Son (Anderson), 47
Winesburg, Ohio (Anderson), 47–50
Wings of the Dove, The (James), 31–2
Winner Take Nothing (Hemingway), 73
Wise Blood (O'Connor), 129
With the Procession (Fuller), 18
Wolf, The (Norris), 16
Wolfe, Thomas, 62, 96–7, 99, 112–16
Wolfe, Tom, 158–9
Woolf, Virginia, 87, 127
World According to Garp, The (Irving),
  164
World I Never Made, A (Farrell), 106
World Is a Wedding, The (Schwartz), 140
World's End (Sinclair), 28
Wouk, Herman, 128
Wright, Richard, 98, 103–5, 133

Yeats, W. B., 127
Yekl: A Tale of the New York Ghetto
  (Cahan), 18
Yellow Back Radio Broke-Down (Reed),
  160
Yellow Book, The, 18
You Can't Go Home Again (Wolfe), 16,
  115
Young Lions, The (Shaw), 128
Young Lonigan (Farrell), 105
Young Manhood of Studs Lonigan, The
  (Farrell), 105

Zola, Emile, 7–9, 16